Eschatological Rationality

Eschatological Rationality

Theological Issues in Focus

Gerhard Sauter

A Labyrinth Book

Baker Books

A Division of Baker Book House Co
Grand Rapids, Michigan 49516

Published by Baker Books
a division of Baker Book House Company
P.O. Box 6287, Grand Rapids, MI 49516-6287

Labyrinth Books is an imprint of Baker Book House company.

Printed in the United States of America

Library of Congress Cataloging-in-Publication Data

Sauter, Gerhard.
      Eschatological rationality : theological issues in focus / Gerhard Sauter.
         p.   cm.
      "A Labyrinth book."
      Includes bibliographical references and index.
      ISBN 0-8010-2112-X (pbk.)
        1. Theology, Doctrinal. 2. Eschatology. I. Title.
BT80.S19   1997
230'.044—dc20   96-24115

For information about academic books, resources for Christian leaders, and all new
releases available from Baker Book House, visit our web site:
http://www.bakerbooks.com/

For my friends
in Oxford, Durham, North Carolina, and Princeton

Contents

Foreword

Gerhard Sauter has served as one of the principal theological voices of the Evangelical Church in Germany in the latter half of the twentieth century. However, he is less well-known in this country than his German colleagues, Jürgen Moltmann and Wolfhart Pannenberg, principally because his writings, unlike theirs, have not been available in English translation. Happily, that situation has begun to change with the release earlier this year of a translation of one of his major theological treatises by another publisher and with the publication by Baker of the important collection of essays you have before you.

The translation of his essays into English is particularly appropriate, since many of them were given as lectures in England and the United States. Sauter has taught as a visiting professor at Duke University and Princeton Theological Seminary. He has energetically pursued theological dialogue with Christians from a wide variety of countries and from a broad spectrum of Christian traditions. His own theology, as he is quick to acknowledge, has profited from these discussions and he has attempted to integrate what he has learned into the rigorous traditions of German Protestant academic theology in which he was formed and from which he speaks and writes.

Gerhard Sauter was born in Kassel, Germany, on May 4, 1935. His father was pastor of a congregation and an active member of the anti-Nazi Confessing Church. His father's ancestors were originally Swiss Mennonites who had been driven out of Switzerland in the seventeenth century for their faith and had settled in southwest Germany. His mother's family was also deeply rooted in the Church. Her father had been a missionary to China with the *Basler Mission* during the last years of the Manchu dynasty and had lived through the Boxer Rebellion.

Like his father before him Sauter decided to enter the Christian ministry and prepared himself for ordination by studying philosophy and theology at the universities of Tübingen and Göttingen. Both universities had excellent theological faculties and Sauter was able to study Church history with Hanns Rückert and Ernst Wolf, Old Testament with Walther Zimmerli, New Testament with Joachim Jeremias and Ernst Käsemann, practical theology with Martin Doerne, and systematic theology with Otto Weber. He wrote his doctoral dissertation with Otto Weber on the theology of the Kingdom of God in the elder and younger Blumhardt.

Sauter was ordained in 1962 as a pastor of the Evangelical Church in Hesse. During his years in parish work, he wrote what Germans call an *Habilitationsschrift,* a kind of second dissertation that anyone who aspires to be a university professor in Germany must write. He chose for his topic "The Future and Promise: The Problem of the Future in Contemporary Philosophy and Theology." His second thesis was accepted in 1965 and he was appointed as a docent on the theological faculty at Göttingen. In 1968 he was simultaneously offered positions as professor of theology at the Kirchliche Hochschule in Wuppertal and at the university of Mainz. He accepted the call to Mainz, where he replaced Wolfhart Pannenberg, who had moved to a new position in Munich. In 1973 he moved as well, accepting a call to Bonn to become professor of systematic and ecumenical theology and director of the Ecumenical Institute.

Sauter was absorbed for many years in editorial work. After the death of Ernst Wolf he assumed the editorship of an important series of theological books Wolf had founded called the *Theologische Bücherei.* He edited as well such significant theological journals as *Verkündigung und Forschung* and *Evangelische Theologie,* including a periodical he founded himself and named *Glaube und Lernen.* Moreover, in addition to his work on periodicals, he produced critical editions of the writings of several important Protestant theologians, the best known of which is his edition of Karl Barth's *Christian Dogmatics* of 1927.

But Gerhard Sauter is not merely an editor, important as that work has been and continues to be; he is also a creative theologian who writes and has written important books and articles in systematic theology. In the early sixties Moltmann (then at Wuppertal) and Sauter (then a pastor), working independently of each other, wrote books about eschatology, examining the relationship between the

10

promises of God, which in the nature of the case are future-oriented, and the hope of the Christian community. But whereas Moltmann's theology of hope was directed primarily toward a political hermeneutic, Sauter was and remains more interested in the implications of promise and hope for Christian spirituality and for the possibility of rational speech about God. Eschatological speech, which is concentrated on the promises of God, is for Sauter a paradigm for all theological speech about God of whatever sort. He has pursued these themes and ideas in such books as *Was heißt: nach Sinn fragen?* and *In der Freiheit des Geistes.* He has also pursued them in the essays in this volume, which offer the reader a generous sampling of important issues in his theology.

As it happens, Gerhard Sauter and I were in Göttingen at the same time, in the academic year 1964–1965, when he was a pastor finishing his *Habilitations-schrift* in systematic theology and I was a graduate student from Harvard writing my dissertation in Church history. Although we were both in contact with Ernst Wolf and may even have sat in the reading room of the Theological Seminar at the same time, we never met. We met for the first time more than a decade later in 1979 when Sauter was a visiting professor at Duke and I had the privilege of initiating him and his family into the mysteries of the proper celebration of the American Thanksgiving holiday. It was the beginning of a long professional association and a warm personal friendship. I am therefore delighted to have had anything to do with the production of this book and to commend it to a new circle of readers who believe they have been called to love God with their minds as well as with their other powers.

David C. Steinmetz
Duke University

Preface

After a guest lecture on "Contextual theology" at Duke Divinity School a black graduate student came up to me and asked: "What makes you expect today an intercultural theological discourse is possible at all?"

A good question—but not easily answered! The reference to a common tradition and its cultural consequences as a link between Europe and North America seems rather dubious when we examine it more closely. The Reformer's discovery of the freedom of faith as well as the Enlightenment have left quite different marks in North America, Great Britain and Central Europe. In 1931, Dietrich Bonhoeffer called North American religion a "Protestantism without Reformation." Conversely, there is no European counterpart to the "American revolution" in the sense of a historical event with its heritage: a religious interpretation of culture in terms of civil religion.

If there are no common traditions—do the ethical and political problems of today concern all of us as citizens of the "global village" and therefore provoke a genuine theological dialogue? Certainly: the ethical and political problems need to be solved on a world-wide scale. But they alone do not give reason to a theological and consistently ecumenical dialogue.

However, I do not think that we should confine ourselves to this alternative. I will rather try to demonstrate that theology as expectant God-talk and the struggle for theological clarification give rise to the hope for a dialogue and for a community surpassing boundaries. Who else but God alone can create real human community?

This hope has also been confirmed and reflected by a continuing dialogue with American and English theologians. Accordingly, the lectures and essays following in this volume have grown from an intensive communication, which started more than fifteen years ago. As visiting professor at Duke Divinity School in Durham, North Carolina, during several sabbatical terms in Princeton, New Jersey, delivering lectures in Eastern Europe, England and the United States, and most recently as an external member of the Faculty of Theology, University of Oxford, I have received helpful and inspiring questions about and comments on my theological work from students and colleagues.

Thus, the ecumenical discussions disclose a complexity overcoming boundaries familiar to German theology: concerning the relation between dogmatics and ethics or between theology and philosophy. This disclosure will be taken into account primarily in the essays "Suffering and Acting" and "How Can Theology Derive from Experiences?" The chapter "Jesus the Christ" addresses questions arising from the Jewish-Christian dialogue—which touches on a tragic sore point especially in Germany.

In order to uncover different approaches to theology, I have decided to present my point in the form of statements and essays rather than in a monographic exposition. Moreover, the openness to dialogue seems to correspond to the Anglo-American way of doing theology, which has often stimulated me; this openness is met by the essay form.

Therefore, the chapters of the book do not represent parts of a "system"—as it is usual especially in "continental theology"—but rather a special way of thinking, behind which the coherence of the themes becomes visible. This attitude is explained in the chapter on "Eschatological Rationality." That essay has been written for the ecumenical anthology *Outlines of Theology* representing different ways of doing theology today.

I am very much indebted to my colleague Professor David C. Steinmetz of Duke University for not only suggesting this volume and supporting its publication, but also for reading the translation and helping me to avoid misunderstanding. I am deeply grateful for his friendship and encouragement. I appreciate as well Dr. Lyle D. Bierma's attentive involvement in the translation process of some of these essays. I also offer my thanks to Nancy L. Zingrone, formerly assistant director of the Labyrinth Press, for her editorial help.

If this volume, by reflecting the intent and the effort to think towards a shared subject, contributes to a theological discourse which overcomes the various boundaries, it will have accomplished its goal.

Gerhard Sauter
Bonn , May 4th, 1995

1

Jesus the Christ

Messianism and Christology

"Are you he who is to come, or shall we look for another?" This was the question (according to Matthew 11:2ff., Luke 7:18ff.) with which John the Baptist sent his disciples to Jesus of Nazareth.[1] Jesus replied by pointing to his works among those who embodied the defectiveness of creation, the blind, lame, lepers, the deaf, the poor, and even the dead: all those who were in need of the gospel. These are, as Matthew points out, the "deeds of the Christ," messianic signs. Whether John's disciples have received a sufficient answer to their question is left open by Jesus. But he does bless those who take no offense at what he, Jesus, is and does: salvation is experienced by everyone who "hears and sees" that here salvation becomes apparent.

The question "Are you he who is to come, or shall we look for another?" has not died. Recently, even in the Christian world where it had long lain dormant, signs of its revival have been multiplying. Obviously it has not been answered finally and unambiguously by Peter's confession at Caesarea Philippi, "You are the Christ!" (Mark 8:29). Jesus' question, "But who do you say that I am?"[2] addresses itself anew to church and theology at a time when messianism is re-

1. This chapter was originally delivered as a lecture at Cambridge on January 27th, and at Oxford on January 28th, 1982. An earlier version was published in the *Scottish Journal of Theology* 37 (1984): 1–12.

2. For an explanation of the category "messianism," see Carsten Colpe, "Das Phänomen der nachchristlichen Religion in Mythos und Messianismus," *Neue Zeitschrift für Systematische Theologie und Religionsphilosophie* 9 (1967): 42–87.

emerging, with new strength and in a host of different forms. What shall we answer? The messianic idea, which has begun to realize itself for many Jews in a new experience of history, brings to mind the "yearning for the right" (as Martin Buber has characterized the prophetic message)[3] as well as the apocalyptic sensitivity to the incongruence of God's age and ours—all of which also finds an echo among Christians. But the Jewish sociologist of religion, Gershom Scholem, interprets messianism (past and present) with polemical undertones, directed against a Christian theology that perverts a longing for the salvation of the world into an assurance of salvation for a few pious souls. "Judaism has always held fast to a notion of salvation as a process that happens in public, in the arena of history, and in the medium of community. In other words, it takes place primarily in the visible world, and cannot be conceived of without this visible manifestation. Christianity, on the other hand, views salvation as a process in the spiritual and invisible realm, in the soul: in the private world of the individual. It effects a hidden transformation, to which nothing in the outer world need correspond."[4] Yet, as the following Jewish anecdote illustrates, to conceive of the arrival of messianic salvation is (tantalizingly) far from simple:

> The wife of a rich merchant rushes breathlessly into the room, and announces that the Messiah is coming into town.
> "That puts the lid on it!" groaned her husband. "We've just bought some land and built a house, business is picking up—and now we're supposed to give it all up to follow the Messiah!"
> "Don't tear your hair out, it's not that bad," the wife replied comfortingly; "just think of everything our nation has been through: slavery in Egypt, Babylonian captivity, Haman's persecution, two thousand years in exile, all the pogroms. With God's help we should survive the Messiah too!"[5]

That is the other side of the coin: the visible can never have the last word.

3. Martin Buber, *Pfade in Utopia* (Heidelberg: Lambert Schneider, 1950), 19.
4. Gershom Scholem, "Zum Verständnis der messianischen Idee im Judentum," in idem, *Über einige Grundbegriffe des Judentums* (Frankfurt a.M.: Suhrkamp, 1970), 121–167, esp. 121.
5. Jutta Janke, ed., *Von armen Schnorrern und weisen Rabbis* (Berlin: Verlag Volk und Welt, 1981), 8f.

Scholem's rejection of Christian internalization, of a Christian abandonment of world-transforming hope (compare Ernst Bloch),[6] however, is now paralleled by Christians' own self-critical reflections. They ask, or are asked, what has really changed within the world or for the sake of the world through Jesus of Nazareth. The traditional interpretations of the life and fate of Jesus Christ as a turning-point of world history, as the final source of its meaning, or even as the end of all history, seem no longer sound. Christian philosophy of history has failed to find some way of continuing to locate the fulfillment of history's purpose in Jesus of Nazareth. This vacuum is now being filled by messianism. Messianism does not reconcile God's action with existing reality: rather, it stresses God's opposition to the world, the incongruence of divine reality and history as we know it. It is precisely this incongruence that is applied as a key to understanding history—to an understanding that leads to inaction. Precisely because messianism does not set out to reconcile our present with all its paradoxes by doing history under Christian auspices, it promises a better, forward-pointing explanation of events from which the consequences, in terms of a desire actively to form history, have not yet been drawn.

The cross of Jesus is explained in a corresponding fashion. From the perspective of messianism, it is a sign of resistance against religious or political structures, insofar as they stand between God and humankind; insofar as they hinder us in our efforts to establish an immediate relationship with God, the environment, and one's self; and insofar as they further all kinds of alienation, increasing human suffering beyond all bounds by demanding that it be accepted as part of human existence.

For Jürgen Moltmann, for example, the reason for Jesus' death is "his deadly conflict with the public powers of his time,"[7] his intervening for the sake of the humiliated and insulted, the powerless power of his solidarity with the oppressed. Moltmann's Jesus of

6. Ernst Bloch, *Das Prinzip Hoffnung* (Frankfurt a.M.:Suhrkamp, 1959), esp. 575–582, 1327–1333, 1453–1464, 1541–1544; idem, *Atheism in Christianity: The Religion of the Exodus and the Kingdom* (New York: Herder & Herder, 1972).

7. Jürgen Moltmann, "Theologische Kritik der politischen Religion," in *Kirche im Prozess der Aufklärung: Aspekte einer neuen 'politischen Theologie,'* eds. Johann Baptist Metz, Jürgen Moltmann, and Willi Oelmüller (Munich: Chr. Kaiser Mainz: Grünewald, 1970), 37. See also Jürgen Moltmann, *The Crucified God* (New York: Harper & Row, 1974), esp. 126–159.

Nazareth is indeed "he who is to come," but in a new sense: he is the one who has to come to us as the Messiah again and again, to stand against the old world. Even if on Good Friday he died once and for all—an event which could be experienced as the death of God himself—nonetheless he dies again day by day with the dying and suffering people of our world. His death continues thus until he is revealed as the Messiah who finally abolishes suffering and death in this world. Only as the Messiah who is still to come can Jesus be he, besides whom and after whom we need not wait for another: this is the consensus of Christian theology and messianism today. In this kind of Christology it is the mission of Jesus that forms the focus of interest—it is concerned exclusively with Jesus' *work* and its success.

The Christ-Title and Christology

Christian theology seems to me to be ill prepared for the controversy that is emerging at this point because the word "Christ" (the Greek translation of the word "Messiah") has generally been understood only as part of the proper name "Jesus Christ." This is already the case in the New Testament: exegetes maintain that one should not pay too much attention to the "Christ" title, since it plays only a minor role in the tradition-history of predicates given to Jesus of Nazareth in the process of doctrinal development. True as this may be, however, it falls short of explaining the *meaning* of the attribution. What does it mean that Jesus was called "Christ" so emphatically as to turn the "Christ" title into a proper name, indeed in an exclusive sense? From now on no other person can be named "Christ" in the same manner as Jesus. The attribution of the Christ title is then of the utmost importance, not only for tradition-history, but also for theology. The word "Christ" does not lose its character as predicate by merging into the name "Jesus of Nazareth." It is intended to convey a specific meaning; this "meaning" is always present when the name of Jesus Christ is mentioned.

But what *does* the "Christ"-predicate in the name of Jesus mean? That he embodies God's salvation; he is *God's new work*. God has here created something which transcends all previous messianic expectations, more than transcends them, makes them obsolete. The fact that we call Jesus of Nazareth the "Christ" does not mean that he is *a* Messiah, or that he—as one person among many—first acquires historic significance through this title. Nor does it mean, on the other hand, that a previously unattached title is now attached to an historical bearer, whose character is derived entirely from the given predicate. Jesus is not any messianic figure; rather, he is "*the* Christ." Christology has to unfold this name to answer the question: Who is Jesus—Jesus Christ—Who is Christ? The answer is taken from the Jesus event: Christ is the new work of God. Christology, then, is not the doctrine of Jesus as a Messiah (not even as the most important Messiah), but the doctrine of Jesus *the* Christ. The Christ-title demands more of Christology than a comparative historical note; it demands messianic theology, a judgment about the knowledge of God that emerges from the Christ-history.

Modern theology, as I see it, has paid scant attention to this question. There are exceptions, such as Martin Kähler, Adolf Schlatter, and Paul Tillich—the last, evidently under Kähler's influence, speaks emphatically of "Jesus as the Christ" and begins his specific discussion of Christology as follows: "Christianity is what it is through the affirmation that Jesus of Nazareth, who has been called 'the Christ,' is actually the Christ, namely, he who brings the new state of things, the New Being. Wherever the assertion that Jesus is the Christ is maintained, there is the Christian message; wherever this assertion is denied, the Christian message is not affirmed."[8] Here the question of the messiahship of Jesus is put, at least implicitly, as the criterion of the relationship of Christianity to messianism. The problem is treated similarly by Schlatter in his dogmatics, where under the heading "The royal office of Jesus" he speaks of the unique meeting of present and future in the person and work of Jesus Christ; of his oneness with God, in which the uniting of present and future brings the fulfillment of divine prophecy.[9] Kähler, finally, understands the messiahship of Jesus as the "super-historical foundation and content" of the history of the old and new people of God.[10]

What are the consequences for a Christology whose prime assumption is that Jesus as the "Christ" is the "Messiah of Israel" and the world? It does not follow that Jesus is the answer to a ques-

---

8. Paul Tillich, *Systematic Theology*, vol. II (London: SCM Press, 1978), 97.

9. Adolf Schlatter, *Das christliche Dogma*, 2nd ed. (Stuttgart: Calwer Vereinsbuchhandlung, 1923), 287f.

10. Martin Kähler, *Die Wissenschaft der christlichen Lehre von dem evangelischen Grundartikel aus im Abrisse dargetellt*, 3rd ed. (Leipzig: A. Deichert, 1905), 93f.

tion that determines its own answer, to a quest for redemption that can only be "fulfilled," even if its fulfillment may produce some variations on what was expected. Jesus Christ cannot be comprehended within this sort of scheme of "promise and fulfillment": as the fulfillment of God's promise, he is not the product of Jewish (or modern) expectations; rather, these are judged by God's work in him. Doctrinal development has concentrated instead on a different problem: the unity of true God and true man in the person of Jesus. It has been concerned with the relationship of divinity and humanity, of immortal life and mortal existence, of eternity and time; and discussion has therefore centered on the relationship between the two *natures*. This pattern of thought has recently undergone heavy criticism: it is said to presuppose an antithesis of God and man, whereas the Christian message speaks of a dynamic movement of God towards humankind, of a loving union in which God abandons His distance from the world and becomes involved in our fate. But does this criticism really touch the heart of the problem?

It seems to me that, underlying this critique, there is a particular concern with the anthropological aspect of the messianic question (which we may also see as being taken up in a different way into classical Christology). The *historicity* ("Geschichtlichkeit") of humanity is the thought underlying most of the modern critique of patristic Christology, especially of the two-natures doctrine: the experience of rapid change in the world shaped by humankind, of a history in which there are no final states, in which to survive means to keep moving. Being human means: to be in the process of becoming; for this reason the concept of *"becoming human,"* of a process of self-development, is a thought that implicitly dominates many Christological schemes. A third motif is the idea of *identity* arising through change; the idea that a life comes to fruition only by exposing itself to a multitude of changing impressions, so that the subject can find itself in a dynamic interrelationship with these—or lose itself, if it will not thus risk itself. This idea is at work, for example, when it is said today that in the Christ-story, and especially in Jesus' death, God has put His divinity at stake to bring about the salvation of humankind from the fate of death. One can speak in this sense about the death of God as being the foundation of theology which would then be a theology of the crucified God. This is the fundamental

Christological concept of Eberhard Jüngel.[11] Jürgen Moltmann, too, starts out with Good Friday to give messianic meaning to God's salvatory actions: Jesus, the man of God, dies because of the desires of the political and religious powers-that-be to prevent humanity from becoming human. But because they are not capable of destroying Jesus totally the messianic story begins in which we stand and which waits for the full and universal realization of the humanness of all people.[12]

Nevertheless, if we want to speak of Jesus Christ in such a way as to expound the Christ-predicate, then we will have to ask first of all what the cross of Jesus means as a messianic reality. Only then can we be in a position to examine the anthropology that also determines the development of classical Christology as well as its critique in our time.

The Messianic Significance of Jesus' Death: His Consent to the Will of God

The cross is the pure form of Jesus' message—which he himself is: the message that God is at work in Jesus, and being at work in him, is in him. Jesus' work is his person, and his person is wholly work, though only, indeed, in that unity which we call "Christ."

This thesis attempts to summarize the reply of *theologia crucis* to the messianic question. It is not meant as yet another addition to the latest attempts to depict Jesus' death as the execution of a zealot, a messianic revolutionary. I consider it unlikely that anyone could now reconstruct the historical, political, or religious factors that led to Jesus' death. Nor, even if this were possible, should a "Theology of the Cross" set out to give theological interpretations of occurrences that are historically more or less doubtful—and still less of the intentions supposedly bound up with them. The message of the cross as a judgment and act of *God* upon Jesus is not bound to this context. In my opinion, the only point of departure we can take from Jesus' trial and execution is Jesus' claim that he would destroy the temple and rebuild it in three days, that is, that he would establish a new worship, and above all, his claim to unity with God. This unity

---

11. Eberhard Jüngel, *God as the Mystery of the World* (Grand Rapids: William B. Eerdmans, 1983).

12. Moltmann, *The Crucified God*, esp. 127f., 178, 186f., 327–329.

was manifest in all of Jesus' life and work. Some had responded with opposition and hate, others with trust and faith. The temptation narratives already make the point: Jesus has come to do the will of God. But he does not do this by setting himself up as the infallible representative and agent of God's will in his own right. Rather, he prayed and hoped that God's will be done. His Gethsemane prayer shows him still incessantly *searching* for the will of God. Jesus accepts that God's will may be different from his own when he prays that God's will be done, even if it contradicts the instinctive human desire to be spared the depths of suffering. Deserted by his friends and driven into a corner, he consents entirely to God's will. But even such wholly unassuming consent to the will of God had already become offensive to the pious. It appeared to challenge the natural order of relationship to God as well as the strict distinction between God and humanity that regulated all religious and political life. Jesus' condemnation and death are then, in terms of the totality of the New Testament picture, quite objectively an expression of opposition to the unity of Jesus with God. This man was to be separated from God by death—his opponents wanted to make a formal declaration and proof of his mere humanity in the passive helplessness, isolation, and destruction of dying.

Jesus accepted the will of God. He put all his trust in God, receiving his future from God's hands, giving his life to God. That was his faith, his hope, the power of his love: that he placed himself absolutely and unreservedly in God's hands. The work of God, for Jesus, was always present in what he experienced. That is why he committed himself into God's hands on the cross, why like the Psalmist in the loneliness of death he turned to God.

But here we must pause. How do we receive Jesus' dying shout, that great cry reported in the Gospels? The evangelists apparently understand it in a number of ways: Luke as the returning of life to God ("Into thy hands I commend my spirit!"; cf. Psalm 31:6), in a prayer that is given new meaning through Jesus' sonship, which comes to expression in the name by which God is called—"Father." For John (19:30), Jesus sees his life and work as finished, completed, and now finally offered to God; Matthew (27:50) and Mark (15:37) only mention an inarticulate scream. Is this the voice of utter despair, of the utterly God-forsaken, terror of death making itself heard as the last word of the man it has reduced to mere powerless humanity?

This is the usual interpretation in contemporary theology. But would not then those who consigned him to death have been proved right? And perhaps they did understand his prayer "My God, my God, why hast thou forsaken me?" as a proof of his God-forsakenness, supported indeed by the belief that Jesus, under the judgment signified by his crucifixion, no longer had any right to call upon God. But Jesus cried out the words "My God!" in full awareness of their significance. *These words are themselves theology,* only in them can a *theologia crucis* find a sufficient foundation. The common thread of the various evangelists' versions of Jesus' last words is Jesus' declaration of his unity and life of fellowship with God: the same, which the church later sought to describe in speaking of "true God" and "true man." The ensuing silence of Jesus on the cross is the death of the voice of God, of God's Word itself. Neither man alone nor God alone, but the God-man himself dies. The cross of Jesus does not mean the death of God, but that his Word ceases to speak. But with Jesus' death-cry, in which perhaps his prayer of Psalm 22 seeks full expression, the Spirit that was the power of his life of fellowship with God ascends, to represent him before God.

Martin Luther, in commenting on the text "Abba, Father" (Galatians 4:6), interprets the work of the Spirit as the articulation of our "unspeakable sighing" in distressed alienation from God: when we can no longer act, we exhaust our remaining ability to express ourselves in the "weak sighing" (Romans 8:26) into which we compress all that we can still say or feel. But even as it fades this utterance penetrates heaven and earth by the power of the Spirit of God. In God's ears it becomes, as Luther says, a gigantic shout filling heaven and earth. What says nothing to human ears is comprehensible and clear beyond the clarity of words to God; for He, and He alone, understands, hears, and answers our last gasp as a cry for redemption.[13]

I do not want to expand these reflections on the Trinity here; one would have to speak not only of Good Friday and Easter Sunday but also of the day in between, which is generally ignored by theology, on the assumption that cross and resurrection tell it all. But only the descent of Jesus into the kingdom of death, what used to be called the *descensus ad inferos,* makes it clear that Jesus' resurrection is no mere revival, no triumph of eternal life forces over transience, but

13. Martin Luther, *In epistolam S. Pauli ad Galatas Commentarius* (1535), WA 40.I:579–593, esp. 581, 28–31; 582, 31–33; 586, 17–28.

God's own victory over death. That is the meaning of the old dog-matic affirmation that we can live because Jesus, true God and true man, died. Thus dying he receives the name "Jesus Christ," as whom he speaks to us, having ceased on the cross to speak in any other way. This name, as Jesus' own name and exclusively his, speaks of the unity of utter consent of the man Jesus of Nazareth to the ultimate work of God in him, by which obedience unto death gains victory over all death. Therefore, from now on, all hopes, and above all every messianic hope, are focused on this death and on what it achieved for our lives. Salvation is perfection only in God, not in our picture of a perfected world. Jesus' life and death are messianic pointers to the promises of God, bringing about salvation even in a still imperfect world, calling and enabling people simply to let God act. Thus the way forward becomes visible: not in the claims of the Kingdom but, even when these are as nearly as possible fulfilled on the level of human action, under the sovereignty of God as pointing beyond itself to his promises. Jesus' excommunication on the cross was meant to exclude him from this: thus his death becomes the question, addressed to Israel and the world, of the manner of God's faithfulness to His promises. God's own answer to the excommuni-cation of Jesus is His incorporating humanity, as well as the whole creation, in the existence of Jesus Christ. The hidden God acts only in His fellowship with Jesus, and He calls all people into this fellow-ship: that is the messianic reality of the cross.

Christ and the New Creation

The reorientation of messianism to Christology is plainly not without consequences for human existence. I have already men-tioned the proliferation of recent attempts to discern an authorita-tive picture of authentic humanity in Jesus of Nazareth. Despite the intended dependence upon the historical authority of Jesus, such an-thropological perspectives rarely get more out of their picture of Jesus than the criteria of humanity which they put into it. Messianic ideals are imposed on Jesus, humanitarian goals inspired by the de-sire to overcome all obstacles that stand in the way of human fulfill-ment—and of God. But do such views of Jesus, and such attempts to imitate him, do justice to what Jesus tells us, above all in his great cry on the cross? It often seems to me that modern portraits of Jesus have opened a new chapter in the quest for the historical Jesus, with just the same distortions (and anachronisms) as in the eighteenth and nineteenth centuries; only Jesus is now no longer the enlightened man, or the leading moral personality, or even the religious example. Rather, his ideal quality lies in his rebellion against inhuman conditions, his struggle against the exclusion of social and religious outsiders, his stand for the God of ordinary people against every kind of property owner. Such "biographies" must be regarded critically, if we are to let Jesus Christ, the man in unity with God, determine the fundamental shape of the humanity to which we are called.

But this outline cannot be discerned from Jesus' visible human existence. His cross contradicts a merely historical view of his life, because in it the incarnation of God is revealed: Jesus is true man to the last and no superman, no supernatural being, no demigod beyond the grasp of death. Messianic expectation has to come to terms with this: this is the messianic reality. Jesus remains fully man in his unity with God, right up to that cry in which he hands himself over to God the Father. But at the same time, the incarnation of God is present in this death, freeing us to be human—no more and no less. The cross of Christ therefore forbids us to turn "incarnation" from a solely Christological predicate applied to the history of God with man into an anthropologically developmental concept, a "human destiny" which has yet to be attained. Many forms of messianism, especially secularized ones, retain only this evolutionary concept, which tells us that "true humanity" has still to be achieved through the attainment of certain necessary conditions: it is in process of "becoming." Theologically, however, "becoming" has to be seen as "being made" (cf. Luther's *fieri*),[14] experiencing life as a created being. Becoming is not an uninterrupted progression into a better future but the transition from nothingness and lostness into a life of fellowship with God.

For humanity the messiahship of Jesus means that God and world are no longer radically divided, like the apocalyptic heaven and earth; that earth need not be destroyed to make way for heaven-on-earth; that everything need not be changed in order to produce a world in which humankind, together with all of nature, can truly

---

14. See for example: *Annotationes D. M. Lutheri in aliquot capita Matthaei* (1538), WA 38: 568, 37: *"Christianus enim non est in facto, sed in fieri."* Cf. WA 7:336, 32; WA 17.II:116, 32–44; WA 56: 223, 5–7; 441, 13ff.; WA 57:102, 16f. Or: *Operationes in Psalmos* (1519–1521), WA 5:400, 10: *"Impius nititur operibus in deum currere, Iustus autem studet fide ex deo venire et nasci."*

live. Its meaning for the new humanity, for participation in the new creation, in the history of Jesus Christ is rather this: that our hope, being formed by the fullness of God's will in us, need not seek self-fulfillment in such vain apocalyptic yearnings. God's will to be with us is the promise given to the "new humanity," and the source of the fullness and the fulfillment of life.

"God with us"—even: "God within us." Thus Paul spoke of the Spirit of God, of God's new reality entering into us, to open us to receive hope for the future of humanity and the world (Romans 8). Paul is without doubt thinking in terms of messianism. The new presence of the Spirit is God's answer to the messianic question: "What is God's new work in the world?" To live with Jesus Christ, the Messiah of Israel, is to be seized by the Spirit of God. The filling with the Spirit is the beginning of God's future. God gives to us thereby as much of himself as we can take. Present and future cannot be distinguished as sharply as our grammar would have it: the future as the approaching not-yet, disappearing through the elusive moment of now into the past, the no-longer. That the future of salvation enters into us means rather that we already have all we need to live with God. To decide what we need from now on belongs to the power and fruit of the Spirit. The Spirit of God shows us what we really lack—not necessarily what we want, not necessarily what, as we judge, could be or should be. We are in no position to decide for ourselves what we lack, no matter how many wants we feel. What we lack—and above all, not what one or another of us may think to be unfairly withheld from him but what we all, what the world needs we can only know when we are released from our consuming anxiety for the fulfillment of our own desires. We can only hunger and thirst for righteousness (in the words of the Sermon on the Mount) if we have let God's justice have its way with us. We can only seek peace when we have received peace with God. Seen in this way, the exposition of the predicate "Christ," in the name "Jesus Christ," is both the criterion of Christology and the answer to the messianic question of our time.

2

"Exodus" and "Liberation" as Theological Metaphors

A Critical Case-Study of the Use of Allegory and Misunderstood Analogies in Ethics

In December 1977, Israeli politicians and journalists were allowed once again, after such a long time, to visit the Egyptian pyramids.[1] It was during this visit that a saying of their Prime Minister Menachem Begin went around: "Just think! Your forefathers built these marvelous works!" What memories does this reminder call forth? Does it express Israel's unyielding self-assurance, which not only runs along the traces of its own history all over the Middle East but also asks yet others to pay attention to them? Should the representatives of modern Egypt perhaps be told that they stand in a different sort of continuity with the great dynasties on the Nile from the Jews? Or does Begin's reminder also revive the ineradicable knowledge of Israel's helplessness, which in the gray dawn of its history drove its fathers to the granaries of Egypt and made them there dependent on their providers, until the time came when Yahweh led them "out of the land of Egypt, out of the house of bondage" (Exodus 20:2)?

It may be possible to understand why the spokesmen of the state of Israel refer to the Exodus tradition, particularly when one considers that the Jews have viewed themselves as exiles for centuries and,

1. This chapter was originally given as a lecture for a seminar on "Exegesis-Hermeneutics-Ethics" to the theological faculties of Bonn and Oxford: in Oxford, March 13th to 17th, 1978.

27

for that reason, have interpreted the founding of the state of Israel as a repetition of the Conquest. But can Christian theology draw similar conclusions?[2] It is not accidental that Christianity does not know of a "theology of the Conquest"—unless it is in the sense of the final home of God's people into which they can "enter" and in which they can "find rest" and "dwell" (Hebrews 3:11, 18; 4:1ff.; 12:22; 13:14). In the theology of the ancient church, this eschatological question was transformed to a large extent into a soteriological one, and the Exodus story was once again recalled. A particularly informative paradigm for this is the oldest preserved Christian Easter sermon, the Passah-Homily of Melito of Sardis (from the second half of the second century). This sees the passion of Jesus Christ foreshadowed in the Passover of the Exodus (67) and discerns in it the redemptive liberation of believers "out of servitude into freedom, out of darkness into light, out of death into life, out of tyranny into the eternal kingdom" (68).[3] At first sight, Augustine deviates from this typological interpretation, but he agrees with it at the decisive point of comparison. He speaks of the transition of man into the world which God prepared for salvation and in which one follows the way to eternity.[4] These two examples, however, are very isolated ones. The remembrance of the Exodus out of Egypt has not played any further special role for Christian theology, except for occasional biblicist reminiscences. For example, such memories have helped the

2. Cf. Heinz-Wolfgang Kuhn and Henning Schröer, "Exodusmotiv" III. and IV., Theologische Realenzyklopädie, vol. X (Berlin/New York: de Gruyter, 1982), 741–747.

3. Méliton de Sardes, *Sur la Pâque, et fragments*, SC 123, ed. Othmar Perler (Paris: Editions du Cerf, 1966), 96–99; Méliton von Sardes, *Vom Passa*, ed. Josef Blank (Freiburg: Lambertus, 1963), 118f.

4. See, for example, *In Iohannis Evangelium Tractatus* II.2 CChr. SL 36, ed. Radbod Willems (Turnholti: Typographi Brepols Editores Pontificii, 1954), 12, 25ff.; Friedrich Kaulbach, *Einführung in die Metaphysik* (Darmstadt: Wissenschaftliche Buchgesellschaft, 1972), 69ff. In his *Einführung* Kaulbach explains this and other Augustinian interpretations of the Exodus as laying the foundation for a Christian metaphysics. See also Rudolf Berlinger, "Der Name Sein: Prolegomena zu Augustins Exodus-Metaphysik," *Wirklichkeit der Mitte, Festgabe für A. Vetter* (Freiburg/Munich: Alber, 1968), quoted in *Einführung*, 70, n3. The antithesis to this metaphysics is the contemporary Jewish theology of the Exodus, which with similarly unmistakable metaphysical elements, retains a total view of Being as History. See A. H. Friedlander, "Die Exodus-Tradition. Geschichte und Heilsgeschichte aus jüdischer Sicht," in *Exodus und Kreuz im ökumenischen Dialog zwischen Juden und Christen*, eds. Hans Hermann Henrix and Martin Stöhr (Aachen: Einhard, 1978), 30–44.

American Black Churches identify their own fate with the early history of Israel.

Recently, however, the signal word "Exodus" has suddenly been heard from all sides of the theological scene. Exodus is becoming a leading motif in Christian theology, especially in a type of ethics that understands itself (with numerous variations) as a "Theology of Exodus." The Exodus story appears here as a prototype for the emergence of believers in the world. The Gospel is now the message of liberation *par excellence,* directed to all the oppressed, and to all people who, although seen as oppressed in different respects, are unaware of their condition. With the Exodus principle there appears a new, universal understanding of the history of God with humanity which interprets this history as a process of liberation. Compared with the two examples from the early church already mentioned, such an interpretation appears to be that of a "salvation history," in the ethically enlightened sense of "history." On examining this view more closely, we have to ask whether allegorizing has been employed: that is, has one theological meaning-complex been transposed onto another level of understanding? This question will lead us to the discussion of several major problems of theological hermeneutics and ethics. How can total views of reality be obtained with the help of biblical images? How can situations be interpreted and ethically illuminated in terms of such pictures?

Biblicism and allegorizing have something in common, at any rate today: namely, they take up isolated biblical texts or concepts which represent condensation of traditions and imaginatively "translate" them without regard for the biblical/theological context of the statements at issue. For this reason, we want first of all to deal with the unusually tension-filled stream of tradition which introduces us to "exodus" and "liberation" as biblical metaphors. By "metaphorical" I mean, provisionally, a manner of discourse that allows a genuine and unified state of affairs to be expressed again in language but under different historical circumstances.

"Liberation"—A Theological Metaphor for "Exodus"?

In the Old Testament we learn about the Exodus particularly from the Commandments laying down and stressing Yahweh's exclusive claim (e.g., in the introduction to the Decalogue, Exodus 20:2ff. or in Judges 6:8ff.), and from laments that invoke God as liberator of the people from their enemies (e.g., Psalm 74, esp. 12ff.). Only once (Deuteronomy 12:9) are God's wandering people addressed. They have "not yet come to the place of rest." However, one can hardly read a perpetual journeying out of this, even though the Deuteronomist admonishes later generations not to regard themselves as already having arrived. There are thus no grounds for speaking of a monotonous "Exodus-principle" which causes a wholesome restlessness but at the same time involves the stress of continuously setting out and making transitions.

As a rule, there are four elements that are referred to in the memory of the Exodus: the leaving of Egypt; God, who leads His people out of menace; the way of testing and preservation; the promised land. Taken together, these elements characterize "exodus" as a metaphor, as distinct from other memories of liberation experiences[5] and from memories of Israel's election at the beginning of her history.[6] In this comprehensive sense, the Exodus becomes the core of the old confessional form which Gerhard von Rad has named "the small historical creed" (Deuteronomy 26:5b–9).[7] It speaks of Israel's time as a stranger in Egypt, of her becoming a people, of her helpless lament in tribulation, and of the miraculous deliverance and the gift of life, the Promised Land.

How does this rather complex statement relate to the short formula, "Yahweh, the God, who led us (Israel) out of Egypt," which is encountered in the most varied contexts even up until the time of Daniel (cf. Daniel 9:15)? Martin Noth regards this as a statement of the "primal creed of Israel" and assumes that the whole Pentateuchal tradition developed out of it.[8] I cannot discuss this reconstruction of the tradition-history in detail here, a reconstruction that has been strongly contested once again recently. (In order to assess its theo-

---

5. For example, Genesis 15:14, where the Exodus is portrayed as a judgment on Egypt that ends with the departure of an Israel richly laden with presents. In Exodus 14:5, there is the comment that Israel simply "had slipped away."
6. Especially noteworthy is the indication of Yahweh's having "found" Israel in the wilderness (Hosea 9:10, perhaps also Jeremiah 31:2f.); see Robert Bach, *Die Erwählung in der Wüste*, Theological Dissertation (Bonn: University of Bonn, 1952).
7. Gerhard von Rad, "Das formgeschichtliche Problem des Hexateuch" (1938), in idem, *Gesammelte Studien zum Alten Testament*, 3rd ed. (Munich: Chr. Kaiser, 1965), 11ff.
8. Martin Noth, *Überlieferungsgeschichte des Pentateuch*, 3rd ed. (Stuttgart: Kohlhammer, 1966), 50–54.

logical significance one must consider not only the problems of dating and the long-standing predominant questions of form criticism concerning the *"Sitz im Leben"* of these traditions but also the function of the narrative in the formation of the tradition.) We must ask what was really being said when the Exodus was spoken about. How is God spoken about when the Exodus is remembered? It is not enough to answer that a miraculous act once took place, in the remembrance of which "Israel" assembles again and again and on grounds of which she can continue to respond to "her God." This is because the further question must be asked as to the real basis of the constitution of this Israel which calls on God and speaks of Him as her Savior. The narratives that have been collected mainly in the book of Exodus, and just because these "narrate," speak differently about the way Israel is constituted than the hymnic references in the Psalms and elsewhere to salvation, liberation, and redemption out of Egypt.[9] Again, the prophetic language about the Exodus and the time of wandering in the wilderness also differs from this.[10] First, I will attempt to sketch the thematic differences and the shifting emphases in these groups of texts.

The stories of the Exodus depict the life-crisis of the forefathers both in Egypt and on their way to the Promised Land. The forefathers were not only helpless nomads who once had to pay for their physical survival in times of extreme need by suffering immeasurable oppression. Under slavery they not only lost control over their own labor and the fate of their children but also all feeling for the risk of a life's responsibility to itself. They lost their spirit of adventure; they vacillated between self-pity and rebellion. Scarcely were they rescued and risking their first step into freedom, surrounded by the danger of an unknown way, when they began to long to return to the fleshpots of Egypt, that is, to live in security even at the price of dependency. It took many detours and trials before Israel became acquainted with the foundations of her life. Israel had to be taught to trust completely in the guidance of her God and to acknowledge

9. Gerhard von Rad, *Theologie des Alten Testaments*, vol. I (Munich: Chr. Kaiser, 1957), 179f.

10. Walther Zimmerli, "Der neue Exodus" (1960), in idem, *Gottes Offenbarung* (Munich: Chr. Kaiser, 1963), 192–203; cf. also Zimmerli's exegesis of Ezekiel 37 in BK.AT, vol. XIII (Neukirchen: Neukirchener Verlag, 1969).

Him not just as her benefactor but as her Lord, one who grants His people the necessities of life.

Exodus does not only mean the deliverance from bondage. It is also the story of the salvation that comes from being guided and tested. Exodus is certainly the breaking of fetters and the giving up of a secure life which has become a prison. However, Exodus is not the transition from a situation which has become alien into a new status, into a *status viatoris*, into a life of perpetual wandering. On the contrary, the meaning of life given by God and in His presence is decided on the way to the Promised Land. For this reason the departure from the land of bondage is the first step in the history of God with His people. This is a step that *can never* be repeated because it must not be repeated, since everything depends on *remaining* on the way of the promise. Therefore, Exodus is not allowed to become a paraphrase for a change of situation[11] such as the grasping of a freedom which would be dialectically opposed to a condition of subjugation.

That the exodus metaphor is not limited to liberation from slavery can be forcefully gathered from the message of the exile prophets Ezekiel and Deutero-Isaiah about the new Exodus (Ezekiel 20:32–44; Isaiah 43:14–21; 48:20–22; 52:9–12). Both prophets speak to the remnant of a people who have been enslaved again. This decimated Israel is also supposed to be "led out." But no more than the old Exodus does the new Exodus merely terminate a situation of imprisonment. On the contrary, it is indeed no longer quite so easy to see whether the exiles in Babylon regarded their deportation as subjugation, even though they certainly complained bitterly about their separation from their homeland. Religious assimilation appears more likely to have become a danger for them. For this reason, as Ezekiel made known, Yahweh wants to lead His people once again into the wilderness, in order to speak and debate with them di-

---

11. Ernst Käsemann obviously understands it in this way when he writes concerning Romans 4:17 that hope is "the exodus out of the realm of the calculable into the horizons of a future lived under the saving will of God and opened up by his word." See idem, *An die Römer*, 3rd ed. (Tübingen: J.C.B. Mohr, 1974), 117. A modern variant of the idea of the *status viatoris* is heard when Eberhard Jüngel calls man a "creature of chance." "As a creature of chance he is simultaneously worldly and spiritual, whereby his spiritual existence is no duplication of his worldly existence, but is precisely a *being-underway-in-the-world*, which follows the word of God, an eschatological journeying which makes him first and foremost an historical being." The quote is from Eberhard Jüngel, *Zur Freiheit eines Christenmenschen* (Munich: Chr. Kaiser, 1978), 83.

rectly, "face to face" (Ezekiel 20:35). The Exodus is determined by the goal lying at the end of the way and thus *not* by what it has left behind. God will reveal Himself as the living God who gives the dead new life. As in earlier times, it is the wilderness where God wants to meet His people, because there they cannot confuse His miraculous gift of life with anything else. As the place of dread, moreover, the wilderness is where the distraction of rendering homage to other deities comes to nothing. The Exodus, understood as a short formula for the saving activity of God, continues to refer to the passage through the wilderness, the place of God's disclosure. Ezekiel proclaims judgment upon belief and unbelief, a "sifting" of the people, for the new time of wandering through the wilderness. Deutero-Isaiah speaks about the disclosure of God's glory in the wilderness (Isaiah 40:3–5). Both prophets, however, no longer speak of a new conquest of the land but instead of the return to the homeland.

The third complex of statements, the hymns of deliverance, liberation, and redemption, cannot be reduced to a common denominator. Occasionally, one gets the impression that the Exodus out of Egypt may have been used as an established formula to describe the conquest of every desperate situation in which the pious man, or the community of faith, has become helpless and is in danger of falling into the hands of a foreign power. In such reminiscences, the liberation from slavery frequently takes second place to the miracle of the Red Sea, in which deliverance from the enemy's hands took place. There, however, it is not now so much a matter of overcoming foreign domination as of warding off the pursuers who harass Israel and want to overrun her. The view of the history of the Fathers thus links up with the mythology of deliverance from the grasp of chaos. The sea which barred Israel's passage and then swallowed up her pursuers, takes on the same meaning as the primal sea from which God's act wrested the creation.[12] What has taken place in this combination of motifs? Was the historical act of liberation by Yahweh to be extended beyond history and into prehistoric times in order finally to identify exodus and creation?[13] Which of the two events was then "explained" by the other? It seems to me that one does not get very far with such attempts at interpretation. One presupposes thereby that an archetypal event can be localized, perhaps in terms

12. G. von Rad, *Theologie*, vol. I, 179.
13. Ibid., 180.

of salvation history, or transhistorically, mythologically. This event would then repeat itself, or man would have to enter into it repeatedly and afresh.[14] But does the Old Testament talk about and recount its story like this? When those who were praying gratefully remember the deliverance from their enemy's hand, they speak of God in a particular way. They invoke God as the liberator, because they know what "liberation" is and, as a result, long to experience it once again. In some hymns God is no longer addressed only as the "deliverer of Israel" but also as the creator of the whole world, who guards this world against Chaos. God does this in such a way that He permits something relating to the whole of reality to happen to a part of reality (and His people have to see themselves as this part) and thus brings about His universal salvation.

We can see then that "liberation" is much too vague a word to be able to become a theological metaphor. Liberation is ambiguous; the conceptions of it can all too easily arise from abstractions of experiences which one perceives as changes in one's situation. Israel has experienced what "becoming free" means in the Exodus. On that occasion she experienced God as liberator. Whenever Israel speaks of the Exodus from now on, she does so in order to expect God as the one with whom she has become acquainted, and in order to deepen this hope through the experiences in which she encounters God as liberator—although not without disappointing misleading expectations and destroying idealized pictures. Nevertheless, the exodus metaphor has been shown to be complex enough to prevent the emergence of conceptions that are too rigid.

The association of the Exodus metaphor with other metaphors was also helpful, since these metaphors were no longer necessarily tied to the history of the Exodus from Egypt. However, they could capture the situation created through God's guidance through life and His preservation of life. Above all, the metaphor of *space* must be mentioned here. It stems from the experience of nomadic life but did not disappear together with it. The Psalmist praises God, who has "set" his foot "in a broad place" (Psalm 31:8; cf. 18:19, 36; II Samuel 22:37; Isaiah 49:20). At his call to become the bearer of blessings, Abraham is "led out" of his tent, so that he could look at

---

14. See, for example, Thomas Mann's portrayal in *Joseph und seine Brüder* of the circular repetition of the life-creating situations in the mythical anamnesis of the generations. Cf. esp. the chapter "Abraham."

the vastness of God's world. This step into freedom shattered the fetters of his hopeless self-reflection (Genesis 15:5). And is it not also a type of exodus, leading first of all out of a prison but belonging to the way of the Gospel, when Peter leaves first his prison, but then also his home, in order to take another step as a disciple of Jesus (Acts 12:7ff.)?

Liberation in the New Testament

As we turn now to the New Testament, we notice that the entire tradition-complex of the Exodus, the deliverance from the hands of one's enemies, the wandering in the wilderness, and the Conquest are almost entirely absent except for the brief paraphrase in Hebrews, where the Exodus is placed in the context of the Old Covenant testimonies of faith (11:27–29). But it is especially noteworthy to see how the Exodus is treated here. It is mentioned as a prophecy of Joseph's (v. 22); then we hear, however, that "In faith Moses left (κατέλιπεν) Egypt . . . " (v. 27). The Exodus concept also denotes Abraham's way of faith (11:8) and then, above all, the way of God's new people to the place of Jesus' crucifixion (13:13)—a new definition of the place where faith is to be lived! The allusions to the Exodus of Israel in the context of the theological explanation of the sacrament of baptism (I Corinthians 10:1ff.) and the Lord's Supper (the Passah-Haggadah) should also be mentioned. At the Lord's Supper there is a new way of speaking both of God's gift of life and of the time of salvation. The liturgy of the Lord's Supper is also characterized by the central assertion of the Passah-Haggadah—"We are free, and this can be seen in what we are doing and how we are thus placing ourselves at the side of our fathers who are ready to depart." Is it the old freedom that is being experienced here, or has another, a new liberation, been experienced? Or is the Exodus once again being comprehensively interpreted, as in the Old Testament hymns, so that the powers of sin and death from which the Lordship of Christ liberates have taken the place of the historical tyrants?

Up to this point we have observed that the Exodus metaphor cannot be defined by means of the dialectic between freedom and slavery. In that dialectic, freedom would be understood as the conquest of circumstances forced upon one. That would have meant one had to begin with the oppression that could be experienced, in order to be able to become aware of freedom. If this held good for the Old Testament, it would be even more true for New Testament discourse about Jesus Christ, the liberator. Conversely, one could almost say that only in the light of his act of liberation does the servitude in which we live become visible. But this is not developed by means of such a dialectic of freedom and bondage. Revealing and determinative is rather Paul's line of argument: "For freedom Christ has set us free; therefore, do not submit again to a yoke of slavery" (Galatians 5:1).

Here Paul uses the state of liberation as his point of departure and, on the basis of the freedom thus created, distinguishes the state of freedom from the threatening subjugation, the foreign yoke. The freedom granted makes it possible to make such a distinction and thereby define the limits of "freedom." Freedom is not some indeterminate thing; it is also not formless, as it is for us today when freedom is customarily interpreted as an unlimited self-determination that always receives its concrete form anew from within, from the free subject, in the struggle with what is humanly possible. The English language has a conceptual distinction at its disposal which provides additional help in understanding what takes place here. It uses "freedom" to designate the indeterminate kind of freedom which grows out of radical human self-determination in contrast to "liberty," which is concrete, determinate freedom.[15] Only this freedom can become the theme of ethics, because the problem of an ethics of freedom is the boundaries within which the acting subject can be limited by no other factor, whereby this "field of action" remains related to limitations by which it has to be measured. Liberty implies what can take place with reference to others, without being determined by this possibility. So liberty is to be understood, anthropologically and ethically, not by means of the antithesis of self-determination and determination by others, but as a definite realm for possibilities of decision and action. This understanding contrasts with a mode of acting that suggests autonomy whereas one is in fact subject to a subtle determination. Subjugation under a foreign will can commend itself precisely in that one hopes, by participating in a world-pervading power, a universal will, or in a destined context of meaning, one hopes to gain a more comprehensive view of life that promises to explain the meaning of one's own life and its fulfillment. Whoever inquires in this way about the "Kingdom of Free-

---

15. See, for example, *The Concise Oxford Dictionary*, 6th ed., s.v. "freedom" and "liberty."

dom"[16] will always dialectically relate it to the "Kingdom of Necessity," in order to explore the dialectical relationship between world and self and to subject the impenetrable or other-determined conditions in the world to one's own self-conscious decision.

The Pauline distinction between freedom and bondage, however, does not correspond to the insight into this dialectic, which itself wants to be understood as an achievement of that freedom of thought which manifests itself in the grasping of relationships. The distinction between freedom and bondage originates rather in the fact of freedom's *being granted*, a freedom which shows up the concrete oppositions in the experienced world. It is not a question of what might be possible if this or that were attained or carried through. What is supposed to be discerned is what was made possible and what contradicts and excludes something else. This understanding is not the same as the perception of the boundaries of freedom and the defense of a boundless freedom. This understanding says what exists over against that which, on the basis of the freedom granted, does not exist and therefore has no power over man. It does gain power over him, however, in the very instant this man relinquishes his freedom. There are, therefore, two elements in this understanding of concrete freedom. There is the affirmation of the liberation which compels one to characterize freedom's opposite and thereby virtually to state its boundaries. Intimately and indissolubly bound to the affirmation of liberation is also the overcoming of the erroneous view that freedom is definable only in act or process, depending on the extent to which the acting subject can assert himself in relation to the determining conditions of his world (including that of an alien will, however this manifests itself). The knowledge of freedom as the basis of every decision and every act does not consist in carefully considering the power relationships between myself and the total of the other or others, but in making use of the space I have received in which to live. In what way can one speak of this particular freedom? Galatians 5:1a is an example of what Martin Luther called "assertion-language." This *assertio* is a direct way of speaking in that it "dispenses with methodical confirmation, because every such confirmation would add nothing to what is being said, but

16. For the history of the concept, see Ludger Oeing-Hanhoff, "Das Reich der Freiheit als absoluter Endzweck der Welt: Tübinger und weitere Perspektiven," in *Freiheit*, ed. Josef Simon (Freiburg & Munich: Alber, 1977), 55–83.

would be redundant in relation to it (i.e., it would surround what was spoken only with other expressions, without being able thereby to ascertain and elucidate its content)."[17] Assertion-language consists to this degree of complete, self-contained statements.

Disclosing Specific Experiences

Did Paul mean by his declaration of freedom something other than the Old Testament confession "God liberates" or the prophetic announcement of the new Exodus? Or did he merely say afresh what they had already said and refer it to the liberation which took place through Jesus Christ? In order to answer this question, it is not sufficient to make comparisons of different occurrences of the freedom motif within the tradition-history, thus tracing the later understanding of freedom back to the earlier and, where applicable, setting the limits of the later by means of the earlier. We must, rather, consider more precisely what is taking place when God is said to be the liberator of Israel as well as what is happening in the other statements under consideration and in the Pauline language.

In Egypt, Israel had become acquainted with Yahweh as a liberator. That is what the traditional Exodus declaration says. At the Red Sea and in the wilderness, Israel had first experienced God as liberator. This kind of "God-talk" had proved its validity. Now when God continues to be confessed as liberator, this depends alone upon the fact that one may reasonably expect God to be a liberator. The Exodus metaphor is employed in view of the new act of God and only to this extent can it speak afresh of "exodus" and "liberation." The use of these metaphors, therefore, does not depend upon situations (in this case, upon experiences of bondage and its conquest) that can be repeated at different times but represent certain uniform conditions as a point of departure. Just as one can not depend on God *because* one perceives some particular condition in life as repressive, one can not speak of an exodus *because* one perceives some fetter or other has been broken. The Exodus out of Egypt does not simply repeat itself in different circumstances. Rather, the expectation of God

17. Gerhard Sauter, *Wissenschaftstheoretische Kritik der Theologie: Die Theologie und die neuere wissenschaftstheoretische Diskussion. Materialien—Analysen—Entwürfe* (Munich: Chr. Kaiser, 1973), 272; cf. idem, "Dogma—ein eschatologischer Begriff" (1966), in idem, *Erwartung und Erfahrung. Predigten, Aufsätze und Vorträge* (Munich: Chr. Kaiser, 1972), 42ff.

as liberator is fulfilled in such a way that individuals become acquainted afresh with the way in which the bondage that threatens or has threatened them consists of separation from God's promised community. The introduction and the employment of the Exodus metaphor tells how we come to experience God. The statement "God liberates" contradicts the view that freedom may be obtained through becoming sure of oneself. In another situation the statement may reveal previously granted freedom or expose self-deception in the distinction between freedom and bondage. "God liberates" will, above all, convey a freedom that is granted in no other way than in its being spoken. As Paul's linguistic practice shows, certain experiences of freedom are disclosed by uttering the metaphor. (It is not that freedom is produced, but that one avails oneself of the freedom which is given by God and defined by His opposition, i.e., "freedom from the law.")

All these ways of application, however, are based on the metaphor that was introduced as their valid basis. But this introduction cannot be fixed to a historically unique situation (quite apart from the difficulties of making such a statement about traditions whose origin for us, in many respects, lies in darkness). The use of the metaphor, therefore, is not the repetition of the originally discovered meaning of a word.[18] The validity of this way of talking simply does not depend on the fact that an original situation is regularly repeated in some form. It is based rather on knowledge of God. God has shown Himself to be the God one is able to call upon from now on, because He has promised Himself as the God He is and will be. The possibility of speaking about "Exodus" and "liberation," therefore, rests upon the expectation of God based on this event, an expectation that aims at knowledge and experience of God. Nevertheless, the possibility does not refer to the human capacity to speak repeatedly, anew, and creatively of "freedom." Nor does it refer to the capacity to experience how this mode of discourse succeeds, that is, in view of the reality which is thus grasped, as well as in view of other individuals, who acknowledge this linguistic disclosure of reality.

I will now define further these linguistic theories and hermeneutical considerations about metaphorical discourse by comparing them

18. For the distinction between "the situation where language is introduced" and "the situation where language is used" see Kuno Lorenz, "Der dialogische Wahrheitsbegriff," Neue Hefte für *Philosophie* 2/3 (1972): 111–123.

critically with analogies and allegorical interpretations. The concept of analogy, as it is often used today in connection with historical theology and ethics, has two levels: First, by "analogy" one means the correspondence between historical events in their similarity which also allows the detection of a diversity. By demonstrating the analogies, the notion of a historical continuum arises, on which not only are typical situations constantly recurring, but also, on closer examination, temporally and objectively different events can be seen as comparable, for otherwise they could not become known at all. Analogy, therefore, is an historical epistemological principle.[19]

Second, analogy is a principle for speaking of God. Who God is and how God acts can only be said in words which "correspond" to that which we also say about individuals and their history by means of these words. Here, too, "correspondence" does not simply mean similarity, but comparability. God's act and man's act indeed remain "substantially" different, but they are not unrelated to one another, for otherwise the work of God could not be recognized and articulated.[20]

This dual principle raises a great many theological, linguistic, and epistemological questions which cannot be discussed here.[21] For the present the key issue is that the predominant trend in the practice of interpretation has become that of obtaining analogies through the synoptic view of different processes which are reduced to the common denominator of a situation or action. This common denominator for "Exodus" and "liberation" is the experience of independence from the previously existing conditions of one's life, the release from the fetters that kept responsible action from developing. Redemption appears as emancipation, and in this regard many incidents of the past and the present seem to "correspond" whenever (in spite of all

19. Ernst Troeltsch used the concept of analogy in this sense in his discussion of methods in the science of history. See his "Über historische und dogmatische Methode in der Theologie" (1898), in *Theologie als Wissenschaft*, ed. Gerhard Sauter (Munich: Chr. Kaiser, 1971), 107ff. Wolfhart Pannenberg has taken up this view and modified it in "Heilsgeschehen und Geschichte," in his *Grundfragen systematischer Theologie*, vol. I (Göttingen: Vandenhoeck & Ruprecht, 1967), 22–78, 46ff.

20. Karl Barth has called special attention to this in his interpretations of analogy. See Joachim Track, "Analogie," *Theologische Realenzyklopädie*, vol. II (Berlin/New York: de Gruyter, 1978), esp. 640ff.

21. See the synopsis in Track, "Analogie" and Wolfgang Kluxen, "Analogie," *Historisches Wörterbuch der Philosophie*, vol. I (Basel/Stuttgart: Schwabe & Co., 1971), 214–227.

historical and other differences) the transition from a condition of bondage into a life of self-determination occurs. Seen from this point of comparison, numerous events and trends in history appear uniform in that they repeat the same structure. Above all, such a point of comparison grapples with the conditions and possibilities of human acts, histories and traditions and interprets them in such a way that the interpreter discovers in them his own problems of action and the questions of his contemporaries.

This interplay between the understanding of the present and historical understanding is, to be sure, a characteristic of every hermeneutic of history. However, in our case, history is also stylized into a sequence of analogous situations. Something like this can be seen particularly clearly in the prevailing exegesis of biblical narratives within the church. They are reduced to structurally invariable features, which one believes can be recognized in the present. To resolve them in this way, one hardly ever examines the extent to which unsolved problems of the present are reflected back into the past. The analogy is now based on a methodical reduction, one that makes possible the simultaneous exposition of tradition and the interpretation of some contemporary situation. Each contemporary and historical situation becomes a virtually repeatable unit of action. The perception, then, coincides with the repetition of already discovered possibilities of action. "Interpretation" and "praxis" appear to stand here in striking accord.

This practice of exposition takes itself to be a continuation of the historical-critical interpretation of text and reality. In fact, however, it is very close to a way of understanding from which Christian biblical exegesis has freed itself only after a hard struggle, and to which the historical-critical method has long considered itself superior, namely, allegorizing. In the allegorical understanding of a text, units of meaning defined by the textual context are transferred to another level of meaning. The reality which is represented in the text is duplicated through the interpretation of particular words or statements. As examples of such allegories one could take the previously mentioned interpretation of the Exodus by Melito, who sees Good Friday foreshadowed in the Exodus and finds the "truth" of Old Testament history stated in the history of Christ. There is also the Augustinian understanding of Exodus as a transition into the "state" of the life prepared by God. Here the impression arises that the concrete features of the Old Testament accounts have been overlooked in favor of a "timeless," transhistorical and symbolic content. The art of paying careful attention to the literal sense of the text, that is, to what the text says in plain words and without additional aids for understanding, has apparently been replaced by the arbitrariness of an imagination which believes it can discover comparisons in all dimensions of reality.

However, is this really hermeneutical arbitrariness, or does this arbitrariness not appear much more in other principles of interpretation? It is again time to ask this question and yet not to answer it with the criticism which has been developed during the history of biblical exegesis, especially in the hermeneutics of the reformers and in the development of the historical-critical method. Indeed, it has long been clear that precisely in the appeal to a supposedly unequivocal, because historically ascertainable, meaning of Scripture, a lot of extraneous interpretations are offered. The classification of the meaning of Scripture in terms of different levels of understanding (as Luther saw in his confrontation with the fourfold meaning of Scripture) is theologically problematic, not because a multiple dimensionality of understanding arises but because a text's theological content of meaning is transposed into possibilities of interpretation that no longer express theological insights but only express the many-sided explanatory activities of the interpreter. Once the levels of understanding have been established, everything is permitted within that framework. Accordingly, although the reformers' rejection of allegory was not intended to curtail the hermeneutic imagination, it exposed itself to the question that an *interpretatio christiana* has always included. Is a text to be taken as God's communication to humankind? Does it understand itself as divine speech? Or does the interpreter explain by means of arbitrarily chosen texts the reality which he has already categorized in advance?[22]

Therefore a mode of interpretation is to be called into question that considers only socio-historical causes and effects as explanatory arguments. Thereby reality would be reduced to these conditions. Certainly, hopelessness in our history and expectations of salvation are apparent everywhere and to a previously unknown extent. But

22. Wolfgang Raddatz, Gerhard Sauter, and Hans G. Ulrich, "Verstehen," in *Praktisch- theologisches Handbuch*, ed. Gert Otto, 2nd ed. (Hamburg: Furche, 1975), 602–633, esp. 609f.

that cannot be the reason why the stylization of biblical texts into uniform, repeatable situations (in our case, under absolute domination of a principle of liberation) is so dramatic and confusing. On the contrary, hermeneutical arbitrariness begins where one believes that one knows history from the outset and where the interpretation of biblical texts serves only as an additional legitimation that retrospectively baptizes this pre-understanding.

Can the analysis and application of metaphors help avoid such arbitrariness? In my opinion, this only succeeds when, in the understanding of metaphorical discourse, we do not cover up the unsettled problems left over after the criticism of allegorizing. Even metaphor transfers meaning. This transfer is not only from one historical situation to another but also between different levels of meaning or dimensions of reality. Precisely because of its fruitful semantic nonclarity (in contrast to a defined concept), a metaphor shows that the words which we use in everyday discourse "mean" more than they usually imply. To this extent, there is no fundamental difference between allegory and metaphor. Traditional allegorizing was a threat to faith because it postulated a specific level of understanding (in theology this was both spiritual and transhistorical), that assumed as given a self-contained and established world of meaning. In contrast, the theological problem of metaphorical discourse consists first of the fact that this way of speaking undertakes to extend language: words which are familiar to us simply assume a variety of meanings. Second, one sees the creative character of human discourse appear in an original way. This is the reason why so many philosophers of language and theologians are presently interested in metaphors, because here the linguistic disposition of man in relation to reality as a whole can be made understandable.[23]

23. Friedrich Nietzsche turned his attention to this problem when he called the "instinct to form metaphors" the "fundamental instinct of man" that gives rise to man's world through language (linguistic conventions). See Nietzsche's "Über Wahrheit und Lüge im aussermoralischen Sinne" (1873) in idem, *Werke*, vol. III, ed. Karl Schlechta (Darmstadt: Wissenschaftliche Buchgesellschaft, 1963), 319. Here Nietzsche sees the consequence of the death of God: there is nothing preceding language in reality. The background portrayed by Nietzsche should be given its full significance, when today—to some extent with reference to Nietzsche, but not as he meant it—the possibilities of metaphorical language as an extension of language and as an "enrichment of language" are being rediscovered. See Paul Ricoeur and Eberhard Jüngel, "Metapher: Zur Hermeneutik religiöser Sprache," *Evangelische Theologie*, Sonderheft (Munich: Chr. Kaiser, 1974); Eberhard Jüngel, *Zur Freiheit eines*

However, this understanding is precisely not the theologically justified intention of metaphorical discourse. For if one always sees a fresh and original view of humankind's relation to reality in the introduction and use of metaphors, then it is no longer possible to test the truth of this discourse. If one understands this discourse, and indeed all discourse, as fundamentally creative, then every proposition is always true, if it can be stated. That means actually, if it "gets across," if it is understood and achieves resonance. From a linguistic-theoretical point of view, the pragmatic dimension of language, its actual usage, is made absolute. If the pragmatic approach became the only valid one in theology, rhetoric would triumph over theological thought. But precisely because theology must preserve the consciousness that we do not have God's reality at our disposal when we use language: theology cannot engage in or limit itself to a supposedly creative discourse that easily conjures up reality. Rather, the theological endeavor must aim at clearly and unmistakably grasping—but not regimenting—the metaphors introduced by the experience of faith. Theological hermeneutics, therefore, should not allow itself to be limited to language-games, but must clarify what can be theologically said with metaphors in all their richness of relationships, and that means "pragmatically": to clarify what reasonable expectations are expressed by them.

Thus, the criterion for the theological effectiveness of metaphors is not their "originality," which enables them to say something surprisingly new with the rich associations of their words. Rather, metaphors must contribute to the passing of theological judgments upon the network of relationships encompassing our experiences and their linguistic representation. The possibility of applying a metaphor does not limit the perception of the mutiplicity of the possibilities of understanding. (In our example, the metaphor is that of God known as the One who leads people out and into a secure living space.) However, such a possibility does not allow "understanding" to be restricted to the creative discovery of meaning-relationships instead

---

Christenmenschen, 40–49. However, Hans Blumenberg takes up Nietzsche's linguistic and critical intention and encounters in the reconstruction of metaphors what can still be said, but cannot be any longer known and understood. See his *Paradigmen zu einer Metaphorologie* (Bonn: Bouvier, 1960), esp. 19f. In this discussion, the question of the limits of our language as the limits of our world has not yet been taken up. For contrast, see Paul M. van Buren, *The Edges of Language* (London: SCM Press, 1972).

of to a knowledge which is always a specific perception and, therefore, tied to some limited aspect. Understanding is determined by the metaphor's limited possibility of application. In the case of the Exodus metaphor, this is attained by means of the association with the metaphor of space.

The Exodus-Story as Political Allegory

Theological understanding and ethical judgment are equally threatened today by a combination of allegorizing and analogical constructions. As I have already said, analogies are created by stylizing a situation given in the tradition into a pattern of experience, in order to be able to adopt this model for other situations. In relating to one another in these situations the only thing establishing the correspondence is the pattern of experience that can be consistently discovered. The historical diversity of the situations may certainly be taken into consideration here, in order to avoid the impression of a complete uniformity. Such a construction of analogies is further extended by means of allegorizing. This becomes particularly obvious in the adoption of the biblical Exodus motif in political ethics. In this case, exodus as an *allegory* signifies the universal conquest of every alien rule as it is embodied in the most varied experiences of liberation. Allegorical interpretation does not take place, therefore, by extending the significance of traditional situations of liberation in such a way that other experiences of liberation are included, such as emancipation from the prevailing economic and distributive system. An allegory is always created when the "true meaning" of a linguistic expression is located on another level of meaning than is expressed by means of the introduction and application of these words. Allegorical interpretation means to break through linguistically characterized human experience and search out the deep or underlying meaning through which one can find the foundation of history, the world and reality as a whole. Picking up our theme again, we can understand "Exodus" and "liberation" allegorically, when we use these words to grasp the problem of the relationship between individuals and reality. All experiences of freedom should then point to this primary relationship.

Exodus as an allegory for radical liberation requires an historical basis, a standpoint from which all subsequent history can be explained. Such a connection is achieved through the *analogy* as I have described it above. Conversely, the transference of the Exodus event into new historical situations first acquires its religious profundity when allegorical interpretation is employed. The connection between allegorizing and the construction of analogies thus depends upon the conviction that, on the one hand, there is a continuity of meaning between past situations and the present and that, on the other hand, there is a correlation of meaning between God's actions and humanity's. Therefore, the once historically manifested will of God can be portrayed in human action. In God's actions there are always human possibilities entailed that can be unfolded by means of allegory.

Three examples from recent times will illustrate this connection between analogy and allegory, that is, biblical exegesis employed with the aim of a total ethical mobilization. Jürgen Moltmann speaks of the "Exodus church" as a new form of the Church.[24] This progressive formation of a community stands in contrast to the old ecclesiastical structures which have long since become institutionally rigid and no longer respond flexibly enough to the social and historical challenges of the present. However, the Exodus community is by no means a faith community which sets out to journey into an unknown territory in order to experience a new encounter with God.[25] Similarly, one cannot compare this community with a church propagating its faith, whose missionaries move out of a familiar religious and cultural environment in order to proclaim their message in an alien environment and to expose themselves there to the still unfamiliar acts of God. The Exodus community in Moltmann's view, rather, is a religious movement which does not derive its power from the preservation of the traditional faith, but which seeks to achieve harmony with the dynamic motivating forces of contemporary history. Moreover, the "exiles" place themselves at the head of these motivating forces and set history in motion by means of the anticipatory realization of a better future. Exodus means here something necessary for survival. A hope-filled humanity or the bearers of hope

24. Jürgen Moltmann, *The Theology of Hope* (New York: Harper & Row, 1967), 304f; cf. also idem, *The Church in the Power of the Spirit* (New York: Harper & Row, 1977), and idem, *Neuer Lebensstil: Schritte zur Gemeinde* (Munich: Chr. Kaiser, 1977).

25. In the history of the Church there have been three sects who have called themselves "exodus communities" because they were expecting the return of Christ at a certain place and wanted to start on their way to that place. See Hermann Stocks, "Exodusgemeinden," *Die Religion in Geschichte und Gegenwart*, vol. II, 3rd ed. (Tübingen: J.C.B. Mohr, 1958), 832.

are out of step with their own time; their present is dominated by the inertia of tradition, especially when the tradition is tied to institutions. These hope-bearers know about the coming God. "God" signifies the basis for their being out of step with the present world. The God of hope is to be found in the repeated experience of the conquest of history by its future, and nowhere else.

In Gustavo Gutiérrez' *Theology of Liberation*,[26] because they are under foreign domination, the exploited and oppressed classes of Latin America become the successors of Israel. This solidarity with Israel leads, therefore, directly into liberation. However, there is no God here who demands the freedom of His people from the tyrants. Rather, those summoned to Exodus represent that part of humanity which, by achieving its self-determination, becomes shapers of history. Individuals change into their own history the circumstances that, until now, have ruled over them.[27] Only those who take this step remain faithful to the Gospel; what is more, the Gospel testifies to them, and that means they alone have an historical future. In the Exodus, the hitherto experienced boundary between individuals and God is crossed over in God's community with humankind and in the brotherly solidarity of all human beings with one another. However, as Gutiérrez emphasizes, the danger is that in this process God will be forgotten.[28] But this can only be observed in that individuals do not universally take the step into the kingdom of brotherly freedom; they want to immortalize their present state and take the provisional for the whole. But whoever does not think universally and who entrenches him or herself in the particular betrays transcendence. That person never becomes acquainted with the absolute scope of the Exodus. Such a person would also misunderstand his or her freedom if what lies beyond the present remains infinitely and qualitatively different from the human experience of life.

Ernst Bloch plainly stated what is still not made plain by Moltmann and Gutiérrez because of biblical reminiscences.[29] No history of the guidance of God's people by God begins with the Exodus. Rather, the

---

26. Gustavo Gutiérrez, *A Theology of Liberation* (Maryknoll, NY: Orbis Books, 1973), 25ff., 88f., 145ff.

27. Ibid., 208: "True liberation will be the work of the oppressed themselves; in them, the Lord saves history."

28. Gutiérrez, *A Theology of Liberation*, 192.

29. Ernst Bloch, *Atheism in Christianity: The Religion of the Exodus and the Kingdom* (New York: Herder & Herder, 1972), esp. 84ff.

Exodus is a moment in the history of God Himself. The Exodus of Israel shows itself to be the theologically disguised surplus value of the historical giving of meaning and creating of salvation. What is meant by "the coming of God" in the Bible is deciphered in utopian consciousness as the integration of the world into the historical subject. The creative becoming, by means of which the historical subject finds itself, no longer needs to trust in guidance. Rather, it traces every event back to the one who establishes it, that is, to man himself. It is he who sees through the dialectic of the world and man, of necessity and freedom. This dialectical conflict is forced into a productive disclosure of meaning by negating that which is perceived as inadequate and obstructive. By calling upon God, individuals oppose the existing and prevailing world. They understand the dialectic of future and present, of new and old, in such a way that everything truly new is indeed startling and unfamiliar, but not unrelated to the hitherto familiar. Bloch's attempt to use the Exodus renounces every reform of existing historical reality. "God" expresses the essence of radical liberation from traditional norms, a liberation which nevertheless moves about in the world, in a world full of surprising possibilities of salvation.

God "is" Himself the Exodus event. The God of Abraham, Isaac, and Jacob moves out into the Exodus. Over against all further liberations, Israel's conquest of the land becomes unimportant (in which conquest, as the Biblical tradition says, the Exodus reaches fulfillment, and light is shed upon the time of wandering in the wilderness). Instead of this, it is decisive for Bloch that the nomads who left Egypt could only set foot in the "Promised Land" after a long and hard struggle. They had to wrest it from the inhabitants, had to conquer it again and again afresh with cunning and tricks, and had to defend it, except during short periods of peace. According to this view, the struggle for freedom does not cease with the conquest, but actually really begins at that point at which those who have become free accept responsibility for their freedom. This is not how the biblical tradition portrays it, however. To be sure, there is never any secret made of the fact that the promised land had to be captured or that great efforts would be required to maintain freedom in that land. As the prophets saw and said it, however, the threat to Israel's freedom came from those enticing voices in and around Israel, those who sought to remove God's people from the claims of their Creator and from His rule over the right to life. Israel was, and remained, endangered by the abandoning of that which had been the source of its life. This happened no less in the promised land than it had in the wilderness where Israel had not discerned the necessities of life, where she had longed to return to the "fleshpots of Egypt" and to exchange the summons to the community of God for the deceitful security of her former comfortable way of life. The grumbling of Israel, however, becomes for Bloch nothing less than a gesture of constant Exodus; discontent becomes the sign of hope.[30] And therefore, the God "Hope" and not the Creator of heaven and earth, the Lord of history, can be the ultimate authority for a theology of liberation. God is Himself Exodus; God in dialectical conflict with the existing world; the creative new in conflict with the existing old; God as the new in the historical future; certainly an innovating but also a created factor. The action of an individual who is destined for freedom can now only consist in repeating this conflict of God. Through this unanimity in action, that is anything but an acknowledgment of God the Father, the dialectic which has been understood is transferred into praxis. The discerned conflict is put into effect; this is to say it is translated back into theology: one places oneself on God's side and carries out the divine historical will.

Living in the Space of Granted Freedom

We see in these three examples of a religious-political interpretation of the Old Testament liberation story that either an ethical directive is derived directly from the talk about God or instructions for the formation of reality are reflected, as it were, back into the concept of God. Both are a short-circuiting of knowledge and of argumentation.

However, it is necessary to distinguish theologically between talk of God and ethical knowledge. This distinction is valid, not just because one has to distinguish between God and man and between God's actions and ours. (This could happen, for instance, by avoiding every identification of analogous circumstances.)[31] Rather, it is

30. Bloch, *Atheism in Christianity*, 16ff., 27ff.
31. In order to be able to derive ethical statements from dogmatics, Karl Barth and many of his followers understand the difference in the analogy under the catchword "a christological foundation of ethics." See my contribution to the discussion in my article "Was heisst 'christologische Begründung' christlichen Handelns heute?" *Evangelische Theologie* 35 (1975): 407–421.

decisive to utter the words "exodus" and "liberation" as an acclamation of God's promise of life and, in view of this, to make responsible ethical statements. These statements can only serve to outline the living space inaugurated through the promise, as limited possibilities of human action.[32]

It has been shown that the Exodus of Israel is characterized by Yahweh's creating a living space for His people and by His leading Israel into this living space. It is already like this in the wilderness and in all the experiences during the time of wandering in the wilderness when the promises of life seemed to be contradicted. Liberation does not take place, therefore, only between Israel and her foreign lords; it is not just a change in consciousness in Israel's self-understanding, not a transition from a feeling of impotence to one of self-confidence. *The Exodus consists rather in the guiding of Israel into the life promised to her.* Israel's freedom is defined by the living space that is granted and opened up to her; it remains freedom only within these limits. Israel is "granted freedom." Freedom is not explained by the lack of definiteness on the part of the subject which does not need to tolerate an objection when it is a matter of realizing itself, of gaining its own appropriate living space. The freedom of those who move or are led out cannot be understood in a dialectic relationship to "necessity," seen as the essence of the conditions of existence, to which liberated individuals must know themselves to be bound (only they are no longer powerlessly and blindly subject to them). The relationship of freedom is wholly undialectical; it is the living space granted by God. Freedom is given by God, can be taken away by God, and is culpably spoiled whenever individuals cover this living space with self-made or blindly accepted systems of obligations that they imagine give them security. The same holds true for God's people of the New Covenant, who move out to the place of the crucifixion (Hebrews 13:13). There they have their living space in which they are allowed to set foot in hope (cf. 11:39f.) but not to reside permanently (13:14). It is a place that cannot be grasped by any interpretation of meaning.

The living space, in which God has put us and in which we find ourselves when we are addressed as liberated people, is not a presupposition for our actions so that we would have to ask what actions

---

32. For this method of obtaining ethical statements, see my *Wissenschaftstheoretische Kritik der Theologie*, 317–321.

"correspond" to the previous actions of God. Ethical statements cannot be reached at all by way of such correspondences, which establish a principle of analogy between God's being and our world, between God's actions and ours, and express this correspondence equivocally (e.g., God liberates—we are supposed to duplicate this liberation in ourselves and in others). On the contrary, "living space" is a metaphor, associated with the exodus; it plainly prohibits a deduction of ethical statements as corresponding to the actions of God.[33] The living space, in which we stand or are placed, is the possibility of life granted to us. "Possibility" is thereby defined for theological ethics as that from which we are able to live and as what we can do. Possibility is therefore not something undefined, for example, in contrast to reality as that which has already happened or as that which is to be attained by realizing what is possible. Possibility is also not that which is open to our decisions (which in contrast to necessity requires our choice, the choice between possibilities).[34]

The possibility of our life being in God's hands is not one possibility among many. It is not something which first would become reality through our actions. It is something *which has been made possible for us.* That people can exempt themselves from exploiting this possibility of life is quite conceivable; but this would contradict what is possible for us, and as such would not be an enhancement but a denial of our ability to act. For that reason, one may neither put possibility before reality (this dominates in an ethically radicalized world view) nor

33. One hopes that the misinterpretation of this "living space" in terms of geographical-political ideology—the unfortunate results of which are in living memory—has been ruled out. The metaphor of space is discussed in modern theological ethics only by Dietrich Bonhoeffer, as far as I know. See his *Ethics*, ed. Eberhard Bethge (New York: Macmillan, 1955), 62ff., in which it is discussed, however, without reference to the problem of freedom. For a different approach, see Hans Joachim Iwand, *Nachgelassene Werke*, vol. IV: Gesetz und Evangelium, ed. Walter Kreck (Munich: Chr. Kaiser, 1964), 25. By means of the metaphor of space that element of passivity in the Exodus and liberation is expressed which Helmut Gollwitzer has strongly emphasized in different ways in his interpretation of Christian freedom. See, for example, his *Krummes Holz—aufrechter Gang* (Munich: Chr. Kaiser, 1970), 364f.

34. Karl Barth, on the other hand, spoke of "reality" in two senses: an onto-theological reality (the "reality of God") and reality from an ethical point of view ("realization"). This shifting use of language is also found in Bonhoeffer's *Ethics*. From this starting-point, three conceptions begin to clash with one another: possibility as what is not yet reality; possibility as the reality awaiting one's disposal (i.e., it is what can be realized); and possibility as a potency in reality (as distinct from reality and necessity). For ethics, this ambiguity is extremely confusing.

desire to derive possibilities out of reality (which can happen in very different and mutually contradictory ways). Theologically responsible discourse about ethical possibilities fundamentally challenges all ideas of action seen as actualization of things not yet real.

The ethical interpretation of Exodus can be, therefore, only as follows: to live in the space of granted freedom and not to abandon this space on one's own initiative. Precisely in view of the election of Israel and the election of the Christian community, this living space is not limited to the particularity of experiences of liberation. Living space is a promise for all human beings. That includes the fact that we may not deny this living space to any other person. Every form of bondage that denies this living space must be hindered. We are obliged to criticize the manifold forms of bondage under which individuals suffer today. But such criticism can be nothing other than the responsibility of granted freedom. It is not the creation of freedom through the appeal to a possible liberation or in the face of the utopian vision of a kingdom of freedom. The hopeless cry for liberation, evoked by the utopia of freedom and standing under an enormous burden of expectation, would shape new fetters for human action by its unfulfillable longings. Because of demands, which can be met by certain individuals for themselves at the cost of others, our action was in danger of becoming irredeemably paralyzed. Israel is supposed to have understood the command to be free differently. That is to say, all members of its own people who had fallen upon misfortune and become dependent, as well as foreigners, and not least, the animals, have been granted that right to life which is created by God and which guarantees living space for all.

Accordingly, theological ethics has to determine what space is that which falls to that share of our life's possibilities that should exist in freedom, that is, without objections alien to our calling. This freedom is not so limited by the conditions of existence that we find our standards in them, for that would mean we define our standard by that which we have wrested from our conditions of existence. The ethical task does not consist of transcending the conditions of existence which we do not control ourselves with a view to self-determination, but in accepting a life which is to be perceived as a life that has been granted to us.[35] This is why Martin Luther describes the at-

---

35. This is the difference between transcending as an incessant movement of life and the making of a transition as the entry into God's world.

titude of the man who is entangled in self-reflection and imagines himself to be free as that of the *homo incurvatus in seipsum*. This individual exhausts all the powers of his existence in theoretical and practical reflection on what he is for himself and on what stands in the way of this "being-for-himself." Only when this *circulus vitiosus* is broken is the individual led out into action, actions that will no longer have the sole purpose of self-affirmation. That is the promise of the freedom into which Exodus leads us. Not the least part of this kind of freedom is a form of exodus-discourse, an application of the metaphor which does not require a hermeneutical arbitrariness in order to point to God, but which proclaims the expectation of God and leads to experiences of God.

3

How Can Theology Derive from Experiences?

Problems with Tradition

Relating the biblical message and the dogmatic traditions to the historical "context" of the churches has been one of the main problems of European theology for over two centuries, arising from the crisis of church authority.[1] This crisis was itself the outcome of a particular conflict, the confrontation between scientific thought and church institutions during the Enlightenment. The underlying cause of the conflict was a realization that Biblical truth was no longer adequate for understanding and coming to terms with the modern world. Therefore there was an increasing suspicion that Biblical truth was something alien, a piece of the past whose relevance to the present could only be appreciated with considerable difficulty. This conflict involved many people in specific controversies between science and the ecclesiastical authorities. It not only set many problems for the theologians, involving them in a great deal of hard work, but also presented them with a creative challenge, compelling them to reflect as theologians on the problem of experiences. This conflict also compelled European theology to look more closely at the nature of "experience," that is, to strive to understand more precisely and an-

1. This chapter was originally delivered to a consultation of the World Council of Churches in 1974 at the Ecumenical Institute in Bossey (Switzerland) and first published in *Doing Theology Today*, ed. Choan-Seng Song (Madras, India: The Christian Literature Society, 1976), 70–89.

alytically individual and group experiences as they related to traditions, environments, and political situations.

As I see it, "continental" theology, both Catholic and Protestant, is still very deeply marked by this controversy even today, not only in terms of its themes but also, and even more so, in its methods. In more recent times, of course, it has been theologically impossible for Christian groups to escape the conflict by separating from each other and founding new churches on the basis of their different historical experiences. On the contrary, theologians have had to try again and again to overcome existing differences between Christian groups, and between the churches and their environment and by so doing to neutralize such conflicts, developing various patterns of theological thinking, and coping with the difficulties that arose by setting them in broader problem contexts. The relatively narrow area of shared life was exploited to the maximum and an intensive method of dealing with conflict was produced by classifying and systematizing conflict experiences. It was only possible to do this, of course, at the expense of countless generalizations and complicated guidelines.

Many European theologians today are forced to admit frankly that they no longer regard this inherited approach to the problem as an appropriate basis for meaningful ecumenical dialogue. We are increasingly reproached for being too abstract and complex in our thinking. These intellectual problems, it is said, can no longer deal with our contemporary range of experience. In a spirit of self-criticism we must go even further than these external critics do, and recognize that, even within the churches, this question of our traditions and how to surmount them which occupies so large a place in our theological work, is a truly existential question for only a limited group. Many Christians, indeed the majority of the people we know, are not seriously troubled by these questions at all. We can no longer expect fresh theological insights if we work on the assumption that the tradition is, in the first instance, something alien to our present time, something that needs hard work if it is to be connected to and translated into the present. Obviously this is still a problem for only a very small number of people, mainly for those who have to deal with the continuing influence of traditions in their daily life and above all, for those who find that their present religious experience is not in accord with the Christian tradition. Only to a very limited extent does the difference experienced between tradition and the present, the distinction between "then" and "now" which has so greatly influenced theological thinking in central Europe and in North America (but which to my knowledge has not been dominant in the Eastern Orthodox Church to the same degree), still do justice to the situation of the churches in the world today.

Revolution in Theology?

Unless I am mistaken, a different question is now coming into the center of discussion: the question of *how* our present situation is to be evaluated theologically and, above all, *who* can enunciate this appreciation in a form binding on the *oikumene*. Not that this question has yet been openly formulated. Perhaps it is still not sufficiently realized that this question underlies many of the difficulties and mutual misunderstandings in the dialogue. The first thing that was noticeable was that the "classic themes" of theology—the Christology of the church fathers, the meaning of doctrine in the individual churches, and the participation of humankind in the eternal being of God—receded into the background. There was much more talk and more heated discussion of recent political, social, and church conflicts, obviously calling for the attention and clarification of Christian theologians but which also affect theology itself and change its character. Many personal experiences were described not simply as illustrations of that which called for common theological reflection. These experiences acquired a credal character: "In those conflicts, in those experiences, God is present, there and nowhere else! If we wish to speak of God, we must repeat these experiences together!" In other words, the common knowledge of God is to be sought precisely there where our diversity is most apparent, that is, in our personal experiences of history. But will this search really bring us to shared experiences? Are we not compelled rather to select just a few outstanding experiences from a present which is still difficult to estimate? Do we first have to make a profession of these experiences in order to qualify as theologians? Do we have to commit ourselves to particular experiences in order to have a common future?

Interest in the "context" of theology (in the social and political nexus of which it forms a part) led to the question: how far does this context itself, instead of remaining external to theology, actually produce theology? In Africa, Latin America, and other areas of conflict in the world there are many Christian groups and churches in which this is not even a question anymore, where this is answered, confidently, in the affirmative. But what is the "ecumenical dimension" of such experiences and the theology nourished by them? I have two reasons for raising this question.

First, we are told of experiences in churches that operate in revolutionary contexts, experiences of conflict, experiences of suffering and disappointment, but also experiences of new freedom and independence, experiences that leave the rest of us no alternative but silent acceptance. Does this mean that there will soon be only two kinds of theologians left in the ecumenical movement: those who have experiences and formulate theology from them and the rest of us who listen to and try to enter sympathetically into such experiences?

Second, if ecumenical discussion is confined to experiences, referring only secondarily to the Bible and perhaps, marginally, to confessional doctrinal traditions, how is the theological significance of these experiences to be assessed? How are we to distill from historical experiences theological insights which are important not just to one theologian or group of Christians but to the whole Christian world family? How are we to avoid the danger that individual theologians may merely be describing their own biographical experience and making themselves the subject matter of theology?

In the first instance these questions arose for me out of the dialogue itself. But I am forced to the conclusion that even the formal difficulties attendant to the description and discussion of experiences can also have a direct theological significance. I therefore regard it as a matter of urgency to draw up strict *rules of dialogue* for ecumenical discussion, to facilitate a more fruitful theological discussion in the future, and to prevent any surreptitious transformation of problems of understanding, problems of psychology and communication, into theological problems. I should like now to make some suggestions about these rules of dialogue, stressing the fact that I cannot regard such rules as mere technical guidelines for dialogue but as actually decisive for the way we do theology.

Other Peoples' Experiences and Our Own

I begin with the fact that in recent discussions this concern with the context of theology and with the experiences that shape it and are the soil from which it grows, has concentrated chiefly on conflict experiences. These constitute quite a specific and restricted area of experience, namely that of emergency situations, ethical decisions, and political choices which, because of their dimension of choice, are immediately recognizable. Religious experiences are sought and expressed within these conflicts. Yet this means it is only possible to speak of God in situations in which we are confronted with inescapable choices, where lines of opposition have been formed, and where controversies are conducted. These are *original* experiences even if such lines of opposition existed and similar conflicts have been experienced in earlier periods of church history. They are new and first-hand experiences because in every such conflict the habitual has to be abandoned. Although fronts may have existed for a long time, although in every age there have been oppressors and oppressed, tyrants and sufferers, the experience of powerlessness and suffering or of victory over them will always be a new experience. The pressure for original religious experience, therefore, the insistence on direct knowledge of God, leads us to lines of opposition. These lines of opposition must be clearly recognizable. We therefore tend to seek the presence of God in the places where the unmistakable lines of opposition are marked out today, lines of opposition that are both ethical and political in character.

Such lines of opposition exist. A large part of the whole Christian family has been drawn into them, involuntarily or by conscious decision. Those who are not directly involved in such conflicts cannot ignore this fact. But where in fact do *they* stand? The answer is, most frequently, that the rest of us must identify ourselves with these experiences; only in this way can we participate in them. The *unity* of the Christian family must come about by *solidarity* and *participation*, and only then will agreement on theological conclusions be possible. This thesis may not yet have been propounded quite so consistently but it is surely presupposed in the fact that so many papers and speeches were devoted simply to a description of a specific, and quite limited, experience.

If this thesis were to predominate, the Christian family would, in future, inevitably split up into churches and groups: those who have experiences because they stand "in the front line" of history, that is, at the point where decisions are made in face of the contemporary political and ethical lines of opposition; and those who are at a different place and can therefore neither have nor formulate such experiences. What for some are original experiences, for others are *sec-*

ondhand experiences. I get the impression that many young Christians and theologians already think in this way, in Europe especially. They no longer believe they are in a position to elaborate experiences of their own and they search for original and unambiguous experiences in the lives of Christians elsewhere in the world. They wish to share these experiences, if not in practical ways then at least intellectually and spiritually, so to be themselves involved in the movement of God's history in our world. For the most part, these young Christians ignore the fact that there is no such thing as participation and solidarity at a distance. They do not see that what they are doing instead is projecting their own personal problems and the difficulties of their churches and their theologies onto these distant fields of conflict in the hope of achieving a solution to their own difficulties. It is for these reasons and with this hope that many of my students interest themselves in the problems experienced by churches living under revolutionary conditions in the Third World. The more intense their hope of thereby importing a "concrete theology," the blinder they are to the real connection between many of the intellectual and spiritual problems of the Third World churches and the political and intellectual conflicts of Europe and North America in recent decades and centuries. Many specifically European experiences today form part of the intellectual background of revolutionary theologies—for example, the criticism of religion by atheistic humanism. Who exported something and who imported it can only be established by a careful study of specific cases. Therefore we must try to formulate experiences that are real and authentic without, however, adopting stereotyped formulas devised to make it easier for people to find their way in our complex world.

It would also be better, therefore, not to speak too glibly of "solidarity." Not that solidarity is not an important and vital part of Christian faith. Clearly there is a proper sense in which Christians participate in "other people's" experience. Such participation rests on that representative experience of which Paul speaks (I Corinthians 4:10; II Corinthians 4:15; Colossians 1:24), the experience of suffering "for the sake of the brethren." Experiences of God in our world are never uniform. We do not all have the same experiences of God; nor therefore of the world or of ourselves. But the diversity of our experiences cannot and should not lead us to divide the Christian Church into one group of experienced and experiencing Christians, and another group of Christians lacking in experience. Nor is it anywhere laid down that the way to achieve unity of faith is by unqualified identification with the outstanding experiences of other individuals. All we can say is that solidarity, participation, and unity become a reality where the experiences of individuals lead to real knowledge of God, to God Himself, by whose presence alone unity is created in our world and people are drawn together. The ecumenical fellowship cannot be created by uniform experiences nor by a world-wide community based on experiences; but only by the knowledge of the ongoing divine history derived from experiences, for this not only transcends each individual experience but also alone makes its theological significance intelligible. This is the only way to avoid equating God's activity in our world with the lines of opposition within our historical situation—with the creation of such fronts, for these are always, in one way or another, human-made and human-defined. Christian prophecy, pointing to God's work in our world and indicating the prospects of decisions for the future cannot, of course, steer clear of these conflicts. But it would certainly be no authentic Word of God if it limited itself to this, if it devoted all its energies simply to retracing and reinforcing existing lines of opposition by giving them a strongly theological tinge. The secret and the authority of Christian prophecy consists precisely in the fact that it distinguishes the spirits, that is, that it is authorized by God to examine and test the lines of confrontation which we as human beings connect with our conceptions and distinctions of evil and good. When we connect conflicts with the question about God, about His will, His good and evil, the result may be not only to intensify such conflicts but also to overcome them.

This gives us our *first rule for the theological dialogue about experiences*: Experiences can only be communicated in a theologically meaningful way if at the same time we make clear their significance for the whole Church. What practical consequences follow from the fact that there are forms of representative experience? How are we to distinguish between, on the one hand, the solidarity of political groups and the mass suggestion of ideas and, on the other hand, the cohesion of the world Christian family amid the painful confusions of our world? How can we get beyond merely verbal, propagandistic, and even financial expressions of Christian fellowship? How can we ensure that our participation in the sufferings of others does not result in a compassion that merely mirrors our own fear of suffering? The fruitfulness of our theological dialogue will certainly be enhanced if significant experiences are not communicated to others in a way that suggests that they have no alternative but to adopt them as articles of faith and to regard them as equally urgent and decisive for themselves. Instead, these experiences should simply be reported so that they can be examined to see what they have to teach us.

But what have previous experiences of conflict taught us? Certainly we have learned that major economic and political conflicts and national problems deeply affect the churches themselves. We realize the intimate connection between religious freedom and the basic conditions of human and social fulfillment. But the only result of this understanding so far seems to have been to make unity among Christians and the theological dialogue itself even more difficult than ever, because many people see the ecumenical organizations merely as an invitation to reproduce the world-wide lines of opposition. If the ecumenical movement fails to develop strict rules of discussion for such cases and to insist on their application, the ecumenical dialogue itself will display, in the not too distant future, the same crisis symptoms we find in the controversy between the civilization of the "North" and the developing areas of the "South," that is, who will play the leading role in world politics in the future. In other words, the ecumenical discussion will become an arena of social and cultural confrontation. Because I believe we cannot steer clear of all this in our theological work in the ecumenical movement, it seems to me all the more important to take advantage of every opportunity, however slight, to transcend the psychological and sociological backgrounds of our thought and experience. Unless the ecumenical movement is attentive to this question, we shall find ourselves involved not in theological arguments but in attacks, efforts to reach compromise, or fending off attempts by the holders of certain opinions to establish a monopoly. We would then become incapable of real theological work.

How Do We Define Authentic Experiences?

Having become so accustomed to valuing "direct" experiences (i.e., events in which our whole existence is challenged, in which decisions cannot be avoided and the issue is one of life or death), we have largely forgotten how difficult it is to have and to describe really *authentic experiences.*

When is it permissible for us to speak of authentic experiences of God? "Authentic" means here: only *God Himself* can insert us into the history that is decisive for our life. However stirring, far-reaching, and world-shaking events may be, if we do not encounter God in them they are not experiences of God, they are merely human interpretations. But again authentic speech is only possible if we *ourselves* are really involved, if we are not merely repeating something others have said or allowing ourselves to be inveigled into accepting interpretations that are perhaps merely illusory. But how are we to determine this? The Bible offers us an important clue here. In the Bible, we have simple narration; incidents are narrated as soberly and accurately as possible, in such a way that a process becomes clear and apparent. There is very little about human feelings, opinions, and explanations, that is, precisely those things psychology and sociology influence us to speak about when we try to account for our everyday life and other people's reactions to it. Equally rarely do we find in the Bible any reflection on the way in which God was able to act and speak in this or that event, the way in which we are to understand and formulate this. On the contrary, the two things—the simple narrative and talk about God—stand in close juxtaposition yet unconnected. What really happens between God and humanity remains for the most part unsaid. This in fact is the secret of the Bible narrative: it remains silent at the point where God alone can speak, at the point where he speaks to the hearer and where he draws us into his own divine reality, and we no longer have to pay any attention to the human storyteller. It will be a tremendous help to us in our discussions today, too, to pay heed to this rule, namely, not to have to push ourselves forward any more when speaking of our experiences. The less we attach profound interpretation to our experiences, the more likely these experiences are to advance our theological understanding as we practice the art of listening and being silent together.

This then is the *second rule for the theological dialogue about experiences*: We will make the theological significance of situations and events really clear only if we leave the interpretation of them to God, while at the same time continuing to make them the object of our persistent questioning. This is most likely to happen if we refrain from attempting to spotlight the world of our experiences and to penetrate down to the last detail but instead respect its hidden depths and dimensions. All we know is the promises and commands of God and these we can only repeat after him, but when we do so our expectancy of a real encounter with the living God also gains fresh urgency and fervor.

Always to be sure in advance where God is present—for example, in the world-shaking conflicts of our time—would be to abandon this tension. Conflicts may certainly seem to be quite clear cut, illuminating for us what has a future and what is fast disappearing into the obscurity of outdated history, but our awareness of conflict is so often stereotyped. We depend for the most part on certain stereotypes of experience, standard patterns of conflict—patterns of power and powerlessness, oppression and liberation, revolution and conservatism. It is therefore difficult in practice to appreciate a particular event, experience, or happening in all its uniqueness and contingency. In our eagerness to explain such an event clearly, we tend at once to look around for typical experiences whose very familiarity can help other people understand new experiences. We theologians have come to regard certain Biblical situations as "primal experiences" and to claim that our own experiences are repetitions of these primal experiences. The Bible talks about people's experiences of God in specific situations: of divine judgment on wicked men, of God's promises in times of political upheaval, and of the validity of these promises over against traditions and social orders, of experiences of freedom amid the disintegration of traditional ritual, social, national, and racial differences. Our tendency, therefore, is to interpret our present experiences in the light of these prototypes, instead of identifying the promises hidden in them and then seeking to discover the specific promise we are called upon to proclaim concerning our own situations. How often in recent years has some revolutionary situation been greeted as an analogy to the Exodus of the Jewish people from Egypt! How often we have made the social criticism of the prophets or the cleansing of the Temple by Jesus the model for our own social criticism! How eagerly we regard Jesus' acceptance of the hospitality of tax collectors and sinners as the model for the solidarity Christianity requires of us with the outcasts of society! But how grievously we falsify the witness of the Bible by making a theology of our own area of experience! How often we first read into the Bible what we hope subsequently to read out of it as an explanation of our own situation! Is it any wonder that after a while the Bible is reduced to silence, ceases to illuminate our minds and serves instead merely as a vehicle to push ourselves forward as theologians and in doing so to become increasingly poor and helpless?

It would be a very serious impoverishment of our ecumenical dialogue if certain biblical situations, turned into stereotypes, continue to be made the sole basis for agreement in ecumenical discussions. To do so would be to ignore the centuries of laborious research into Biblical interpretation that has established the rule that the Bible can only be properly understood when we really try to listen to it. That, instead of merely seeking within it a pattern of our own history—one we already assume we understand—we must let ourselves really be drawn into God's history with humankind, a history already initiated and proclaimed to be full of promise in the Bible. We cannot, therefore, try to compile from the Bible a collection of authoritative situations and experiences, then look for analogies in our own time, and imagine that by doing this we have succeeded in describing authentic experiences.

Authentic experiences which lead us to theological truth can only originate in God Himself. Attention to the Bible will help us to clarify this knowledge of God's presence, to listen to God speaking through the witness of the Bible, and to inquire about Him there. This is a far more arduous and exacting task than using a few biblical passages to explain some contemporary experience. But unless we accept this discipline, and this means knowing how to listen and to be silent when our experiences are not immediately transparent theologically, we will in time view our own situation simply through the spectacles of those few biblical situations we consider decisive and then pay no heed at all to much that is happening in our world. The danger of this is already plain today. Whereas in previous generations, especially in the European churches, attention focused mainly on the spiritual problems of the individual Christian, the center of attention today is the social implications of the Christian life. This is an important corrective, owing much to a more faithful hearing of the biblical message of God's action in and promise for the world. But we are already threatened by another danger: our attention is now focused almost exclusively on God's message to suffering and oppressed human beings. We have become almost incapable of appreciating aright the experience of the troubled in heart and assailed in conscience. In the theological dialogue here we should remember the rule that authentic experiences of faith can only be sought where God speaks to us today—the God who is greater than our hearts, the God who, while leading us into conflicts, cannot Himself be simply one party in a conflict, but who inserts us into the history of His salvation.

The Prophetic Experience of God's Presence

There are two respects in which this rule of dialogue for testing authentic experiences is, I believe, being neglected today: In the course of centuries, "continental" theology has come to be dominated by the view that our historical experiences are so ambiguous that it is better not to try to make any direct identification of God's presence in our world. Our capacity for Christian prophecy, which affirms authoritatively where God is at work in our time and where we are dealing directly with Him, has atrophied. Western Christendom has often been *unfortunate in its experiences of experiences* and has therefore developed a theological technique of passing experiences through so many filters that all that is audible in them in the end is a few general views about God's guidance of humanity, His purpose with the world and lordship over the world. The fear of a possible lapse into false prophecy, the fear of the possibility of worshipping idols and false gods instead of the living God, led to the extinction of prophecy and with it that testing of the spirits that is, in fact, the basis of all genuine experience of God. If we in European Christendom wish to become receptive to the charisma of prophecy, which can only be received from God, we must rid ourselves of an ingrained tendency to seek exclusively for eternally valid theological ideas. We must learn in our theology to work at the "middle distances" instead of settling for nothing less than theological notions which at once embrace all history and all world processes. We must also abandon all large and abstract formulas. We can no longer choose for our discussions and theological study programs that sound correct and impressive only because they are, in fact, meaningless. We must learn to spell out in detail the great words of faith— freedom, hope, love—instead of repeating them as Pavlovian stimuli, we must take the risk of expressing them in the form of limited concrete examples and of using these to test together how much creative power they possess, in order, after a while, to begin our questioning afresh. There is a very close connection between the lack of experiences in our churches and our theological work and the fact that we theologians attach far too great an importance to absolute values and utterances of unrestricted validity, which, not surprisingly, are difficult to extend into the limited world of our daily experience with its constant need for revision.

As for the "young churches," the danger I see here is the opposite one: namely, the danger of attaching the label "experience of God" to their daily experience of being distinct from their environment and from the traditions which have hitherto dominated this environment. Here God is equated with the *new situation* in which Christians find themselves. Life in the community of faith is lived contemporaneously with the reordering of political, social, and religious life. There is no question of abandoning the problem of where and how God is at work, of course, least of all in this situation. Nevertheless, the young churches could perhaps learn from the "old" churches that even these revolutionary situations and new historical beginnings will one day be superseded by new traditions and institutions (even Christian ones!), and that then it will once more be necessary to seek for new religious experiences, only this time the novelty and revolutionary character of the real situation will not be a matter of daily observation. The old churches have learned by experience that, even when there is no longer much change and the scope for reordering life has become much narrower, there can still be new experiences of God. Certainly experience of God is always bound up with the breakdown of old rules of living which have become a barrier between God and humanity. But this crisis is not confined to revolutionary events. It is always precipitated where God opposes man's work because it delays God's future. All of us in the worldwide Christian family must learn, in the midst of the phenomena we take to constitute crises, to ask about *this* crisis, *this* judgment of God, for only on the basis of this crisis can any really new situation arise. Other changes will very soon be out of date.

The Role of Dogma and the Development of Dogma

I felt obliged just now to state my opinion that the ecumenical dialogue would be seriously impoverished if, in addition to the communication of experiences, it restricted itself simply to a few biblical

passages selected in the belief that they were important for our contemporary experience of history. This would also represent a lamen-
table backward step in the light of the history of the ecumenical dialogue so far. For the dialogue has been greatly enriched by the
introduction of the theological findings of the early centuries, the development of the dogmatic tradition in the ancient Church, into the
interconfessional discussion. The Eastern Orthodox Church made
this one of its special concerns and by its efforts has prevented the
kind of intellectual impoverishment to which many areas of Protestantism had succumbed, for example. Of course, it will not be
enough in the future simply to appeal to particular dogmatic statements of the church fathers. It must first of all be made quite clear
that the theological truth contained in the dogma of the Church is
not pointing to some ideal world or to a truth which is unrelated to
our own history but rather that the truth of faith expressed in dogma
very pointedly if indirectly affects the world of our experiences.
Large parts of church dogma are indeed rules for dealing theologically with experiences and are intended so far as possible to teach us
to see and understand our world in the light of divine revelation "to
all times." The dogma does not transcend all experience; it teaches
us how to handle experiences properly by posing the important questions we must direct to our own individual experiences. In its way,
therefore, the dogma helps us to find our way out of our own personal limitations and provides this help very practically by offering
a very comprehensive and ample theological basis for discussion,
making it possible for us to exchange our individual impressions of
a variety of situations and a variety of traditions of thought and
modes of experience.

I believe fresh considerations of dogma to be very necessary for
another reason too. I get the impression that many representatives of
the young churches tend to enhance the importance of their own
fresh experience by regarding the dogmatics of the major confessions
as part of the tradition from which they wish to be distinguished.
These dogmas, they feel, are typical of the European West and also
a remaining vestige of the colonial imperialism they wholly reject.
This is why they concentrate mainly on theological themes which
have hitherto been marginal in Western Christianity and which leave
room for fresh theological insights, namely, for eschatology and
pneumatology.

Now it is in fact true that, in spite of all the theological labors of the Church from the early centuries down to the present day, eschatology and pneumatology have still not been formulated as clearly and comprehensively as the doctrine of God in the Trinitarian theology of the ancient Church and in the confession of Christ in Christology. We still lack *sound rules for speaking of our hope (eschatology) and for speaking of experience of the presence of God in our world (pneumatology)*. There is need today, therefore, for a joint effort in the field of pneumatology and perhaps, in relation to this task in particular, a new theological agreement could be reached in the ecumenical dialogue. The subject of pneumatology is God's presence in the midst of our actions: God's will meets our intentions by confronting them. This way pneumatology formulates the rule how to expect God's advent as Spirit.

Pneumatology as Rule for the Theological Dialogue on Experiences

Since the Uppsala Assembly, it has been clear how vital pneumatology is for ecumenical action and for the theological orientation of the churches. The slogan of Uppsala—"Jesus Christ the New Man"—certainly seems to remain within the old familiar Christology. But on closer inspection it is clear that the new humanity is now no longer to be understood only as God's becoming man in Jesus Christ but also as man's becoming human in history. To the incarnation is added the incorporation of God in the world, in the process of man's humanization and the humanization of his living conditions. We need therefore to realize quite clearly that the slogan "man's becoming man" strikes a new note in Christian theology. It is new insofar as the ceaseless technological and political changes of our historical life are now regarded as "essential" for being human. This affects not just the Church's action but also its existence.

But as straightforward as the slogan of man's becoming man sounds, its theological meaning has so far remained obscure. To be sure, the confession that God became man in Jesus Christ includes the knowledge of the new creation and the new humanity. But the Christology of the ancient Church expressed this knowledge in terms of "transfiguration" rather than in terms of a process of change. Nor can we ignore the fact that the main intention here was to assert that

God makes the destiny of humankind wholly His own cause and does not, in fact, leave this destiny at the mercy of some incalculable process of historical change in which there is no certainty at all whether such change would ultimately lead to a better and truer humanity or to inhumanity. What the Christological dogma says here is that the new humanity is present in Jesus Christ in a final way. This means that our question about humankind's future is also placed (pneumatologically) under a promise, namely, that what is to be fulfilled from God's side in the history of humankind is already clear, unambiguous, and certain. We have no further need to seek it in the mists of our hopes and desires, our imaginings and projections. The new humanity is the presence of God in our world; it is being realized in the common history of God and humankind. The new humanity is therefore a promise which produces a happening, not a utopia which could only present itself to us as a demand.

This then is the theme of the classic Church Christology; God's becoming man as the inauguration of true human existence. Christology spoke therefore of the difference and the relationship between God and man in Jesus Christ; of salvation as both present and future, of man's redemption in the midst of an unredeemed history. Redemption is the penetration of the world with the saving presence of God; it is signalized in the special forms of the presence of God, in the saving power of His gospel and sacraments, in the new possibility of human speech about God and of human adoration of God in prayer and the liturgy. In reference to the salvation of humankind, therefore, Christology brought out the difference and relationship between divine and human *being*.

What we need today—not with a view to abandoning Christology but in order to advance it further—is to reflect deeply on the difference and relationship between divine and human *action*.

I see this as one of the most urgent questions for the churches and for theology today. This is the occasion for most of our uncertainties as well as the source of the most common heresies. We argue about where God's action leaves off and our activity begins. Can we set them off against each other at all? This is not just an abstract intellectual conundrum but an entirely practical problem. For if God's willing and God's doing disappear completely into our tasks and actions, this would mean that the new human existence could only take the form of a performance by which salvation is created. Our true humanity would consist (solely and exclusively!) in the complete achievement of this performance and therefore in the conquest of all division, all inadequacy, every form of alienation in relation to other human beings and to ourselves.

I doubt if anyone in the ecumenical movement could honestly speak in such terms. But many contemporary hopes concerning the new humanity and the new creation, concerning liberation and peace, tend in this direction. Most of us want to maintain the closest possible unity between God's work and our activity, fearing that otherwise Christendom will succumb to a passive role and leave the initiative in fashioning history not to God but to the arbitrary activity of other human beings. In this context even the theme of the Nairobi Assembly in 1975—"Jesus Christ Frees and Unites"—is taken to mean that the freedom given to us by Christ brings us into harmony with God's history, that it unites our action with God's action and thereby creates the worldwide unity of action which transcends the boundaries of Christendom and embraces all those who share (perhaps without always realizing it) in carrying out God's will.

I find here a situation similar to that in the early centuries of church history. The saving presence of God in the confession of Jesus Christ seemed at that time so decisive that it became more and more difficult still to recognize in truth the real God and the real man. Instead, the God-man, Jesus Christ, came to be subordinated either to our image of God or to our ideal concepts of humanity. In its Christology, therefore, the ancient Church had to resist the dream of man's divinization and also to challenge the idea that our human distance from God was in any sense repeated in Jesus Christ. It did both these things by its insistence on the unity of God and man in Jesus Christ. Strenuous efforts and many struggles had to be endured before it became clear that God and man are united in Jesus Christ "without confusion" and "without change" but also "without division" and "without separation." How long will it take us to reach the same clear understanding of our new humanity and of our action in comparison with and in relationship to God's action?

It will certainly not be enough simply to repeat the paradoxes of Christology. For our action can hardly enter the new creation "without confusion" and "without change." There is indeed a close connection between the confession of Jesus Christ the New Man and our experiences of the new humanity. But in our experiences we are confronted with new paradoxes. Equally strenuous debates and intellectual efforts will be needed as those of the early centuries, if we are to be able to speak with equal seriousness and responsibility about God's presence in our world, about the new creation within our history, and about the humanization of human beings. This is the task that confronts us in pneumatology.

It will be necessary for the *future pneumatology* to specify rules by which we can recognize experiences and explain them theologically in our contemporary situation. It will encounter differences here in practice and polarities that are irreconcilable in theory but which, because of the hope that is in us, cannot be accepted as permanent: As human beings we seek to transform our conditions of life. But at the same time we ourselves are also subject to profound changes. At one and the same time we are agents and objects. It is therefore difficult for us to reach any firm judgment as to what in the long run can really be "new" and "lasting."

It is no longer adequate today to think in terms of the alternative: "activity" or "passivity." This alternative no longer matches what we actually experience in the way of possibilities for action. The cry for freedom and self-determination is not just a demand for a better political and social future but also an admission of our present uncertainty about ourselves.

Pneumatology speaks of God's presence: God's Spirit is in us, he enters our existence. Only because this is so is his life a living hope within us. But this hope draws us completely to God's side and God's future. The work of the Spirit precedes our wills and capacities and we are permitted to discover this work. Only "from God" can we do anything—and yet this dependence is not something determined by history but is only fulfilled in our freedom.

It is often asserted today that human beings cannot be defined because this would mean depriving them of their openness. It would mean we should no longer be able to experience anything new. On the other side, the new humanity continues today to be interpreted in terms of fixed classifications: the division of humankind into races, social classes, and so on, whose relationship to one another can only be reversed but not abolished.

But what is the relationship between our limitations and God's new creation that sets aside barriers and leads us across accustomed frontiers? Is it correct to say that "ultimately anything which embraces less than the infinity of God is dehumanizing for man" (David Jenkins)? Could not the very longing for infinity lead to inhumanity?—Surely we share in redemption only as human beings! Redemption draws us into the eternal reality of God. In doing so it liberates us from the desire to become as gods. It unites us in the ability to be wholly and completely *finite human beings*, whose lives are so fulfilled from God's side that they can really and finally entrust to God all their longing beyond this life.

Pneumatology affirms that the *cooperatio* of God and man is indivisible yet without confusion. As human beings, therefore, we cannot assign any ultimacy to our tasks and decisions. We must always be prepared to revise them. We are not at liberty to oppress other men and subject them to ourselves by our action.

This once again makes it possible for the Church to be one and free. We are at liberty to devote ourselves wholly and unreservedly to our *limited* tasks and experiences. We are to communicate them to one another and then together to ask about God's presence in our world and about the history of God in the afflictions of humankind. But none of this in itself is yet an announcement of God's entire action; God's history is not established, much less exhausted, by it.

Pneumatology is in every respect a directive for our *speech*. What we say about God (not just in reference to what he once said but also as we listen to what he has to say to us today) cannot be uttered by us as if we ourselves were God.

Yet we cannot simply express our own opinions. Even our speaking also shares in God's history. We cannot shrug off our *responsibility* for the *response* we make to God's promises. Only to a limited degree are these answers possible—and they will at the same time point beyond all our experiences so far to God's infinite and unlimited future. They will require a far-reaching perspective and yet they will have to argue with the middle distances in view (more than has been the case up to now), without being short-sighted.

4

Being Human
and Being a Theologian

Some years ago I participated in consultations of the Ecumenical Institute in Bossey, Switzerland, on the subject of "doing theology today."[1] We talked about theological traditions and about the
contemporary social and political context of theology and church
and we inquired how the situation in which we live determines our
theological knowledge. There was talk about the revolutionary
change of the world and about the "new man," formed or to be
formed by new changeable, technically or socially influenced conditions. I was especially struck by one impression from these discussions, something that had nothing directly to do with the discussed
subjects; but I learned to see that it is a key question. A Swiss psychiatrist who had been invited as a specialist in anthropological research asked me after every lecture (Europeans, Americans, and Af-
ricans were speaking): "Could you understand what had been said?
I could not. I have been concerned with theology to the extent that I
can understand some terms, questions, and theses. I also understand
that they try here to put together these theological terms with conceptions of our present world. But I am not able to perceive the structure of theological knowledge and theological thinking. What do
those theologians *say*, anyway? Don't they just talk about themselves? Don't they merely present themselves? Do they not show us,
with their intelligent perceptions, with their historical knowledge,

1. An earlier version of this chapter was presented as a lecture at Duke Divinity
School on December 5, 1979, and published in *The Duke Divinity School Review* 45
(1980):50–59.

with their knowledge about the problems of our times, just one thing: *how they themselves react to* that which they call *the modern world?* What is the difference between theology and the self-presentation of the human being which is mainly concerned with coping with the world around us and which uses words like 'faith,' 'love,' 'hope,' 'liberation,' 'God,' and 'Jesus Christ'for it?"

That was the question of a psychiatrist and physician. He was certainly not an enemy of theology. He did not at all believe that faith is just a psychological fiction and religion just mere ideology. He also agreed that theologians, unlike other scientists, could not merely observe and objectify. Those people who want to be true theologians are involved personally in what they talk about. They cannot isolate themselves from that which needs to be proclaimed. But what exactly is the relationship between being human and doing theology? Do theologians expound *something other than themselves* when they claim to talk about God?

It should be noted that this question has nothing to do with the obvious fact that we theologians are all human beings, which to a great extent affects our thinking and doing. We have feelings, hopes, and concerns, aggressions and proclivities; we all have our own experiences, and we are dependent on the world around us. We can all also obtain—by means of a good course of studies, for example—new, perhaps better, insights and new experiences. All of that determines our perceptions and thinking. We cannot cleanly separate theology from it. If we were able to do that, we would not be real human beings anymore. We should not try to *separate* our being human from our doing theology. But we have to try to *distinguish* between them. If we do not succeed in that, then theology would be a *mere expression of being human*. It would have nothing to do anymore with the question of truth and untruth and would then cease to be a cognitive endeavor. What then is theology? What does it mean: being human and doing theology?

Existence as Demonstration?

In German theology this question was asked in a different way but in a similar direction in the year 1933. The answer affected the path of German theology and theological education for a long time afterwards. I want to describe this in order to state more clearly our question. In 1933 Karl Barth put it at the beginning of the so-called church conflict in the form of a programmatic sentence: "Theological existence today!" This title of a little pamphlet of Barth's in 1933 became the title of a theological journal which was published until 1984.

When Karl Barth, in the early summer of 1933 in Bonn, proclaimed the slogan "Theological existence today!" he wanted to address all responsible Christians, but especially the clergy. "Our theological existence," he declared to them, "is our existence in the church, that is to say as called preachers and teachers of the church." Theological existence for Barth means the profession which emerges out of the exclusive attachment to the Word of God and which can only subsist in this connection. It means knowing to whom we belong and to whom alone we have to listen.

Barth's call came out of fear of eventual loss of this theological existence. Barth found a sort of absent-mindedness among many of his theological colleagues as a consequence of their diffused interest in various day-to-day matters. They were constantly preoccupied with reacting to changes in piety and morals, with searching their relationships, with reflecting on the situation of the church, with doing justice to its involvement in the intellectual situation of the time and its change, and with trying to get involved in those that seemed promising for the future. Because of their attempts to speak to the situation, they lost track of the center of faith. To get down to the center, not just to take sides in the present situation: this is the way Karl Barth put the decisive question of theological existence, which sees itself in the face of God and which has to realize this fact, which is incomparable to all other conceivable situations.

Today there are many symptoms that could demand a similar call. Theological work and the practice in our churches are often overloaded with psychological and sociological considerations. The many attempts to impress the importance of Christianity on the world have blurred the outlines of the church. Some focus on the socio-political situation, while others introduce ideas about reality which prevent living experiences of faith. A complete catalog of errors would illuminate a cardinal problem: *the need for orientation*, which belongs to being human, has become an acute crisis. Church and theology receive a multitude of radar-screen impressions from a bewildering variety of directions and often seem to be merely reacting instead of leading the way. Ministers can easily become disoriented because of the diffuse multitude of conflicting signals which they can hardly categorize, let alone sift through.

On the other hand, the call back to the center of the matter and to reflection on theological existence appears as *concentration* on the *essentials of being human*. Human beings are to be brought back to a place where they can gain a perspective on the perception of the world and history. They are supposed to see the relationships that indicate what is essential and meaningful. This task of concentration is pointed to by the term "existence," which Barth derived from a fashionable language trend of his time. "Existence" means the process of life, which cannot be prepared for by any theoretical effort, which cannot be captured by a distant overview of the situation, but which happens at the moment when everything unimportant is disregarded. At the same time existence is the risky enterprise of being human, in the midst of the many voices of the time, so that it fulfills the many historical tasks. In this sense Barth asked with the formula "Theological existence today!" the question whether being a Christian means to be up-to-date and to fulfill the demands of the times, while resisting the lack of concentration that comes about when human beings merely react to a multitude of challenges without really being able to meet them in the knowledge of the total Otherness of the word and will of God.

Without wanting to modify anything that has been said so far, I would nevertheless like to consider more closely the notion of existence and I would like to turn our attention to an anthropological mark that I believe is suspect. This is a crucial question in regard to Barth's formula. Barth demands that we totally expose the ground of Christian existence. In response to this demand the process of existence may become (contrary to his own intention) *a demonstrative gesture which draws all attention to itself* instead of pointing to that to which it wants to point. The notion of existence becomes the mark of a problem of orientation and of its solution by means of concentration and true self-reflection. Theological existence thus becomes expressive *self-presentation*.

A Paradigmatic Way of Life?

I want to consider more closely two examples for this self-expressiveness, for this understanding of theological existence as special, demonstrative behavior. They seem to me to be typical of some tendencies in German theology and in the church, despite the effects of the theology of Karl Barth, which they oppose in part. They have in common the fact that they perceive theological existence as *a life style* that counters the dangers that threaten being human today. I have often also found this view in the United States.

The first example of understanding theological existence as a demonstrative gesture of self-presentation is the *call for concentration*. It starts from the indeed apt observation that our being human today is endangered by diffusions of various sorts. We do not know the center of being human anymore. Our doing and thinking do not live in the distinction between the important and the unimportant anymore. We consume a multitude of offers promising a better and more meaningful life. We lose ourselves in testing these different offers instead of really living from the center of our own existence. We seek our salvation in diffusion. We look for relaxation in a restless journey to ever new impressions, and then we have to realize that we did not recollect ourselves and find ourselves, but instead, have split ourselves even more.

Many of our theologians diagnose in themselves this same widely spread disease of our times. They lack the authority in their professional work that would allow them to select that which is essential for their doing and thinking and to know without many doubts that which is life-fulfilling. But wherever there is a diagnosis, there is also often enough a therapeutic recipe. The pattern of behavior that many theologians follow in their studies is: *concentration as self-reflection*. Concentrating means then: to concentrate on oneself, to listen to oneself, to shut oneself off, and to select from one's many possibilities those which are reflected in the inner self. *I* have the impression that this form of concentration dominates most of what is called "experience" in theology and church today. Experience in this case is nothing else but reflection on the center of all awarenesses, where I find myself and from where *I* can speak. Experience is nothing but the expression of the fact that *I* have searched for and found myself. Existing theologically then means nothing more than training for self-reflection.

Is this really a concentration? Is concentration achieved when one cuts out, selects, and pushes away that which might be disturbing? But concentration and concentrating on oneself means: *establishing a relation to the center,* and to get, from this angle of perspective, a view of an area which is clearly related to that center. Certainly concentration opposes diffusion; it refuses to dwell at all conceivable places. But this cannot be cured by trying to dwell at some arbitrary place, settling down like a spider, there, where one's own set of relationships with the world can be most easily webbed. No, concentration means primarily: finding the *true center*, and from this center one gains the *perspective*, which gives validity to all things, whether they are far from or close to that center. Concentration in other words is undistorted *perception*, not a reduction of impressions to a degree that they can be coped with, without much pain. Concentration shows proportions; it shows realities in their *relative relations*. It is not a refusal of perception by means of confinement to some few, favorite viewpoints.

What is the center from which theological perception is possible? We find an answer to this question in the Gospel of John, where Jesus recalls the strange story of the time of sojourn in the wilderness when the people of God were threatened by serpents and only those who *looked away from themselves* were saved, only those who fixed their eyes on the bronze serpent, the sign of salvation in the hand of Moses (Numbers 21:8f.). With this image of salvation Jesus points to his cross, which is at the same time his elevation to life for all (John 3:14f.). The center of theological perception is this unity of life and death in the crucified one, not only *the suffering but also the glorified Christ*, sitting at the side of the Father. To look towards him means: becoming able to look away from oneself, not being spellbound anymore by the dangers which we—as the traveling people of God—encounter or have created. In other words: *being alive through Christ in Selbstvergessenheit*. Without *Selbstvergessenheit* there is no theological concentration! *Selbstvergessenheit* means: Not until an external reality—God's liberating action—distracts my attention from myself, will I be unexpectedly made to discover myself within that reality.

I do not think I have to protect this *Selbstvergessenheit* from the misunderstanding that I am recommending here a suppression of the I, a supplanting of the self in favor of imaginary "objective" perception, or in favor of a "collective" consciousness. But it is important to realize just how our existence is at stake and that—according to another word of Jesus—those who think they have found themselves have actually lost the true fulfillment of self because they thought that individuals could gain life by themselves and to produce life from their own resources. In any case the focus would be the Self. It seems to me that we have to learn what this means for the perception of theological existence. The letter to the Colossians (3:1–3) gives us a hint: "Since you are now revived with Christ—that is, you have entered life—seek that which is above, where Christ is, sitting at the right hand of the Father. Turn your senses to that which is above, not that which is on earth. Because *you have died*, and *your lives are hidden with Christ in God.*"

That is a description of authentic Christian theological existence, its realization, and the mode of being human that is involved in such an existence. We need to grasp the language of these verses, which are loaded with metaphors: The "above" in contrast to the "on the earth" is not describing an overworld in the sense of a purely transcendent reality, beyond our day-to-day reality. The stress is on the *hiddenness* of the new life in the community of the glorified Christ. Being hidden is not a designation of localities in terms of this-worldly/other-worldly, but a designation of reality. Being hidden designates the manner of *God's presence*, God's life, God's acting. Theology is talking about our *perception of this hidden presence*; theological existence is *participation in this hidden presence*. A demonstrative attitude is then ruled out if such behavior is the expression of self-assertion, even in a blurred manner: perhaps with the good intention of showing that God is totally different from our world, that faith is higher than all reason, that theology is incomparable with all other cognitive endeavors. In all of these points theological knowledge can and easily may get lost in favor of a self-presentation of religious existences, which merely intend to express their own behavior in relation to their environment in its various forms.

I shall now endeavor to draw the anthropological consequence of this kind of theological perception. Knowledge of faith is the *perception of the world in light of the hidden presence of God*, and that means: of the world in its true proportions, in its relations to God's presence. In order to be able to learn to realize this, we have to distinguish between acts of meditation and the process of theological perception. Meditation, contemplation, reflection *correlate to* the rhythm of perception, to the task of ordering, sifting, and testing of impressions. This form of concentration is necessary. But theological perception is a *liberated* perspective, *oblivious of itself*. It is more than focusing the view, concentrating on one single point in order not to have to overwork itself! Theological perception is an unobtrusive invitation for *communal* perception, because that which has to be perceived is not the private idea of something that must be reflected in the eyes of others, but rather the world in the light of the hidden presence of God—the reality which is focused on by all communally.

The second example of the misunderstanding of theological existence as a demonstrative gesture of the expressive self-presentation of the theologian is the *provocation toward "creative" behavior*. It wants to liberate the human being from the confinements of being human which are produced by the pressures that exist in modern society to achieve something. In Western civilization (it is a separate question how far this civilization actually extends!) human beings are absorbed by the world of technology and bureaucracy, by an impressive and oppressive administration of life and its turning of reality into a made and manageable product. We are under pressure to produce, bring about, form, and register something. Only that which we thus set forth is reality for us and others.

It certainly cannot be denied that, because of all this, our being human is distorted and the protests against this are justifiable. But the attitude taken by many theologians in face of this is little more than the expressionistic escape into a counterculture, into a world where unruled activity and free associations are dominating. *Being a Christian then means: existing spontaneously*. In this view church practice has become a sort of playground for supposedly creative—actually simply anarchical—behavior. I speak now about the situation in Germany and its consequences for theology, but I think there are also signs of similar developments in the United States. Many theologians think of themselves as alternative models in face of the achievement society with its criteria of measurable effectivity. They do not want to be mere managers who keep the church organization functioning. In Christian education and confirmation classes, they do not want to impose more knowledge to be learned on their pupils, who groan under the pressure of school anyway. They want their church services (paradoxically, carefully prepared with a variety of technical tricks) to become happenings, where something new and "unpredictable" will occur: a "creative process" that is not disturbed by explanations (and that also avoids sending the church "visitor" back home concerned with questions and responsibilities). I need not continue this enumeration. But I do want to clarify the point that in this understanding and practice of theological existence—in the language of church dogmatics—the doctrines of creation, eschatology, and pneumatology are at stake. Christian hope, which knows about the creative contradiction of God against the world, is misunderstood as the opportunity of making God's contradiction "our own thing," so that we presume to negate everything that exists as the distorted world. Creation is dictated by an idea of creativity that finally deems only chaos as creative, bringing every order into contradiction with life. This is the consequence of an idea of Spirit which forgets that the spirit that only negates is called—according to Goethe and with good reason—the devil, enemy of God. Certainly God breaks the forms behind which human beings hide from God. Spirit is not the principle of formlessness but rather the formation of God's reality in our world.

The Sermon as Paradigm

What do these dogmatic assertions mean for our inquiry about theological existence? That *the sermon* is a test, so to speak, because in the sermon every assertion is necessarily and inevitably related to the human existence of the preacher. This is shown by the human expressiveness in every sermon: experiences of the preacher, intellectual and rhetorical idiosyncrasies, gestures, in short: all aspects of one's ability of communication. Moreover, and especially, the theological structure of a sermon shows one's individual humanness, expressed not only in certain sentences but also in that which the sermon articulates as a whole.

Basically, many sermons speak today about only one thing: that the preacher stands at the *frontline* between yesterday and tomorrow, between the usual and the unusual. Only there—thus it is said, either directly or indirectly—God is to be found, where a borderline between the old and the new becomes visible, so that we can cross over in the direction of a radically new beginning. The preacher has to mark this frontier. He or she is a "frontiersman" who, moreover, has to disclose this frontline. And this takes place by proclaiming God's word as contradiction to all other viewpoints and to day-to-day knowledge. The preacher first has to convince the congregation that it has the wrong ideas, the wrong religious attitudes, the wrong political opinions, the bourgeois habits, that have alienated it from the truth. Certainly, all this can and has to be said in due time and in appropriate context. But such marking of frontiers cannot be the character of a *sermon,* because then it first would have to create a wasteland, and only through a complete deforestation would it gain the space where God could again find a place in the world, whose alienation from God was just so loudly proclaimed. No wonder that such a preacher will grow weary and resign in time. This fatigue is a widespread phenomenon precipitated by a way of preaching that feels it must arouse and stir every Sunday. A theologian who acts like this, wholly apart from that which is said substantially, has eventually to judge everything that he or she actually brings about in this way as wrong, because everything that may be achieved must be seen as belonging to "the world," which has to be changed! In terms of psychology this leads to a process of destruction of all that-which-is, including one's own ego. But since such theologians, too, must go on living, they can merely communicate their own destructive "creativity."

An apparent contrast to this sermon structure and the related way of behavior is the endeavor to *identify* God's presence with a piece of well-known reality. That seems to be affirmative, that is, it encourages the listeners to trust whatever they regard as meaningful or significant. But this strenuous building up of interpretation, too, depends much too often on those who, openly or secretly, want to express their belief that *without their technique* of seeing God and the world as a whole and of describing relationships between them, *God would remain excluded* from the world of our experiences. But is this seemingly positive attitude not just another form of the viewpoint that causes the destructive and self-destructive theological attitude? God's presence seems here—as there—dependent upon those who represent God, who thereby indirectly proclaim the absence of God. The ungodliness of the world is also implied when theologians, by the way they express themselves, make their statements depend on their own personal *credibility.* This concentrating of theology on the credibility of the theologian, on human capacities and behavior—today not usually any more one's morality but more often one's ability to live meaningfully and give meaning—this glorification of personal credibility is nothing else than the perversion of theology into a lifestyle. In common with the critical attitude toward other human beings and their presuppositions, this lifestyle shares the assumption that the environment is removed from the presence of God and has to be brought into God's presence by the special activity of the theologian.

But what would prevent us from considering human beings whom we encounter as those who stand already under the promise of the new humanity, as those who live now (without always knowing it clearly) under the sign of salvation and *in whom God meets us?* Theological perception means: not just accepting this blindly but discovering whether or not it is that way. But we can—right here!— only perceive that which has happened *before* our critical inquiry.

What we theologians need to do is discern the prior truth of God's active presence and thereby to realize ourselves as limited human beings, recipients of God's grace and liberated from our selfishness. That means opening up human life for God's activity, not distorting that reality which God has already erected amongst us.

The old church at the marketplace in Wittenberg, where Martin Luther preached, shows an altar painting of the reformer in the pulpit and the congregation listening to him. But between the congregation and the preacher is the cross of Jesus Christ, and Luther points to this *Deus Crucifixus,* so that his listeners look at Christ and not to the pulpit. What they see is, at first sight, a suffering, dying human being, forever silenced. But in this death the living God is present, who does not give up the Son, the man who hoped alone for God. God does not permit other human beings to tear apart the unity between God and this man. This is the work of God, which should be looked at, which out of the powerlessness of Jesus pronounces the certainty of victory over death and all misery. The cross of Jesus Christ is obviously the sharpest contradiction of any human self-presentation in the interest of individual convictions, even in the form of symbolizing human suffering as a pronouncement on one side of human existence—namely for the longing not to remain in a hopeless state. The promise and task of each theological pronouncement is not to read that into the cross of Jesus Christ, but to perceive in the death of Jesus the living God. Existing theologically means: to be drawn into this event, to experience the history of the life of Jesus in the unity of life and death, and thus—in certain perceptions about our world—to realize that the history of God with humankind goes on: as a continuous history of the passion of Jesus Christ in the expectation of overcoming misery and death. In order to participate in this history, one needs—to repeat it again—the gift of *Selbstvergessenheit,* which liberates us so that we can, by means of our existence, *point* to the God who is hidden in our time and world. It liberates us to become attentive to God and to draw attention to God, without ourselves becoming the center of attention.

5

"Suffering" and "Acting"

Cross and Suffering

"Suffering, suffering, cross, cross; that is the Christian's privilege, that and nothing but that."[1] Thus Martin Luther admonished the rebellious revolutionary peasants of Southern Germany in his 1525 "Admonition to Peace."[2] It was a very crucial and decisive year for the Reformer and the German Reformation (the year, by the way, in which Luther also got married, an event that was part of a crisis only to the extent that Luther viewed his marriage as a sign of hope in turbulent and dark times). The year 1525 brought Luther's confrontation with the humanist Erasmus of Rotterdam on the freedom of will. Erasmus defended the freedom of the individual to make a decision for or against God.[3] In this regard he confined himself to viewing the human being in its diverse possibilities of action. Luther replied that no person can really start with himself. If persons anchor themselves entirely in their own freedom, they forget that they are and remain God's creatures. If, as human beings we recognize, however, that we belong to God, then we let God's activity simply hap-

1. This chapter was first given as a lecture for a symposium on "Theological Anthropology" organized by the Duke Divinity School in Durham, NC, March 24th to April 2nd, 1985.
2. Martin Luther, "Ermahnung zum Frieden auf die zwölf Artikel der Bauerschaft in Schwaben," WA 18:310, 10f.
3. Erasmus of Rotterdam, *De libero arbitrio Diatribe sive collatio* (1524) I b 10: *"liberum arbitrium hoc loco sentimus vim humanae voluntatis, qua se possit homo applicare ad ea, quae perducunt ad aeternam salutem, aut ab iisdem avertere."* "We here understand the free will as a power of human willing through which the human being could turn toward what leads to eternal salvation or away from it."

pen to us. Here the human being functions, as it were, in nothing but passive ways. One does not do anything, but one *becomes* whole.[4]

This was one front during 1525. The other took shape at the height of the Peasant Wars in the spring of that year. The spokespersons of the rebellion banked on the freedom message of the Reformation, the Gospel of the "freedom for which Christ has set us free" (Galatians 5:1). On the basis of this freedom they demanded liberty-space for each individual. They asked for far-reaching political equality on the grounds of a divine justice that allows no unlimited domination of human beings over other human beings. This justice, it was said, might have to be enforced by force, so as to destroy pseudo-privileges or to eliminate social distress caused by such privileges and to establish just conditions. From this angle, the struggle for social justice challenges God personally. Since God's cause is at stake, the cause of the one who makes common cause with the oppressed and the suffering, God must come to their help in the decisive battle against god-forsaken rules.

Those of us who hear these words today might feel ourselves placed right in the midst of our own political and theological struggles. There is no question in my mind that social conditions today are radically different from those of Europe 450 years ago, conditions which were then, by the way, quite varied. There were significant differences in the situations and the legal status of the peasants, the impoverished middle class, and the feudal "under-class" caught in distress—three groups that became allies in the so-called Peasant Wars. But in spite of such differences there exists a common denominator in the confrontations then and now. It is *the question of the rights of the suffering*. The Gospel of Jesus Christ answers: the suffering belong to God. God has sent the Son "to preach good news to the poor, to proclaim release to the captives and recovering of sight to the blind, to set at liberty those who are oppressed, to proclaim

---

4. Martin Luther, *De servo arbitrio* (1525), WA 18:697, 27f., on Jn. 1:12: *"Hic homo mere passive (ut dicitur) sese habet, nec facit quippiam, sed fit totus."* See, however, Erasmus who considers it a superfluous, though formulatable, question *"utrum nostra voluntas aliquid agat in his, quae pertinent ad aeternam salutem, an tantum patiatur ab agente gratia, an quicquid facimus sive boni sive mali, mera necessitate faciamus vel patiamur potius"* (*De libero arbitrio*, I a 8). "Whether or not our will can attain something in what pertains to eternal salvation, or whether it can only let effective grace come upon it, whether we, whatever good or evil we do, do it from sheer necessity or rather suffer it."

the acceptable year of the Lord" (Luke 4:18f.). The suffering are called to God because they need liberation—Luther did not question that. All the suffering certainly belongs to Christ, since God has placed the divine Son on an equal footing of suffering. But does God's standing on the side of the suffering, or rather their standing on God's side, also mean that God takes their side, espousing their cause, so as to assist them in victory over their oppressors? That would imply that the world is divided into armies of the good and the bad, identical with the oppressed and the oppressors, respectively, the suffering and the well-fed and healthy.

What is at stake here is the range of the experience of suffering. It is also the dramatic background of Luther's words I quoted in the beginning: "Suffering, suffering, cross, cross; that is the Christian's privilege, that and nothing but that." Luther had to experience that God's rights and God's activity will be misperceived if replaced by the utopia of a definitely just world order. The world can be catapulted into dreadful discord and strife, even with the best intention of making it just.

Luther, with his appeal to see God's justice in the cross of Christ, by no means took sides against the suffering. He did not betray the poor of his day and deliver them to their oppressors. But he felt that human beings at that time were tempted to misperceive God's action towards them, and in the world, and to avoid God. They wanted to create a world conforming to God, since they believed that God's kingdom had been ousted from their world and would have to gain entrance again through the work of their hands. They demanded their God-given rights and forgot in the process to ask where God's right might be found in the first place. They intended to fight human suffering and they thought that, in the process, they would encounter also the suffering of God. They wanted to start a crusade against the godless and yet—so Luther thought—meanwhile they depreciated the cross of Christ. The proclamation of the freedom for which Christ set us free was no longer heard. It had turned into a battle slogan, even a weapon, in the struggle for one's own rights. Both parties, the rulers and the ruled, thus claimed God's rights. Both sides increased the suffering which had arisen from social distress.

The sole issue thus was no longer to tackle the need, to assuage suffering, and to get rid of injustice. Luther saw that what was at stake was *the meaning of God's action creating rights for human be-*

ings and the meaning of the human search for justice as well. Whoever searches for God's justice will not find it anywhere but in the cross of Christ. There God has revealed the divine justice. It is justice that is given and that we humans merely receive. We do not create it. Luther calls this justice *iustitia passiva*. It is justice that God effects in us, in justifying us and placing us in the divine life, the divine rights, and divine truth. The concept of *iustitia passiva* stands in contrast to the entire traditional theological-philosophical language where God's justice appears only as *iustitia activa*. "Active" justice means that God *is* just in that He punishes the guilty and rewards merit. The *iustitia activa* does not overcome human failings and human wrong. It underscores what is right and what is wrong.

Luther's new insight into God's rights and God's justice as *iustitia passiva* was his "Reformation discovery,"[5] and only from here can we understand what Luther wants to say when he claims: "Suffering, suffering, cross, cross; that and nothing but that is the Christian's privilege." In virtue of the cross, rights and suffering inseparably belong together. We cannot *merit* God's justice; we can only *suffer* it. Suffering thus receives a new quality without being religiously enhanced or glorified. Without experiencing the reality of God in the midst of suffering there will be no rights, at least not for the Christian. God's justice is God's salvific action: God judges by painfully distinguishing between what human beings want to have and what they are to become. God saves by not demanding of any person anything he has not first received from God.

It is in this regard that Luther stresses cross and suffering as the Christian's *right*. I need to explicate the point by saying that we get our rights before God only through suffering, if we seek God's rights as the rights of all humans and the world as a whole and thus confess that we do not view "rights" as status-quo maintenance of dogmatic positions. Luther never doubted that for Christians suffering is something that "serves them right" if they stand on the side of Jesus

---

5. Luther describes it in the preface to the first volume of the edition of his Latin writings (1545), WA 54: 179–187; for juxtaposition of *iustitia activa* and *iustitia passiva* see ibid., 185, 19f. and 186, 6f. As to the issue itself see, for example, Luther's lectures on Galatians (1531), WA 40.I:41, 3–5: "*Christiana iustitia est mere contraria, passiva, quam tantum recipimus, ubi nihil operamur sed patimur alium operari in nobis scilicet deum.*" "Christian justice is completely different [from all other forms of active justice, that is], passive, which we merely receive where we effect nothing, but let someone else, that is, God work in us."

Christ, since here human enmity against God, persecution, and martyrdom can strike them as they struck Jesus.

Even so, Luther did not say something like, "Suffering, suffering, cross, cross; that is the Christian's fate," which might mean that those who suffer should take it on the chin, or in fact, even feel honored because they are suffering like Jesus. Ernst Bloch in his book on Thomas Müntzer (one of the theological opponents of Luther in the Peasants' War) has misquoted and misunderstood Luther to promote this type of pious justification of suffering. Luther supposedly said that cross and suffering is the Christian's fate—Jesus thus being "mixed up with the lowliest suffering" so that the defenseless and the powerless received false comfort and their resistance was weakened.[6] Behind this reproach lies the conviction that suffering must be transcended by social equality, that is, relationships that are more just. In this instance "cross" at best can function only as symbol of the contradiction to the thus far rather painful world.

This view, however, disregards the fact that *suffering* implies a *new beginning* in a completely different vein, since *God's activity here meets human activity*. We discover this in the cross of Christ. This cross has been erected by human beings. Humans laid hands on Jesus. They nailed his hands to a cross, so that he could not move. His arms remain stretched out defenselessly in intercessory prayer. The time of action has come to an end in the cross. Here Jesus delivers himself into God's hands. He calls upon God exactly as one whom the pious wanted to separate from God, to ban from this world as a rebel against God and an orderly world. This is the last we hear and see of Jesus. What remains is pure hope in God, distinct from all wishes and expectations.[7]

6. Ernst Bloch, *Thomas Münzer als Theologe der Revolution* (Frankfurt a.M.: Suhrkamp, 1969), 133.

7. Martin Luther, *Operationes in Psalmos* (1519–1521), WA 5:166, 11–18, on Ps. 5:12: *"Sola vero passiva vita purissima est, ideo et spem et gloriam operatur, atque in hoc oportet, nos conformari imagini et exemplo Christi, regis et ducis nostri, qui per activam quidem vitam incepit, sed per passionem consummatus est, omnibus scilicet operibus eius tam multis tam magnificis adeo in nihilum redactis, ut non solum coram hominibus sit cum iniquis reputatus, sed et a deo derelictus. Adeo scilicet omnia a nobis auferenda sunt, ut nec optima dei dona, idest ipsa merita, reliqua sint, in quibus fidamus, ut sit spes purissima in purissimum deum . . . "* "Only the truly suffering life is fully pure life. Thus it produces hope and glory. For it we have to be conformed to the image and example of Christ, our king and leader, who started out with an active life but was perfected through suffering. All his many and magnificent

God has acted in the suffering Son of Man. This is the message of the resurrection and his exaltation to the right hand of God. God has taken him into the divine life and become newly active through this suffering and dying human for all other humans. He has become so real that they can now recognize God. It is not apart from the cross of Jesus that God becomes recognizable, but exactly through it. Where merely a corpse is visible in complete and final *passivity,* faith sees a *passion* in which Jesus suffers God's power of life. In this suffering, which from our perspective cannot be distinguished from the passivity of a human being forced to let things happen, Jesus Christ becomes an "other," a new creation (II Corinthians 5:7). He enters into unity with the Father so that God will no longer be found just anywhere but in the suffering of the Son. Here the Creator becomes the co-suffering fellow human. "God can only be found in cross and suffering," says Martin Luther in the Heidelberg disputation of 1518.[8] *To understand suffering theologically* thus means *to fix one's eyes on the cross of Christ and to begin to live and think in terms of his passion.*

We are being prepared for the suffering of Christ (the *passio*) on account of the prayer in Gethsemane: "Father, if it be possible, let this cup pass from me; nevertheless, not as I will, but as thou wilt" (Matthew 26:39). Suffering can open us up for the question of God's will. If this happens, God's will and our will, God's promises and our wishes, meet in suffering, very painfully at that. Suffering is not just there to be "suffered." It is not fate that would compel us to become dumb, so as not to challenge it some more. Those who pray need to ask how they can, whatever happens to them, *let happen* as the will of God. Acquiescence means letting God's will happen, not to resist the will of God.

This is a different way of acting than what we are familiar with in the formula of "activity versus passivity." "To need God is the high

---

works thus came to naught, so that he was counted not only by men among the evil-doers but was also forsaken by God. Everything must be taken away from us that much, so that not even God's best gifts, that is, the merits remain for us to trust in and the purest hope be directed toward the purest God."

8. Comment on Thesis 21, WA 1:362, 28f.: *"At Deum non inveniri nisi in passionibus et cruce."* For the interpretation see Walther von Loewenich, *Luther's Theologia Crucis,* 6th ed. (Bielefeld: Luther-Verlag, 1982), 20–22. See also Hans Joachim Iwand, "Theologia crucis" (1959) in idem, *Nachgelassene Werke,* vol. II: *Vorträge und Aufsätze,* eds. Dieter Schellong and Karl Gerhard Steck (Munich: Chr. Kaiser, 1966), 381–398.

est perfection of the human being," said Kierkegaard.[9] We need to add: to submit to God's will is ground and telos of human freedom. Everything that happens to us comes, however secretly, from God. However, everything that happens to us is not always identical with God's will. These two statements, however paradoxical they may seem, are valid theologically at one and the same time. They create a tension we cannot suspend or annul, certainly not on grounds of an anticipatory interpretation of suffering.

We do not know *how* God is present in all that happens to us. But we trust *that* God encounters us in all things, demonstrating the divine power in our lives. Thus hope springs from suffering. Only on the road of suffering, in undergoing suffering, do we become the creatures of God, in whom and through whom God sustains rights as Creator and Redeemer. We do not have these rights as a matter of course in the *fact of human life*. We cannot bank on them or claim them in battling others.

I have drawn out a few lines that I find Luther only hinting at.[10] Luther took as a point of departure the suffering *(passio)* of Christ and returned to it time and again. He concentrated in that regard on the history between God and human beings. That which happens between God the Father and the crucified Son pertains to all human beings and to all their suffering. Luther was never able to disregard this fact when he spoke of the suffering of the world (of whose forms of expression, causes, and challenges he had relatively little to say). Perhaps the diversity and the constant presence of this suffering was so much a matter of course for him that he did not feel called upon to stress how he himself was subject to it. Yet we need to show more clearly than Luther did how human beings encounter their suffering and that of others, and how they experience it. I will return to this point.

What is sufficiently clear at this juncture is the anthropological result of this theology of the cross. Luther comprehended it in the notion of the *vita passiva*.[11] *Vita passiva* means life that is primarily *un-*

---

9. This is the title of one of Sören Kierkegaard's *Edifying Discourses* (Copenhagen, 1844).

10. For their Christological basis, see "Jesus the Christ," chapter I above.

11. For this term within the context of Luther's theological development see Christian Link, "*Vita passiva*: Rechtfertigung als Lebensvorgang," *Evangelische Theologie* 44 (1984): 315–351. See also Wilfried Joest, *Ontologie der Person bei Luther* (Göttingen: Vandenhoeck & Ruprecht, 1967), especially 37–39, 302–310.

dergoing suffering and that cannot exist without this suffering. One "suffers" God's activity in that one lets God act upon oneself and receives this activity gratefully, even though it might be painful. For without suffering human beings cannot become what they are intended to be in virtue of God's rights. *Suffering and becoming belong together.* Through suffering the human being is transformed, moved, drawn toward God—yes, torn by God out of one's old ties and set on the road of the new creation.[12] Suffering means to will what God wills, not obstinately or in resistance, but in assent to God's will. The human "Yes" emerges from the freedom with which God endows us.

In his lectures on Romans (1515–1516), Luther described suffering God's activity as conception. In the annotation (scholium) to Romans 8:26 ("God's Spirit helps us in our weakness; for we do not even know how to pray") he says that in the coming of grace and the glory of God we behave "passively as a woman in conception, for we are the bride of Christ. Therefore we may ask and pray before (we receive) grace. But when grace comes and the soul is to be penetrated by the Spirit, it ought not pray nor act, but simply submit quietly."[13] This last cue appears to me especially revealing. It lifts out suffering from any non-action and does not permit simply pitting the *vita passiva* against human willing. What is excluded is that human beings can become *creatively* active in order to realize what they "have

---

12. See, for example, from Martin Luther, *Operationes in Psalmos*, WA 5:177, 12f., on Ps. 5:12: *"Velle enim illud, quod credere, sperare, diligere iam diximus, est motus, raptus, ductus verbi dei. . . . "* "The willing that we have called faith, hope, and love is being moved, overpowered, led by the word of God. . . . " *De servo arbitrio*, WA 18:753, 33–35; *"Deinde ubi spiritu gratiae agit in illis, quos iustificavit, hoc est in regno suo, similiter eos agit et movet, et illi, ut sunt nova creatura, sequuntur et cooperantur, vel potius, ut Paulus ait, aguntur."* "What is more, where [God] through the Spirit of grace works in those that [God] justified, that is, in his kingdom, he impels and moves them. They follow and labor, having become a new creature, or, rather, as St. Paul says [Rm. 8:14] they are moved." Luther previously has included all creatures in the "movement of God's omnipotence." See Hans Joachim Iwand, *Nachgelassene Werke*, vol. V: *Luthers Theologie*, ed. Johann Haar (München: Chr. Kaiser, 1974), 97–101.

13. WA 56:379, 2–6: *"Ad primam gratiam sicut et ad gloriam semper nos habemus passive sicut mulier ad conceptum. Quia et nos sumus sponsa Christi. Ideo licet ante gratiam nos oremus et petamus, tamen quando gratia venit et anima impregnanda est spiritu, oportet, quod neque oret neque operetur, Sed solum patiatur."* For an interpretation see Martin Seils, *Der Gedanke vom Zusammenwirken Gottes und des Menschen in Luthers Theologie* (Gütersloh: Gütersloher Verlagshaus Gerd Mohn, 1962), 78f.; Joest, *Ontologie*, 313f.

coming" because they are creatures of God. Where human beings allow God to act upon them and through them, their cooperation begins in pausing and keeping quiet. They no longer propel themselves ahead in their time, carrying along everything around them as if in a current. God's future happens to them; God's advent does not simply interrupt the course of human life—so that human beings could continue with business as usual after a possibly fruitful interruption—but opens human life for God's promise.

Thus, the *vita passiva* is not a mystical ideal of piety.[14] Yet also this theology of suffering, in terms of Luther's conviction, is quite distant from the theology of the cross, for it builds on human achievement, that is, on some negating activity. Thus it again depends on active life, the *vita activa*, although it orients itself in the negative of all values that generally pertain to this particular ideal of life. For Luther, therefore, it is not the *suffering image* of the captive, tortured, and dying Suffering Servant that is determinative for his theology of the cross. It is solely the *crucified* as such: Jesus Christ (the suffering Son of Man, identical with the exalted Son of God!) draws his own into *his* suffering, his continuing history of suffering which no one can really picture beforehand. The *vita passiva is not a self-chosen suffering, but the co-passion with Christ,* who communicates to us humans the activity of God that leads the world to salvation.[15]

The human beings to whom suffering happens through the power of God's Spirit *become* what they are *allowed to be* and *ought to be.* This would never happen to them if they would *remain* who they *are,* locked up in themselves, even in a permanent activism.

14. Link, *"Vita passiva,"* 317–324. For Staupitz see David C. Steinmetz, *Luther and Staupitz: An Essay in the Intellectual Origins of the Protestant Reformation* (Durham, NC: Duke University Press, 1980), 75–78.

15. See especially Luther's interpretation of Ps. 8 and Ps. 22 in *Operationes in Psalmos,* specifically WA 5:273, 15–277, 29; WA 5:287, 12f. (cf. "Summarien über die Psalmen und Ursachen des Dolmetschens" [1531–1533], WA 38:20, 31–35); WA 5:600, 23–30 (cf. WA 38:25, 6–12). These and other pertinent texts are interpreted by Horst Beintker, "Gottverlassenheit und Transitus durch den Glauben. Eine Erschliessung der Anfechtungen des Menschen Jesus nach Luthers Auslegungen der Psalmen 8 und 22," *Evangelische Theologie* 45 (1985): 108–123. The difference between Luther's Christological theology of the cross and mystical suffering theology is emphasized, as well as in something of a critique of Walther von Loewenich (see note 8 above) by Rudolf Hermann, *Gesammelte und nachgelassene Werke,* vol. I: *Luthers Theologie,* ed. Horst Beintker (Göttingen:Vandenhoeck & Ruprecht, 1967), esp. 69.

Suffering—A Borderline Experience of the Active Life

Thus far I have pursued several foundational ideas that run through Luther's entire theology, even though they do not always take the limelight and were not always carefully attended to after Luther's days. On the whole, Luther was hardly able to assert himself with his interpretation of the message of Christian freedom that grows in distress, that can be tested in steadfastness and that proves itself in hope (cf. Romans 5:3f.). His opponents of 1525, the humanist Erasmus on the one hand and the religious social-revolutionists on the other, found greater response in the long run. On the bottom line, Luther's two protagonists are rather similar to each other. This does not pertain as much to their political ideas and social convictions as to their image of the human being and his existence in the world. Erasmus and the theologians of the Peasants' War (for example, Thomas Müntzer) see the human being as an agent in a world that is a single network of cause and effect. God has made the world that way, so that human beings are moving toward God, if they do the right thing. They have been created for and called to the realization of the divine purpose which has been embedded in the world or which still needs to be brought into the world. They must move around in it and move it ahead, since it still leaves much to be desired. Only the restlessly active person—active in thought, in extrapolating reflection, and in prayer as well as in deed—can discover the traces of God.

This particular perspective on the proper way of life is the *vita activa,* the constantly effective and self-propelling activity. *Vita activa* need not immediately involve restless activism. It moves first of all as an inner dynamic responding to everything it encounters. The *vita activa* is active from within its own center and in various ways. It moves incessantly in interpersonal interaction and is sustained by it. At the same time it elaborates the interaction. It thus helps to tie together the giant network which we call our "world reality." The philosophy of Western culture, political philosophy in particular, takes this network as its theme as Hannah Arendt in her study of the *vita activa* has convincingly shown.[16]

The way of life of the *vita activa* considers "suffering" only as interference, as a big tear in the fabric of the world and as injury of

---

16. Hannah Arendt, *Vita activa - oder vom tätigen Leben* (Stuttgart: W. Kohlhammer Verlag, 1960).

one's action center. This suffering might be a fruitful interference, in particular when it calls forth resistance and rouses new life dynamics. More frequently, though, it appears only as a brake on life: It interrupts life processes and possibilities of formation; it blocks activity or paralyzes it. Thus, human beings must try with all their might to become capable again of acting so as to overcome any resistance which holds them back. They have to stand up especially against their own sloth, indolence, or weakness which drags them down, as it were, and keeps them from getting ahead. They must watch out and, if need be, they must do battle so that they themselves determine the balance between rest and activity as well as between reception and action. They will want to *experience* life and not merely undergo suffering, experience suffering only to the extent that it stimulates an experience that is stronger, deeper, and more far-reaching than mere occupational therapy.

I want to show, in reference to Reinhold Niebuhr and Paul Tillich, how widely this image of a human being existing in action in the world has determined the Christian image of the human being, covering large periods of Christian history. I can speak more concisely at this point more so than with Luther, since Niebuhr as well as Tillich operated with a rather neat (and somewhat schematic) thought structure. What is more, both spoke relatively seldom of suffering (unless I have overlooked something). This does not have to mean that, for them, suffering is marginal or irrelevant. The ethicist of culture and social critic Niebuhr as well as the religious socialist Tillich probably preferred to understand suffering as a task of social ethics, thus within the framework of the *vita activa*. Suffering for them hardly turns explicitly into an anthropological theme.

In his development of a Christian anthropology Reinhold Niebuhr mentioned the transference to Jesus of two outstanding Old Testament figures: the all-earthly evil overcoming triumphant heavenly "Son of Man" (Daniel 7:13) and the "Suffering Servant" (Isaiah 53). As Messiah, Jesus unites both figures in himself in that he bears the sins of the world and overcomes them. "It is God who suffers for man's iniquity."[17] God vicariously stands up for human beings where they have injured God and thus missed their destiny, that is, in the abuse of their freedom. The human being is born as free spirit,

---

17. Reinhold Niebuhr, *The Nature and Destiny of Man: A Christian Interpretation*, 2 vols. (New York: Charles Scribner's Sons, 1941–1943), II:46.

not subject to nature. Human beings are to realize this freedom in moving into ever-new spaces, never satisfied with what they have discovered and thus far achieved. Freedom incessantly makes us set out to new frontiers, having to overcome fear of the unknown as well as uncertainty over the limits of its possibilities.[18] Human beings discover from their fear that they are finite and that within their limits they will never find rest. If, however, human beings fix their minds on what they have accomplished, for once they stay put congratulating themselves, losing themselves in their egotism and thus in sin. But they equally miss their destiny in transcending their creaturely limits. They climb too high and lose themselves in the mountainous terrain, being unable to move ahead or back. In both instances we do not come to terms with our limitations,[19] and thus violate not merely ourselves but also others. "All human life is involved in the sin of seeking security at the expense of other life."[20] Sin can be overcome only when freedom is discovered anew. Here the crucified Christ comes to our aid. He renounced absolutizing himself in his limited perspective of historical reality the way all human beings and human communities are wont to do.[21] As a finite being he opened himself to the infinite God and thus gained the freedom that neither flees from self nor enhances self.

Niebuhr's concept is based on the dialectics of freedom and limitation. The dialectics unlock the relationship of human beings to themselves, fellow humans, history, and God. In their destiny for freedom all human beings are equally immediate to God's freedom. The significance of the human being "as a free spirit is understood as subordinate to the freedom of God."[22]

Am I mistaken when I hear resonating in the motif of "freedom under God" one of the dogmas of the American "New Man"? It is explicated in the words of Thomas Jefferson in the Declaration of In-

18. Ibid, I:183. In note 3 Niebuhr emphasizes, in contrast to Luther, that there is no freedom without anxiety and that sin cannot be said to be the same as turning away from God, or as the absence of trust in God; sin, rather, is that which misses the possibilities of freedom, and thus sin can only be grasped from freedom. Anxiety is the price of freedom: " . . . a life totally without anxiety would lack freedom and not require faith."
19. Ibid, I:178, 180.
20. Niebuhr, *Nature and Destiny*, I:182.
21. Ibid, II:62.
22. Ibid, I:92.

dependence: " . . . that all Men are created equal, that they are endowed by their Creator with certain inalienable rights, that among these are Life, Liberty, and the pursuit of Happiness."

Paul Tillich viewed suffering as the "fallout" of freedom. It is a token of the ambiguity of human life, a symbol for that existence that experiences its finitude and becomes conscious of its limits. Suffering can show "the limits and the potentialities of a living being."[23] For example, we human beings have been lonely for a long time. We would like to break through this barrier. But if we seek the other only so that we no longer have to be alone, we miss encountering the other. We discover merely ourselves in the other and thus create new suffering for our fellow humans as well as for ourselves. We read something similar to Niebuhr: "Suffering is therefore overcome by the self-negation of the will's desire to be something particular. In Christianity the demand is made to accept suffering as an element of finitude with an ultimate courage and thereby to overcome that suffering which is dependent on existential estrangement, which is mere destruction."[24]

Fifty years ago at the Union Theological Seminary in New York that heritage of German idealism imported and modified by Paul Tillich—the human being as Spirit, projecting itself into the world—was married to the American pioneer spirit embodied in Niebuhr. To what extent the Christian anthropology here conceived is still determining North American theology I am unable to judge. I might say, though, that the impression still exists in Europe that the American people always move on to new frontiers, whether the frontiers of space or the vast landscape of inner life. In the American view, human beings are considered free only as long as they keep moving. We are, of course, always tempted to disregard the limitations set for us as individuals or in terms of our social relationships. Thus, we need to learn to move within these limitations. The limits of our body and of our mind, as well as those forces that depend on the balance between body and spirit, are the issues here.

As far as it is possible to investigate the cultural background of the concept of the human being in North American theology the same applies to Luther's anthropology. Here is only a hint: If for Niebuhr, for example, it is typical to assess that "life in history must be recog-

23. Paul Tillich, *Systematic Theology,* vol. II (London: SCM Press, 1978), 71.
24. Ibid, II:80.

nized as filled with indeterminate possibilities"[25] (a history-intoxicated modern European, by the way, could utter very much the same thought), for Luther the picture is more that of a widely limited historical world. Human beings not only lived together much more closely then; their lives were also ordered by the institutions of State, Church, family, and a family-focused economy. Although institutions can take away some suffering, they can also create new suffering if one does not, or is unable, to submit to them.

Christian anthropology should not disengage itself from the analysis of such presuppositions. Yet it dare not get shackled by them either whenever it asks to what does God's activity with humankind really amount. It certainly must notice this activity in definite situations and occasions and thus will have to address the issue contextually. If the context becomes transparent to the human condition before God, Christian anthropology, in view of its particularly incompatible conditions, can become open for dialog of theological thought in other situations. Perhaps it can also become helpful for common insights. I wish to take a few more steps in a comparison along these lines.

Dimensions of Suffering

Suffering means: pain, hunger, oppression, unbearable burden, throes of death. As best as we can tell, human beings share such suffering with all animals. Plants also suffer, if they are deprived of light, if the air is polluted, or the water is poisoned. Animals suffer not only in the struggle for existence but also because of us humans as we use them for our purposes. There are animals we use to save our strength. There are animals we claim as our own to overcome our loneliness. There are animals we subject to experiments so that we humans might suffer less, or only for the reason that we might live even more unreasonably than thus far, or that we might look a little more beautiful.

Where is the borderline between natural and artificial, or even unnatural suffering? Which pains must we suffer just to stay alive? Which pains do we produce for ourselves that we might also rid ourselves of again? The distinction no longer seems clear today. The

25. Niebuhr, *Nature and Destiny,* II:207.

thought and actions of generations in Western civilization were, and still are, bent on limiting our natural suffering more and more. Ideally it ought to be eliminated entirely. Pains were anesthetized, new frontiers were opened up, maladies in body and soul were covered up by all kinds of cosmetics, the hopelessly ill were surrendered to euthanasia. Today we need to recognize that the limitation of natural suffering produces other forms of suffering. Human beings who are no longer deprived of anything and therefore no longer need to struggle for anything suffer boredom. Human beings who no longer know restraints, and thus no longer need to show consideration for others, become ill from the loneliness they themselves have created.

The realm of inescapably natural conditions of life seems evermore to dwindle. Yet at the same time new sufferings are added. It now becomes all the more important to ask what kind of suffering will be brought about if human beings want to live better and happier and in less limited ways. Each birth brings pain. Each truly great physical or intellectual achievement depends on self-chosen restrictions that are often quite painful but are compensated for by the expansion of bodily and intellectual maneuverability.

Yet what price did people have to pay for the cultural monuments on which we now look with pride as the great achievements of the human spirit, human creativity, and religious awe? The tombs of the Egyptian kings, for example, were erected by innumerable slaves who were killed in the process. Many temples and churches—certainly not all, for quite a few emerged from the gratitude of people who had been freed from suffering—and most of the ostentatious buildings we sightseers today enjoy cost their builders an amount sufficient to support their subjects. What infinite suffering does our standard of living, our technological progress, and our security bring? What price for those who had to pay for all of this with their economic dependency, their impoverishment, and their insecurity?

Human, all-too-human, need is discredited if it translates into needs that have to be satisfied at any cost. One's real vulnerability and continuing dependency on others are thus forgotten. Needs begin to develop a logic of their own. They can become independent and thus appear to transport the needy beyond their limits, at least in terms of their wishes. Human beings (according to Reinhold Niebuhr) disown their nature and destiny whenever they transcend their limits. In suffering, they reach beyond what they are now. They want to *be* more and *acquire* more merely in order to live. But this wanting more can unexpectedly turn into a denial of one's own suffering, so that others have to suffer also. Those guided by their desire for limitless self-realization will get stuck in their egoism and thus bring suffering on others as well as on themselves.

These are the insights of Reinhold Niebuhr's and Paul Tillich's thought. Suffering is created and increased through the limitless self-interest of individuals, social groups, nations, and cultures—today we would also add in relationship to other forms of life on the planet we inhabit together. Actual suffering, however, shows us being addressed by the limits of all life forms. We are addressed by the suffering of others as well as by our own suffering, if we choose not to close our eyes to it but regard it as indicative of the global community of all living beings. In this perspective, the interdependence of suffering turns into a challenge of the *vita activa* of each individual—as we recognize that our planet is also a battlefield littered with countless victims of the *vita activa*.

Suffering physical and psychological pain shows us that we are *beings in need*. Much clearer than does any intellectualization, our own suffering makes clear what we need: food, warmth, space, security, and care from others. From the suffering of others we can also sense that perhaps we have *used* them in order that we ourselves might survive. We might even have *abused* them in that we tried to live at their expense. Also in this manner—through the suffering of our fellow humans—we remain needy and cannot be content.

We would gain a great deal if we would only recognize this need of ours in the light of increasing suffering in our world. Apparently we cannot exist without causing suffering. But do we have to live in such a way that we increase suffering? Increased suffering occurs if humans do not pay attention to the *limits* involved in their needs. These limits connect every human being with the needs of others who arrive at the same limits. If we pay attention to our common limits we can keep suffering *within* limits. That does not rid us of suffering, of course, but it sees to it that suffering does not increase—something that surely happens when extreme and far-reaching efforts are made to rid us of suffering. These efforts only transfer or repress suffering so that it unexpectedly surfaces again at some other place.

How does this borderline experience relate to Luther's talk about suffering in view of the cross of Christ? One might understand both as complementary, God taking on all the world's suffering and also human resistance against all conditions that create suffering. Yet in this instance Jesus Christ's cross will turn, as it often happens today, into God's expression of sympathy that sensitized humans and empowers them for a more intensive and extensive activity. Luther, however, did not find it possible to use an ethical perspective to see through what was happening on the cross. What happened here to God's Son, and for all human beings, takes place again anew wherever people are confronted with the living God, and wherever the crucifixion intervenes between them and their activity.

From the human perspective, this intervening of God means suffering, letting God work—really letting it happen to us, not merely being shook up and taking it on the chin, as though God's intervention was an overpowering fate. From the human angle it is *one* reflection of *knowing the cross of Christ,* a knowledge that is far more comprehensive. That which has happened between God and the Son who was destroyed by humankind, opens itself up to all the suffering of the world and addresses this suffering. In Jesus Christ's cross our perception of suffering is refracted as through a prism that lets light fall on several levels.

What drove Jesus Christ against the wall, what made him suffer did not come to an end on Good Friday (Colossians 1:24). It was not exhausted by the pain of torture and his death struggle. As terrifying as his suffering was on Calvary, it can hardly comfort the countless who have had to suffer much longer and endure yet more cruel deaths. How could the suffering of one person, even though one descended from heaven, encompass the many forms of creaturely suffering! There is distress that can increase our energies of resistance until they explode. But distress can also gradually consume a human life, so much so that one cannot even protest. Then there are pains that become unbearable because they do not appear in any reasonable relationship to whatever we can still achieve in spite of our suffering. Or there is the silent pain of the handicapped who can become victims of those seemingly kind benefactors who, because of their projection of the whole person, overtax the limited opportunities of existence, thus creating new oppressions. Finally, there is the suffering of a frustrated life, imprisoned, caught in endless repetition, a life that in complaining and sighing seems to cling only to itself and no longer looks beyond itself—and yet, probably unconsciously, reaches for something new. (This is the way Luther interpreted the word of the Apostle in Romans 8:19, the creation waiting with eager longing "for God's sons to be revealed.")[26] How can suffering that has been left speechless be articulated?

The cross of Calvary does not provide a meaningful interpretation applicable to every imaginable suffering. What occurred on Good Friday was grasped as the *innocent suffering and dying* of the Son of God—the innocent self-sacrifice of the perfect high priest who was without any personal sin (the way Hebrews 7:26f. puts it). The suffering is not called "innocent" because Jesus Christ, perhaps innocently, became a victim. It is rather God's judgment that pronounces it "innocent." Here God does not just note whether or not the person's faults catch up with him. It is rather that God so reveals the divine justice that herein the guilt of the whole world is revealed. God does not manifest the innocence of a just person suffering in order to cleanse this person from some crime done to him. God has made the sinless Jesus, the one who in no single action abandoned communion with God and yet who found himself at the hour of death abandoned by all, "sin for our sake," as St. Paul puts it, "so that in Him we might become the righteousness of God" (II Corinthians 5:21). This action is the "praxis passionis divini," to use Frederick Herzog's term.[27] The cross of Jesus Christ is intended as a means for human beings to maintain their rights. God is involved in the cross in such a way as to enable humanity to participate in God's justice whenever they let themselves be drawn into the death and the life of Christ: in Baptism whenever the old self dies; in the Lord's Supper in which the death of Christ is proclaimed; and in the forgiveness of sins.

In other words, Jesus Christ's suffering and the suffering of humanity together with him happen because of the coming of the kingdom of God. This implies not only that at the cross and at the "word of the cross" (I Corinthians 1:18) human beings who do not

26. WA 56:371, 28–31: *"Igitur optimi philosophi, optimi rerum speculatores fueritis, Si ex Apostolo didiceritis Creaturam intueri expectantem, gementem, parturientem i.e. fastidientem id, quod est, et cupientem id, quod futura nondum est."* "Therefore you will be the best philosophers, the best scientists, if you have learned from the apostles to perceive creation as waiting, groaning in travail, that is, as something that rejects what it is and longs for what as future it is not yet."

27. Frederick Herzog, "Praxis Passionis Divini," *Evangelische Theologie* 44 (1984): 563–575.

want to owe God anything begin to resist, and who, therefore, intentionally or unintentionally, bring suffering upon themselves and others. Suffering for the kingdom of God also means that it has to be received and suffered as God's will, since only in this way does it remain God's project and not become subsumed under human projections.

What "God's activity" implies we grasp once and for all on Calvary and on the way from Good Friday to Easter—through the infinite silence in the face of death's finality during these three days. Christian theology can be nowhere but *in via* toward the place where God's life breaks through the world of death, yet not in such a way that this world is torn to pieces or turned upside down. Rather, in the world "the life through faith" is created. The person just through faith shall live (Romans 1:17).

God's justice shares itself as *iustitia aliena,* alien justice, coming from outside us and making us partake of God's rights, a *iustitia passiva.* What happens here does not fit into any traditional pattern of rights and justice, also not as a matter of course into the Old Testament affirmations of God taking sides with the socially disadvantaged and those unprotected before the law. God's promise to them certainly has not been canceled. We also cannot give up the perspective sharpened by injustices suffered—the "perspective from below,"[28] as Dietrich Bonhoeffer calls it—a view that can assess the miserable condition of the world in a manner less biased than an eye trained in affluence.

The perspective of the Crucified One (in this regard and above everything else) is the view of one abandoned, in fact, ostracized by humanity in order to distance him from God and God from him. It is the perspective of God-forsakenness. On these grounds Christianity had to learn what justice is—the justification of the godless. Christianity cannot cease learning this lesson as long as the history of Christ's passion continues. (What this yields for the socio-philosophical view of justice as distributive justice,[29] presently prevailing in

28. Dietrich Bonhoeffer, "Der Blick von unten," in *Gesammelte Schriften,* vol. II: *Kirchenkampf und Finkenwalde,* ed. Eberhard Bethge (München: Chr. Kaiser, 1965), 441.

29. Frederick Herzog has developed this for North American liberation theology in his book *Justice Church: The New Function of the Church in North American Christianity* (Maryknoll, NY: Orbis Books, 1980).

church and theology cannot be elaborated in this context.[30] One pointer must suffice. God's justice does not issue in equalization between what God has to demand for Himself and what human beings can achieve. God sustains the divine rights in taking upon Himself unbearable guilt. In this way God creates the "right relationship" that helps human beings measure what they owe other creatures and what they can do about it.)

"Suffering" thus can no longer be seen as merely an alternative to action. Are we not already, and have we not been for a long time, caught in a stereotype that allows only acting and not-acting, movement and rest, energy and lethargy? As far as our action is concerned this stereotype would allow only productive activity, the realization of ideas, and the transfer of intentions into reality. Suffering apparently can be neatly fit into this stereotype, that is, as a conflict with reality that allows the resistance energies necessary for life to increase, but that also compels those who suffer to accept unavoidable life conditions so as to avoid getting ground up by them and which, under the most favorable conditions, helps the sufferers retain the balance between resistance and submission.

Where does Jesus' prayer in Gethsemane and on the cross have its place in such a schema in which Jesus' silence before Pilate at the moment of truth made Jesus withdraw from the justification of the power that crucified him, and thus says everything that needs saying for the unmasking of self-destructive power—what has to be said in silence in order that this "power above right" unmasks itself?![31] I could go on: in transferring suffering into the relationship of persons with themselves have we not also reshaped faith, love, and hope as motivations for action, or even relegated suffering to pure irrationalism? Suffering that allows itself to be called to Christ's cross does not persist in opposition to action, but resists the unbroken will, the will that does not want to suffer God's will for the world and thus also resists God's action. "Not only action, but also suffering is a way to freedom," Bonhoeffer writes. "In suf-

---

30. See Gerhard Sauter, "Gerechtigkeit" and "Recht" in *Evangelisches Staatslexikon*, eds. Roman Herzog, Hermann Kunst, Klaus Schlaich, and Wilhelm Schneemelcher, 3rd ed. (Stuttgart: Kreuz Verlag, 1987), I:1074–1083, II:2693–2706.

31. The ethically and politically extremely illuminating interpretation of Jn. 18:33–19:11 I owe to Paul Lehmann, *The Transfiguration of Politics: The Presence and Power of Jesus of Nazareth In and Over Human Affairs* (New York: Harper & Row, 1975), 64–70.

fering, the deliverance consists in our being allowed to put the matter out of our own hands into God's hands. . . . Whether the human deed is a matter of faith or not depends on whether we understand our suffering as an extension of our action and a completion of freedom."[32]

Suffering the action of God is *first of all pausing for thought and standing up to the question of what the will of God is* in what actually happens in the vast and impenetrable network we call "reality." Therefore, "suffering" in the shadow of the cross is paired with steadfast patience. It is to be distinguished from a mere surrender to *letting it happen.* It is tied to the question of what we would *suffer* as God's will. It is something positive, something that makes us feel grateful. Certainly this is often, in fact as a rule, not at all something we would welcome, if it is removed from suffering. Thus, Luther did not tire of stressing that God's activity is *hidden* from our view. That does not mean that God plays hide and seek with us, that He works only invisibly so that it would take a special religious sensorium to be able to trace this mysterious rule. No, God's hiddenness is the form of God's activity, the expression of the sovereignty of the living God, the ability to attain divine rights.

For this reason we are called *time and again* to recognize the cross in our human reality. However clearly the cross of Christ stands out on Calvary we have to hear ever anew from Christ's Word and Sacrament that the Cross unmistakably tells us what we need for life and death. We have to let it be communicated to us instead of trying to determine its locale in the present by using a general outline of what it means to suffer, however religiously profound, and seemingly modeled in terms of Christ's suffering, this outline might be. Once more from the words of Luther in an early interpretation of the penitential Psalms on Psalm 32:8 written in 1517, God says, "I will instruct you and teach you the way you should go." "Behold, this is the way of the cross. You cannot find it, but I must guide you as though you were blind. Therefore not you, not any human person, not any creature, but I, I myself, will instruct you in the way you should walk. Not the work you choose, not the suffering that you understand, but what goes against your choosing and thinking, that is, against your grain, that's it. There

---

32. Dietrich Bonhoeffer, *Letters and Papers from Prison* (New York: Macmillan, 1967), 206.

follow, there it is I call, there be a pupil, there is the time, there your
master has come. . . . "[33]

"Suffering," the way I have formulated it above, *also* means to fix
one's eyes on the cross of Christ and to begin to live and think in
terms of his passion. *Theology begins with the "reading" of the passion of Christ as the context of all suffering in the world.* Theology
does not come to terms with it as long as there is suffering. (The context is not clear in and of itself. Only in virtue of the text the context
becomes clear. It envelops the text and makes it speak.) Such reading
begins with painful experiences. Whether or not God's action is experienced will be known in the transformation of suffering and in
suffering itself not having the last word. This kind of "reading" has
an existential side and a theoretical side. The existential side states
that suffering befalls us not merely because suffering belongs to life
but because, in view of the immeasurable suffering in our world, we
need to reflect on the rights of the suffering. This implies "pragmatically" that the ontologically evident statement, "Suffering is part of
life," dare not become an excuse. In any case, theologically, it dare
not turn a profound interpretation of immeasurable suffering into an
intellectual form of grasping the concept. Descriptions of suffering
may be measured by whether or not they make the cross of Christ
speak so that it can be heard as Christ's presence dealing with us in
God's name. Christologically "Suffering is part of life" can only
mean that undergoing suffering mediates between God and the
human being. On account of what happened on Calvary, in virtue of
the promise of this cross, in undergoing suffering God and the
human being become engaged with one another. It is precisely this
involvement which gives rise to a new relationship: God encounters
human beings and persons encounter each other.[34] Theoretically
(that is, not speculatively but *in the truthful perception of the world
in the light of the cross*) this again leads to a *vita passiva* as the place
in which theology begins to understand how activity can be conceived and performed theologically, namely, as nothing but the hearing and understanding of God's activity in Word and Sacrament, not

33. WA 1:172, 1–7.
34. In "How Can Theology Derive from Experiences?" above, chapter III, I suggest viewing the relationship of God's action and human action on the basis of the
Christological dogma of Chalcedon, the unity of God and the human being "in two
natures, inconfusedly, unchangeably, indivisibly, inseparably."

limited to both, but pervading the world, audible and visible in Word and Sacrament.[35]

Finally we need to state that *whether the cross of Christ determines the place of suffering as the life form of faith* (perhaps we now may add: also the *thought* form of theology!),[36] there is no way to localize cross and suffering in our world in "revelatory places." This concern that suffering evokes in us, the fellow-feeling it entails, the compassion that is not always "fear of suffering" (the way Ernst Bloch once put it) but which moves us to actively sharing—all this could tempt us to discover those places where suffering overpoweringly speaks to us. God thus would have to be found, demonstrated and exemplified at the edge of survival and death.

Luther had already defended against an attempt to mark off God's presence from a godless world and the battle for survival on the side of God from the woeful defense of godless—even though religiously armored—world dominion. That was my point in the beginning of this essay. It is an example of the recurring temptation of theology—in the understandable longing for concretization—to look for evidences and thus to answer questions that have yet to be posed and to which theology needs to open itself, that is, questions pertaining to God's own action. These questions are detoured or blocked off if one derives from memories of the "great acts of God" models for further experiences of God. By making present prefigurative events one intends to delimit the area in which God can further be found. The fact is, however, that in this manner historical reality is stylized, strait-jacketed by stereotypes that reduce the complexity of our perception so as to gain a sharper profile more quickly.[37]

The Christian tradition knows highly impressive stories of creaturely suffering and the liberation from such sufferings. There have been numerous attempts (and there still are such attempts today) to "read off" the continuity of God's action from the repetition of such experiences, and to discover therein expectations that would ad-

---

35. See Herzog, "Praxis Passionis Divini," 574: "Without the premise of God's praxis, human praxis turns into a prison" since it evades the "theopraxis, that is worship, the Eucharist, in which 'Unheilsgeschichte' (history of corruption and destruction) and 'Heilsgeschichte' (salvation history) meet."

36. The excellent study of Arthur C. McGill, *Suffering: A Test of Theological Method* (Philadelphia: Westminster Press, 1982), also points in this direction.

37. For further reflection, see "'Exodus' and 'Liberation,'" chapter II above.

vance the issue at hand. Situations of suffering, however, can be *"contexts of discovery"*[38] which can help us perceive, for example, that human beings experience help—human help perhaps—that makes them ready to look for God's help. Or we can discover from situations of suffering that suffering involves being present for others in special ways. Or the profile of suffering together with Christ (the way St. Paul outlines it in II Corinthians 4 and 6) can become clarified as vicarious suffering.[39]

All these discoveries are highly important. But they cannot offer *reasons* for what can happen alone from God's side, what can be confirmed as a sign of God's faithfulness. Whoever ponders suffering will continue to inquire throughout all their experiences of whom they speak. We have to look hard in order to discover what we have been told and what has been offered to us—and what we will never find if we envelop our reality in a cocoon of traditional stories.

An example: Frederick Herzog notes[40] that one of the decisive discoveries of Black Churches in North America occurred when slaves grasped that the God of Abraham, Isaac, and Jacob, who had led Israel out of slavery into freedom, was also their God. The Exodus story spoke to them as an oppressed people within a "Christian society," and they rediscovered themselves in Israel's experience of suffering. They also understood the crucified Christ, suffering for the sins of the world, as the central figure of this history. Their worship services concentrated on the event of the redemption of humanity under the aegis of the Cross, seen as one with the liberation of God's people then and now.

Whoever states this problem in terms of traditional criticism will discern the influence of an Old Testament piety of Anglo-American and Calvinist provenance. The notion of election kept alive in this tradition has, however, also brought forth imperialistic aberrations. Is not a *theology* of the cross needed at this point, distinct from a religiosity of suffering that shapes experiences of injustices, and the

---

38. See Gerhard Sauter, *Wissenschaftstheoretische Kritik der Theologie: Die Theologie und die neuere wissenschaftstheoretische Diskussion* (Munich: Chr. Kaiser, 1973), 356.

39. For this point and further New Testament references see Erhard S. Gerstenberger and Wolfgang Schrage, *Leiden* (Stuttgart: Kohlhammer, 1977), 155–162.

40. Herzog, "Praxis Passionis Divini," 571.

deprivation of rights in new forms of community? A true theology of the cross does not serve a narrative self-identification, a reembodiment of an ancient lifestyle. Rather it trains human beings wherever they move or stand in the perception of a life before God. It tells them what God has promised to do for them and what God will cause to happen to them in the presence of Christ.

Luther's new discovery was not always protected from misunderstanding as an ideal of life, and as an admonition against preaching long-suffering when critical discernment of competencies in action would have been called for, not to mention silence when the power of others moved toward irresponsibility. Whenever Luther spoke of suffering he wanted to proclaim the justification of sinners who must die (not mortify themselves) in order to live by the power of God. This passing away and becoming takes place in all we do and in whatever happens to us. Luther formulated it in a highly dialectical way in the Heidelberg Disputation (1518): "Through the cross works are nullified and Adam is crucified who would rather be edified through works."[41] The issue here, as we have seen, is not a strategy of human action but the liberation of action from self-edification, from self-justification. Will human beings accept the benediction that they are not a project that has to be made concrete in deed upon deed but that they are being worked on, as it were, formed in the image of Christ? Do we produce ourselves—or do we allow ourselves to be "edified" and thus live out our full creaturely, needy form?

We encounter this question not merely in theology but frequently also where human beings suffer from themselves. Suffering finally arises not so much where humans fail in what distinguishes them, but in what *makes* them distinct in one-sidedness and narrowness as part of their genetic heritage. Thus, contrary to their own willing they have to show their full humanity.

I have in mind contemporary literary figures such as Saul Bellow's *Herzog*, Arthur Sammler in *Mr. Sammler's Planet*, or Herman Broder in Isaac Bashevis Singer's *Enemies, A Love Story*. Obviously—yet not inescapably so in every being—the destiny of individuals is not imposed on them as the great telos, as a life plan which

41. Luther, Comment on thesis 21, WA 1:362, 29–31: *"Ideo amici crucis dicunt crucem esse bonam et opera mala, quia per crucem destruuntur opera et crucifigitur Adam, qui per opera potius aedificatur."*

we would merely have to execute. Should action be understood as progressive self-realization, suffering contradicts it. The issue is whether or not we understand its language.

Singer's novel *Schoscha* ends with an open dialog that identifies the suffering of the Jewish people with the traits of suffering in those who cannot realize their life project:

> "If God is wisdom, how can there be foolishness? And if God is life, how can there be death? I lie at night, a little man, a half-squashed fly, and I talk to the dead, with the living, with God—if He exists—and with Satan, who most certainly does exist. I ask them: 'What need was there for all this?' and I wait for an answer. What do you think, Tsutik, is there an answer somewhere or not?"
>
> "No, no answer."
>
> "Why not?"
>
> "There can't be any answer for suffering—not for the sufferer."
>
> "In that case, what am I waiting for?"
>
> Genia opened the door. "Why are you two sitting in the dark, eh?"
>
> Haiml laughed: "We're waiting for an answer."

6

Shifts in Karl Barth's Thought

*The Current Debate between
Right- and Left-Wing Barthians*

At the time of Karl Barth's death on December 10, 1968, an intellectual uprising, later given the rather overblown title, "The '68 Revolution," was fully underway.[1] I do not know Barth's own assessment of this turn of events. Certainly a conversation early in that year provided some clues. Barth asked me about the interest in his dogmatics among my students at Göttingen. He seemed disturbed that so many young theologians were still drawn to Rudolf Bultmann's theology. Clearly, the "Barth vs. Bultmann" debate had received top billing in German Protestant theology since the 1950s. Dramatizing mid-century theological development along these lines, Heinz Zahrnt, in the 1966 survey Die Sache mit Gott, portrayed Barth and Bultmann as protagonists conjuring up ever-new entanglements until Paul Tillich appears as a Deus ex America (shortly before being supplanted in America itself by cries of "God is dead!") to bring this passionate drama to a well-balanced conclusion.[2] Tillich in his *Systematic Theology* had apparently plotted a course between the Scylla of American-style liberal theology and the Charyb-

1. An earlier version of this chapter was delivered to a conference on the occasion of Karl Barth's 100th birthday, May 1st to 4th, 1986 in Stony Point, New York, and as a lecture in Utrecht, Netherlands (May 10th, 1986), Münster (May 27th, 1986) and Bonn (June 11th, 1986).
2. Heinz Zahrnt, *Die Sache mit Gott:Die protestantische Theologie im 20. Jahrhundert* (Munich: Deutscher Taschenbuch-Verlag, 1972), esp. 122–133, 325ff., 335–338.

dis of European Neo-orthodoxy.[3] More accurately, however, both these extremes corresponded to then-current American tendencies which were only subsequently conferred on German theology. The role of the Neo-orthodox could, of course, only fall to Barth because of his masterpiece in dogmatics. Barth appeared as representative of a theology faithful to the Bible and to revelation, carrying all the burden of clumsy concepts and, first of all, anxious to prevent theologians from leaving the shell and finding their own way in the open field of historical exegesis.

Such was the state of affairs in the year of Barth's death. With this event, the assessment (an often highly artificial and far-fetched one) of Karl Barth and his life's work began to alter almost overnight. Many students rediscovered Barth's political statements and found through them ways to approach particular sections of his voluminous *Church Dogmatics.* They found an answer to their questions about the social relevance of theology more readily in Barth than in Bultmann, or in any case they believed that they did. Of course, Barth's moving life story also offers many clues to the shaping of his life's work. During thirty-five years of his life, a period encompassing the shocks of the Third Reich, the war, the postwar period, the Cold War, and the Restoration, this theologian concentrated exclusively on the *Dogmatics,* a work of seemingly antediluvian proportions. But this concentration appeared less interesting than the fact that Barth had taken positions on manifold current problems—not just incidentally, but obviously from the power of his theological thought. It seemed most odd that such an apparently conservative basic approach to theology should repeatedly spawn critical political thought and often clear political opposition.

The Struggle for Karl Barth's Theological Legacy

As it represents an attempt to fully analyze this oddity, F.-W. Marquardt's 1972 work *Theology and Socialism*[4] quickly became the focal point of a controversy. Marquardt considered Barth's early theological works, the first edition of *Epistle to the Romans* (1919)

---

3. Paul Tillich, *Systematische Theologie,* vol. I (Stuttgart: Evangelisches Verlagswerk, 1956), 7 (preface to the German edition).
4. Friedrich-Wilhelm Marquardt, *Theologie und Sozialismus: Das Beispiel Karl Barths,* 3rd ed. (Munich: Chr. Kaiser, 1985).

in particular, as exemplifying conceptually a "contextual theology" (as we would say today). At its center, this theology conceives of "God's revolution" as a principle of change in sociopolitical conditions. Marquardt sought to show that all of Barth's theological reflections emerged directly from the prevailing historical situation which Barth took as a challenge. Elaborating his theological answer, Barth contributed toward changing the situation through the coming Kingdom of God. Thus Marquardt saw the young Barth, according to the center and focus of his theology, as a religious socialist. Even after his split from Religious Socialism in the early 1920s, Barth remained true to his basic approach: God enters into the world in Jesus Christ, both transforming and renewing it. Therefore, the further stages of his theology comprehended as well a broad-based theological confrontation with prevailing political conditions. If we subscribe to Marquardt, we must for each section of the *Dogmatics* search out the sociopolitical phenomenon to which Barth referred; Barth's dogmatics becomes an intellectual movement that entered directly into the realm of political ethics.

Marquardt presented this thesis to a theological conference near Basel aimed at continuing Barth's theological work in a new generation of theologians. In a report on the conference, Max Geiger wrote, "We experienced something similar to the formation of a Barthian 'right-wing' and of a Barthian 'left-wing.'"[5]

These two fronts have haunted the discussion of Karl Barth's theology and its consequences ever since. Max Geiger was not thinking of a baldly political division. He did not mean something akin to opposing parties in a Barthian parliament in which the conservatives sit on the right side and the progressives sit on the left, each striving for the majority and spouting off polemics against the other: the party shouting loudest invariably being the one considering itself the persecuted minority. In any case, Geiger's designations have been taken in this exact sense, as political classifications. Ever since, individual "Barthians" or Barth interpreters are duly sounded out on their political stance, a practice which naturally assumes that every theological position must be located on a political scale as well. But have we then not already put on the political point of view that Marquardt

5. Max Geiger, *Karl-Barth-Tagung auf dem Leuenberg,* supplement to Eduard Thurneysen, *Karl Barth: Theologie und Sozialismus in den Briefen seiner Frühzeit* (Zürich: Theologischer Verlag, 1973), 45.

claimed on Barth's behalf, the theological authority of which we must first examine?

Clearly, Marquardt and his mentor Helmut Gollwitzer would place themselves on the left side of the political spectrum in the Federal Republic of Germany and other countries, as would many among the circle of Barth's students. Yet does this mean that those who understand Barth quite differently from Marquardt and Gollwitzer, say for instance Eberhard Jüngel or Trutz Rendtorff and his friends and pupils who have published "Barth-studies,"[6] belong to the "right wing"? Certainly Marquardt himself never understood the situation in such a manner. He found the labels "right-wing Barthian" and "left-wing Barthian" always misleading. Geiger also described the problem differently: "The one side considers the other to have reverted to a self-satisfied Scholastic methodology of formal abstraction and to an individualist narrow-mindedness that can be interpreted as a hidden but nevertheless effective traditionally bourgeois basic attitude. Inversely, as seen by its opponents, the other side, in its attempts to join Christian belief and socialism, betrays the freedom of theological perceptions and abandons the first Barmen Thesis by building a new 'idol factory.'"[7]

One side, then, concentrated on the structure of theological thought that Barth erected, planning to remain comfortably within its walls for all eternity, needing only to wander about its halls in order to discover whatever was necessary in the way of faith, hope, and love. This unrelenting recapitulation of Barth's thought, insured by the most exact formulations possible, seems symptomatic of an overly self-satisfied approach to Christian existence. The other side considered theology a crowbar with which to pull prevailing political conditions off their hinges, providing the room for and the power to build new structures. I cannot help but wonder whether those who call the first type of interpretation "scholasticism" are not insulting both historical Scholasticism and the great respect Barth had for medieval Scholasticism and for its successors in the post-Reformation theology. But Geiger wished to describe the opposition of pure theological thought that now needs only be translated and exposed to an impetus for theological thought that calls for its realiza-

6. Trutz Rendtorff, ed., *Die Realisierung der Freiheit: Beiträge zur Kritik der Theologie Karl Barths* (Gütersloh: Gütersloher Verlagshaus Gerd Mohn, 1975).
7. *Karl-Barth-Tagung*, 45f.

tion—or more concisely, the alternative of a hermeneutically deepened dogmatics and a political hermeneutics of theology.

Around 150 years ago, at Hegel's death, a similar rift occurred in German philosophy. The legacy of Hegel's thought degenerated into the pro-state philosophy of law of right-wing Hegelians and the revolutionary thrust of left-wing Hegelians. Supporters of right-wing Hegelianism were found in Prussian politics and in the chairs of philosophy at German universities. Left-wing Hegelians like Karl Marx became journalists when academic positions were denied them. The rift certainly corresponded with contemporary political circumstances, but the fundamental reason for the fight over Hegel's legacy stemmed from a contradiction within Hegel's own philosophy. This contradiction becomes clear to us in a famous sentence from the introduction to Hegel's *Philosophy of Law:* "What is rational is that which is real; what is real is that which is rational."[8] This sentence can be read starting with either half. When read from the beginning, it expresses the fundamental unity that comes about through the reconciliation of reality with rationality, a reconciliation that resulted in an intellectually conceived and continually reintegrated reality. Read beginning with the second clause, the statement means that rationality dictates what really should be. Consequently, all that has been up to now is transitional and preliminary to the true reality which lies in front of us and which must be realized by us.

Hegel explains the implications of his dialectical sentence in 6 of the *Encyclopedia of the Philosophical Sciences.* According to Hegel, God alone is true reality; being is partially appearance and only partially reality.[9] In his system of philosophy, Hegel attempted to conceive perfectly God and in this way to grasp all of reality. But what can still happen, how can history proceed, if history is conceived as already fulfilled? In the dialectic between rationality and historical being two possibilities emerge: the incessant incorporation of all further events in a previously conceived reality and the opposite alternative, the attack on existing reality in the name of the

---

8. Georg Wilhelm Friedrich Hegel, *Grundlinien der Philosophie des Rechts oder Naturrecht und Staatswissenschaft im Grundrisse* (1821), *Sämtliche Werke,* vol. VII, ed. Hermann Glockner, 4th ed. (Stuttgart-Bad Cannstatt: Fr. Frommanns, 1964), 33.
9. G.W.Fr. Hegel, *Enzyklopädie der philosophischen Wissenschaften im Grundrisse* (1830), eds. Friedhelm Nicolin and Otto Pöggeler (Berlin: Akademie-Verlag, 1966), 38.

true, utopically conceived reality. Both of these consequences may diverge and even clash, but they still converge in one motive: the creative impulse, directed to political formation. Hegel's system, interpreted on the background of his Philosophy of Law, is thoroughly political, subordinating all realms of life to the only crucial task of reconciling reason and reality, spirit and history. The spirits take leave from one another only if the question is raised: how can such a reconciliation succeed? But it must succeed, both "wings" agree on that.

Examined in this light can the fight over the legacy of Karl Barth's theology be more easily understood? To answer this question we need not push Barth completely into Hegel's orbit. Admittedly, Barth's relation to Hegel is quite complicated.[10] Barth did not consider himself a theological Hegelian. Nevertheless, his respect for Hegel was great, especially because of the significance of Christology for Hegel's thought. To be sure, Barth held Hegel's system to be problematic and theologically questionable, thereby agreeing with Hegel's critic, Søren Kierkegaard. During his entire life Barth denied being a systematic theologian in the strictest sense. Nevertheless, many parallels between Barth and Hegel leap to the eye. Do not both attempt to begin with the reality of God, which reveals itself to humanity once and for all in Jesus Christ? Do not both speak of the Christological perfection of reconciliation that can never be surpassed by anything further in history? Do not both understand God's reality, the reality of the triune God, as perfect and absolute in itself, as unity of divine freedom and love, pervading, embracing, and inspiring the world so that the further course of time can no longer possess any significance of its own? And finally, do not all these parallels indicate that the continuation of Barth's thought faces similar problems as those faced by further development in the Hegelian school?

I would ask, therefore, whether the governing principle of Barth's theology, the dialectic between God and the world, makes Barth's theology as political as Hegel's philosophy. Here, too, I use "political" not in the sense of belonging to any particular political group but rather in the sense of characterizing a way of giving shape to reality. In the following I will address this last question, developing

---

10. Cf. Michael Welker, "Barth und Hegel: Zur Erkenntnis eines methodischen Verfahrens bei Barth," *Evangelische Theologie* 35 (1975): 421–437.

three characteristics of Barth's theology, especially in the *Church Dogmatics*: his thought in *context*, his thought in its *movement*, and the *unity* of his thought. With these remarks I will conclude the comparison between Barth and Hegel. There only remains one annotation: Hegel's legacy has influenced some of Barth's students in other ways than by the affinity which possibility holds true for Barth and Hegel. Since the sixties, the influence of Hegel and of his controversial legacy has been rapidly increasing. This influence also affected the reception of Barth's theology, and it is remarkable that just Hegel's forms of reflection appear most adequate for the interpretation of Barth's intentions. Once more, the tensions within the interpretation of Hegel come into play: The standard may be *either* Hegel's *Science of Logic*, read and used as a universal theory of sense and reference—or the socio-political philosophy of history, radicalized by the left-wing Hegelians. Eberhard Jüngel managed to reconcile Bultmann, Barth, and Hegel—nevertheless, it is not quite clear who plays the lead in the plot. On the other hand, historical materialism is considered as helpful and even indispensable for analyzing the situation as a challenge theology has to accept (Walter Kreck[11] and Helmut Gollwitzer[12]); some of Friedrich-Wilhelm Marquardt's overpointed statements even amount to a complementary relation between Barth's doctrine of God and the "Critical Theory."[13]

There may emerge some points of controversy, but they are less significant than the fact that Barth—comparable to Hegel—obviously did not define the line with sufficient clarity in order to detect future deviances. Of course, Barth would have nothing to do with the "Führerprinzip" of totalitarian leadership, but he actually has exerted leadership to a much greater extent than his colleagues— even if they found adherents, which was exactly the reason why they

11. Walter Kreck, *Grundfragen christlicher Ethik* (Munich: Chr. Kaiser, 1975), 236ff.; idem, "Kirche und Marxismus: Präliminarien eines Gesprächs," *Evangelische Theologie* 35 (1975): 421–437.
12. Helmut Gollwitzer, *Die kapitalistische Revolution* (Munich: Chr. Kaiser, 1974); idem, "Historischer Materialismus und Theologie: Zum Programm einer materialistischen Exegese," in *Traditionen der Befreiung*, vol. I: *Methodische Zugänge*, eds. Willy Schottroff and Wolfgang Stegemann (Munich: Chr. Kaiser, 1980), 13–59.
13. Fr.-W. Marquardt, in *Traditionen der Befreiung*, 276ff.; idem, "Sozialismus bei Karl Barth," *Junge Kirche* 33 (1972): 2–15.

provided certain standards. The validity of these standards was independent from the teacher's personal commitment; they enabled the disciples to find their own way. In contrast, Barth always navigated in dangerous water, always on the alert. Barth determined the position, and he who would not agree had to leave the ship. But who is able to take the helm if such a helmsman is recalled and takes along the compass?

Thought in Different Contexts

Throughout the whole of his work Barth again and again approached theology with a fresh outlook—not only when the major "breaks" occurred in his work: during World War I, between the first and second editions of *Epistle to the Romans,* between the *Christian Dogmatics* and the *Church Dogmatics,* and during the last half of the thirties when political questions of the day troubled him with increasing persistence. Within the *Church Dogmatics* itself, Barth continued to pose questions at every step of the way, in particular at each major division and even within the individual volumes. These inquiries take up a lot of room relative to the whole of the material. This fact becomes especially clear in *Church Dogmatics* IV.4, the "Ethics of Reconciliation," which, apart from the doctrine of baptism, basically does not go beyond laying down groundwork. Only in small part do these inquiries involve a clarification of methodology. They are more important in that they expose the lines of discussion along which Barth was developing.

An impressive example of this development is the comparison of Barth's defense against "natural theology" in *Church Dogmatics* I.1 with IV.3, in which Barth assigned the manifold possibilities for knowledge in our world, the so-called lights, having a relative indicating function in the observation of the one true source of light, the revelation of Jesus Christ. Many interpreters have felt that this section represents a late acceptance on Barth's part of natural theology's intentions, which he had earlier so passionately rejected. Certainly the historical situation had changed: at the beginning of the thirties, the German-Christian heresy confronted Barth, as folk and race received the status of a second source of revelation next to the Bible. It was necessary to give an inexorable "No!" But by 1959, in the midst of a period of church restoration and isolation from social changes, was it not time to be on the lookout for confederates in politics, philosophy, and the sciences, to move beyond the borders of church and theology? This view contains much truth. Barth, with his inborn penchant for contradiction, always took his opponents well into account. He even felt it necessary to define his own position with respect to and distinct from many of his friends. This "no" influenced the "yes" of his argument's positive exposition. Barth also paid attention to the larger intellectual and social context of theology. The political climate played an important role in his assessment of that which must be expressed theologically *under all circumstances*. But how does this affect Barth's theology?

Since the sixties, discussion in ecumenical theology has opposed contextual theology to dogmatic theology. Dogmatic theology concerns itself with traditional dogma and its accompanying questions. Opposed to that, contextual theology emerges from its situation and reflects theologically the position of theology and Church in their place and time. Doubtless, Barth is no contextual theologian; he asserted that "revelation is not a predicate of history, but history is a predicate of revelation."[14] A theology of God's Word cannot grow out of an assessment of the situation as much as this theology seeks to address this situation. Yet Barth is not simply an old-style "dogmatic theologian" even though he did use categories taken from traditional treatments of the salvation story in the construction of his dogmatics to guide its form. As stated earlier, Barth continually tried to renew his approach to theological problems to which he was dedicated and which arose from this constellation and story. This "problem approach" implied Barth's involvement with the world situation. This involvement always drove at a theologically determinant point, which Barth sought to work out as clearly and decisively as possible. At stake in the construction of his dogmatics is *theological priority* over against the questions and perspectives that, at first glance, seem possible in any theological theme but that cannot in specific situations simultaneously possess equal importance without engendering a terrible confusion.

---

14. Karl Barth, *Die christliche Dogmatik im Entwurf*, vol. I: *Die Lehre vom Worte Gottes. Prolegomena zur christlichen Dogmatik* (1927), ed. Gerhard Sauter (Zürich: Theologischer Verlag, 1982), 311; idem, *Church Dogmatics* (Edinburgh: T. & T. Clark, 1956), I.2:58.

I will use natural theology to exemplify Barth's priorities. In Barth's view, natural theology is more than just a problematic subject of theological tradition, but plainly the basic error of modern theology, a source of trouble with incalculable consequences. "Natural" theology is not the opposite of "unnatural" theology; it rather presupposes that God does not encounter human persons in immediate sovereignty, but mediated by the world (not however, *in* the world) in which we have always been found. We have already been found in the world: that is crucial. As humans, we are naturally directed to God and, therefore, we always encounter God as soon as we reflect on our existence in a given situation. Theology, then, only has to articulate what the situation tells us.

In the first chapters of the *Church Dogmatics* (I.1), Barth entered his vehement protest against such a foundation of theology. At the same time, he rejected other possible implications of the term "natural theology." Natural theology, searching for points of contact with the Word of God, can come about through hermeneutic interests. It assumes that we possess "beforehand" preconceptions of words found in the Bible. Our understanding of the statements of faith refers to these preconceptions, as Rudolf Bultmann maintained. The question for natural theology may as well stem from missionary concerns: how can we explain our own views in the face of other religions or in a society that has lost all religion? This characterizes the thought of Emil Brunner. Barth confronted both of these views with the fundamental question of theological epistemology: can we know God from within ourselves or must we not, if we want to argue honestly, start with the presupposition that God created by addressing us with His Word? Barth built his question along strict epistemological and, it must be said, doxological lines. He forced his early comrades (later adversaries) such as Bultmann and Brunner to treat this question as decisive. Barth took the liberty of establishing the theological priorities, regardless of the relative adequacy of other theological problems and without compromise. He no longer tried to find his way in the jungle of hermeneutic and apologetic debates. Instead, his intention was to blaze the trail—also for the solution of other theological problems. He did not at all deny the theological "point of contact," but he inexorably challenged the significance of that "point of contact" for the *truth* of human perception. In Barth's view, we must ask that question at the outset, unconditionally and immediately. Otherwise, we might surreptitiously obtain theological statements which, moreover, on closer inspection will turn out to be borrowed from ideology, philosophy, or elsewhere.

Then by 1959 in *Church Dogmatics* IV.3 had the theological priority changed? No. A careful study of this volume shows quite clearly that Barth argued on the subject of epistemology exactly as he had argued earlier. Epistemologically and doxologically his argument remained: We can only know God because and insofar as God has made Himself known to us. Our knowledge requires an acknowledgment of God's sovereign freedom to approach us. Barth only developed this statement further and thereby shifted the accent. God, in God's self-revelation, is not locked into the Church's tradition(s), no matter how strongly He has bound Himself up with the pronounced Word to which the Church refers. But God acts within the world as well; there we may virtually stumble across traces of God's work. God approaches us in concepts and in actions that at first appear strange, even godforsaken or godless. Yet in the hope of God's universal self-revelation we are free to ask after God. Everything depends on this quest for God. In no case may we confuse any world concept with God's voice; we can take it as a challenge to search for knowledge of God. It is decisive that all these "lights" which illuminate our situation (or perhaps only seem to shed light on our situation) are dependent on the single source of light: God's revelation in Jesus Christ. Barth certainly drops some hints—e.g., "the laughter of children, the scent of flowers and the song of birds"[15]— but there is no need to go further and establish a "point of contact." On the contrary, Barth carefully avoids the identification of theories, models, or movements as authorities for verification or even appeal[16]—with the exception of Wolfgang Amadeus Mozart, of course. So, after twenty-five years, Barth did not finally catch on with Brunner and Bultmann, his old opponents. Rather, he took up theological tasks that, because of his earlier concentration on the one decisive question, he had not wanted to bring to the forefront.

This freedom, to set and adhere to theological priority regardless, distinguishes the whole of Barth's theology. This freedom is not naked "decisionism" in the sense of an arbitrary, at least not argumentatively justifiable decision, as for instance Pannenberg

15. *Church Dogmatics*, IV.3:698.
16. *Church Dogmatics*, IV.3:135.

argues against Barth.[17] Such freedom does not express the freedom of the independently responsible subject as formulated in the history of modern times. Finally, it does not describe the radical autonomy of God which Trutz Rendtorff wants to find in Barth. The freedom evidenced in Karl Barth's theology, and indeed in his entire being, rose out of Barth's habit of obedience to God in act and in thought. This obedience means: theology has to avoid digressions and must not simply state this or that just because it could be stated. Theology must not have false regards for interests or needs whose fulfillment could lead into false paths and pitfalls. Theology should never start with concessions which sooner or later must be retracted for theological reasons; therefore, we should not look for apparent solutions, but rather concentrate on that which can be said in accordance with good theological reasons. We have to start with God's Word—and we have to be aware that this starting point is neither arbitrary nor the zero point of human reflection. If we do not start with God's Word and instead try to arrive at that starting point only much later, it may be too late, even for any honest argument!

To use my own words, Karl Barth, with iron resolution, took the trouble to bring out the difference between the theological *context of justification* and all that comes to theology in challenges, answers, judgments, and problems. This is the subject of his various and different introductions. Theology can make discoveries from many sources (a fact Barth considers in *Church Dogmatics* IV.3). It can learn from other disciplines, from political movements, and also experience much from religious struggles. But it cannot learn from these sources how to do theology. Different *contexts of discovery*—as presented in political and other theories—must not be confused with the theological context of justification. Once this difference is clear, it is possible to be open to various contexts of discovery—above all, in times not dominated by ideological struggle.

Karl Barth spent his life considering such contexts. The difficulty in duplicating his thought and, with its help, to think independently, lies in the fact that Barth never clearly indicated the difference be-

17. Wolfhart Pannenberg, "Die Subjektivität Gottes und die Trinitätslehre," in idem, *Grundfragen systematischer Theologie,* vol. II (Göttingen: Vandenhoeck & Ruprecht, 1980), 103.

tween the context of justification and the context(s) of discovery.[18] In a sense, the distinction was at the heart of Barth's rejection of natural theology: In the first volume of the *Church Dogmatics,* he strictly defined the theological context of justification over against any possible preliminary knowledge of God. In the last complete volume, the christological substantiation is prior to any context, but, Barth concedes, we can derive certain insights from the periphery of the Church's proclaiming the Christ event, insights which are not irrelevant to the form of preaching reconciliation.

This complex of questions, however, remains somewhat mysterious, because Barth comes to a decision corresponding to his method (i.e., the priority of certain questions) and at the same time applies that decision to methodological problems (i.e., deriving theological statements). Barth never described his way of thought or his methodology. He did not make them the object of a metatheory. When others tried to do so, for example, Gerrit Cornelis Berkouwer in his impressive presentation *The Triumph of Grace* (1954)[19] or Kornelis Heiko Miskotte in his miniature *On Karl Barth's Church Dogmatics. Short Preludes and Fantasies* (1961),[20] Barth did indeed gaze at these works of art in wonder— he was equally astonished and a little disturbed to see himself described with such artifice. Barth was afraid of any reflection which might make itself indepedent and overgrow the "theological substance." For that reason, he did not give many clarifications that could have facilitated an exact understanding of his intentions or provide a means to stay true to his intentions while carrying them out.

Thought in Movement

Throughout his life, Barth wanted to be led not by a methodological principle but only by the theological "material in motion." As a dialectical theologian in the twenties who possessed expressionist speech and rhetorical skill, Barth understood how to set his audi-

18. Gerhard Sauter, *Wissenschaftstheoretische Kritik der Theologie* (Munich: Chr. Kaiser, 1973), 355f.
19. Gerrit Cornelis Berkouwer, *De triomf der genade in de theologie van Karl Barth* (Kampen: J. H. Kok, 1954).
20. Kornelis Heiko Miskotte, *Über Karl Barths Kirchliche Dogmatik: Kleine Präludien und Phantasien* (Munich: Chr. Kaiser, 1961).

ences' thoughts in motion. As he once stated, he tried to trace the bird's flight,[21] that is, to stay in motion while presenting the "material in motion." In this sense, in the *Church Dogmatics* Barth remained a dialectic theologian. He never takes up a single definitive viewpoint from which he draws the whole of the theological panorama. Rather, he proceeds with incessant questions, answers, and fresh questions. Raising his own objections, he places himself in dialogues between his own arguments without losing himself in monologues. I quote two highly characteristic sentences: "Dogmatics is scientific not as the exposition of all sorts of material, although it must be that too, but as the movement of this material or as this material in motion";[22] and "The results of dogmatic studies are not really important, truly not the results. Important is the *movement* of the Church, striving for purity of doctrine, denoted by these results."[23]

How does this trend or movement exhibit itself within the vast material of the *Church Dogmatics?* Observed from without (and perhaps not only from without!), this trend shows itself in the way Barth forced his readers to go on ever further with him. Nowhere, not even at decisive points or in the formulation of ground statements that cap off the contents of many other sentences, do we find a stopping off point, somewhere where we can settle down. In Barth's dogmatics there is no yearning for the end of the line. Even if Barth had written the last section of the *Church Dogmatics*, eschatology, no such end point would have emerged. Barth always required that his *Dogmatics* be read as a whole and that no section, however interesting, should be examined with the goal of providing an idea of the work in its entirety. Barth had said more than once to us younger scholars that we should try to lay out something new, perhaps even overtake his *Dogmatics*. However, we should not be satisfied with a narrower span of thought and should not claim to examine something new if we had simply overlooked or neglected

21. Karl Barth, "The Christian's Place in Society" (1919), in idem, *The Word of God and the Word of Man*, trans. Douglas Horton (London: Hodder & Stoughton, 1928), 9.

22. Barth, *Church Dogmatics*, trans. George Thomas Thomson (Edinburgh: T.& T. Clark, 1936), I.1: 324.

23. Idem, *Die Kirchliche Dogmatik*, I.2:860 (my translation). The translation of G. T. Thomson and Harold Knight (I.2:769) reads: "None of the results of dogmatics—really none at all—can be important. The only important thing is the activity of the Church, denoted by the results so far attained, in its striving for purity of doctrine."

some point. But who has the courage to write a new dogmatics that is not only greater in importance but also, if possible, heavier than the 28.6 pounds of the *Church Dogmatics!* But is not Barth's requirement of his readers—to know the whole and to keep it in mind—overly demanding, even arrogant? If the reader cannot lay hold of any section, but can only pause there, does it not become impossible to cite Barth? Incidentally, I have jokingly told my students, "You cannot quote Barth," because for so many statements a countercitation can be found from Barth himself. Naturally, this does not mean that Barth was inconsistent in his thought. Rather, it indicates that his trend of thought, although offering an image of deduction, was not a one-dimensional movement and, clearly, not a progression. Barth's trend of thought makes one thing apparent: theology can only direct its speech towards God. Theology articulates what it has to say only in reference to God. Thus theology is incapable of saying everything at one time. Theology cannot wrap everything up in one concept that it thereafter continually unfolds. True, theology could not manage without concepts, but we must be aware of the risk taken when theology uses them. Concepts must not, so to say, congeal.

Barth's dogmatics has no "material principle" such as proposed by many nineteenth-century theologians: the doctrine of justification or the kingdom of God. Nor does the concept of reconciliation become such a material principle for Barth's theology, although he does state as a basic in I.1 "Revelation is reconciliation" and in IV.3 "Reconciliation is revelation." Such basic statements possess only an indicatory character. They point towards Christ as theology's center, to which theology refers in all of its questions and answers. Jesus Christ stands at theology's center because he stands at the center of the Bible. In expectation and remembrance, the Bible testifies to him, and truly, so that all speech and acts in the name of Jesus Christ, all knowledge won in view of him, only witness to and indicate the Christ of whom the Bible testifies. (Barth elaborates this view especially at the beginning of his lecture on the gospel of John.)[24] Thus, Barth's intentions in his conscious emphasis on "the whole" become clear. The whole does not refer to a complete measure of Barth's work, but to the theological whole which cannot be contained between the covers of one

---

24. Karl Barth, *Erklärung des Johannes- Evangeliums* (1925/1926), ed. Walther Fürst (Zürich: Theologischer Verlag, 1976).

or more books. With the person of Jesus Christ always in view, this whole comes into discussion step by step without ever reaching a comprehensive fulfillment. Said otherwise, the whole of theology results from the arguments of theologians who rely entirely on the Bible. No theologian can bring theological work to completion, as no theologian can reduce the whole of biblical witness to a formula, no matter how comprehensive. Whatever claim a theologian makes using a single biblical text requires supplement and correction from further biblical texts. This trend, always involving movement from particular theological conclusions towards their biblical foundations, gives rise to an impression of the whole. A look through the *Church Dogmatics* reveals that this effort towards "conformity to the biblical writing" gains ever more strength. Exegesis continues to take up more and more room, not in order to provide as many biblical references as possible consistent with Barth's earlier statements but rather to open up and set in motion theological arguments, so that they may become transparent for the reality they only can announce.

This motion is in no case a divine dynamic which enters the world through theological mediation. A few Swiss religious socialists, contemporaries with whom Barth had some contact at the beginning of his career, wished to spark off such a trend. In *Struggle Towards God's Kingdom in Blumhardt, Father and Son—and Further*, Leonhard Ragaz attempts to build along such lines: the kingdom of God is the moving principle of history, destroying politically all static order and destroying theologically all static thought.[25] Never did Barth wish to understand his work or himself in this manner, however often he spoke of trend and movement or however much he set himself in motion. I agree with Eberhard Jüngel when he interprets Barth's concept "the revolution of God" as a taking back of the concept of "revolution" into God's reality.[26] Thus the theologian has no specific call to act as a revolutionary in the name of God. Rather, the theologian is called to ask questions about the truth of God in the middle of a changeable and changing reality. These questions can lead from time to time to revolutionary consequences, not because the theologian, through his calling, is in opposition to the existing

25. Leonhard Ragaz, *Der Kampf um das Reich Gottes in Blumhardt Vater und Sohn—und weiter* (Erlenbach-Zürich: Rotapfel-Verlag, 1922).

26. Eberhard Jüngel, *Barth-Studien* (Zürich/Köln: Benziger/Gütersloh: Gütersloher Verlagshaus Gerd Mohn, 1982), 123.

state of things; rather because the asked-for truth of Jesus Christ pushes against opposition, since this question does not grow out of our world and its frame of reference. Discussing the implications of this view for ethics, Paul Lehmann, in *The Transfiguration of Politics*, gives arguments which touch in many respects on Karl Barth's own interpretations.[27]

Back—or rather forward—to trend or movement in Barth's dogmatics: this trend in my view indicates a true historicity. Barth never reflected upon historicity as such or upon his own historicity, his own place within the larger scheme of things. In this he differed from Hegel. Barth also differed from Hegel in not claiming to alter himself within a trend of thought: Barth did not claim to frame the object of his thought within the changes of the subject and its thinking. For Barth historicity meant simply to go on, not to halt, not to search for one point from which one can view the whole and place oneself within it.

Once more, I should consider a question, which as well might have been asked in the discussion of my first catch phrase "thought in context." Why did Barth not take pains to clarify all these aspects? In each individual case, the contours of his "thought in motion" must be laboriously reconstructed. These contours first clearly enter into view as the extensive and complicated combinations of concepts, statements, and arguments are considered. Moreover, Barth does not care to develop his theology in a stepwise fashion and on different levels corresponding to different tasks and states of knowledge. Such reconstruction and stratification simply did not interest Barth. He wanted to enter into the movement itself as difficult as it was to concentrate on a living center that cannot be pinpointed.

Barth's dogmatics cannot be slotted as a "dogmatic school" in the old sense, something that starts off with the basic statements of theology and from there attempts an architecture of the "material." Therefore, Barth had a distaste for theological "schools" and for "students," even his own students, in whose work he always detected coarsening and distortion and often also banalization of his own thought. Even so "schools" and "students" should not be looked down upon as from some superior height. Schools and their teachers develop talents and skills and incite more than an imitation

27. Paul Lehmann, *The Transfiguration of Politics: The Presence and Power of Jesus of Nazareth in and over Human Affairs* (New York: Harper & Row, 1975).

of brilliant thought. A sovereign rejection of the school method, such as Barth's, leaves open only the possibility of occupying the master's position. Difficulties then arise surrounding the legacy, such as those I have discussed at the beginning of this article. Barth desired nothing of the kind: he simply wanted to train us to think theologically. Dogmatics for Barth was, so to speak, the gymnastics of theological thought. Yet for that purpose perhaps a few more methodological supports than Barth provided are required.

Thought out of Unity

Even so did not Barth affect the foundation of a school in that he constructed his dogmatics—truly, all of his theological thought—with Christology as the starting point? Did he not tirelessly enjoin that Christian theology could only be founded on Christology and that this foundation alone can and must be duplicated (but not itself newly grounded)? Karl Barth was reproached for thinking "Christo-monistically," an accusation passionately rejected by Barth's friends.[28] The formula "Christomonism," when correctly understood, is neither a slogan nor a profanity for a Christological enthusiasm which pares down the field of vision (if this were so we would have to call it "Christomania"). Rather, the formula characterizes a philosophical and, in a stricter sense, systematic program. "Monism" is the ultimate foundation of all reality from one principle, in contrast to a dualism which assumes two final reasons, opposed to each other, which explain reality. How does Barth relate to both of these ways of thought?

Karl Barth looked for the unity of theology in the act of confessing Jesus Christ. He tied all that theology has to say (particularly about the Christian life and Christian actions in the world) to this confession. On this point Barth was rigorous and inexorable, a stand easily seen in all of his work: not "Natur und Gnade" (against classical Catholic theology as well as against Emil Brunner) but rather Jesus Christ as "the one Word of God, whom we are to hear, whom we are to trust and obey in life and in death";[29] not "Theologie und Philos-

---

28. Ernst Wolf, *Barmen: Kirche zwischen Versuchung und Gnade* (Munich: Chr. Kaiser, 1957), 96.

29. "The Barmen Declaration," I. Thesis, in *Creeds of the Churches*, ed. John A. Leith, 3rd ed. (Louisville: John Knox Press, 1982), 520.

ophie" in the sense of "Glaube und Vernunft" or "Glaube und Verstehen" (Rudolf Bultmann) nor "Gottes Gebot und die Ordnungen"
(against Paul Althaus and against Emil Brunner) or "Gottesherr-
schaft und Eigengesetzlichkeit der Welt" (against the Neo-Lutheran
doctrine of two kingdoms) but rather the rule of Christ over all areas
of our lives (II. Barmen Thesis)![30] This *cantus firmus* "Christ alone"
gives the theology of Karl Barth a unity which comes through loud
and clear. Many seem to feel that this unity is sometimes monotonous; it impresses others as a powerful feat of reduction which concentrates everything on one point, thereby unleashing new power.

At this point, no doubt, Barth comes to meet one of the widespread tendencies of our time, one which certainly possesses a socio-
political background as well. The more involved various external relations become, the more power they develop to offset each other to
the point where state and culture can hardly bind them together, the
stronger the decay of morality, religion, and knowledge into pluralism becomes, the more often each individual must exist in different
systems of orientation, hardly experiencing a feeling of unity—the
more pressing the search for a central point that promises to provide
a clear outlook on the world, and on life in the world, will become.

It seems as if Barth's "Christological foundation" followed such
a search. For in terms of ethical, and especially in terms of political
decisions, Barth recognized no "situational exigencies" and no com-
promises with political rationales. Rather, he simply asked the question of faith: "In our actions, are we trusting in God alone or are we
not?" Yet this question of faith differs totally from a universal formula for the world. Barth insisted on a Christological foundation
precisely because he wanted to protest against every explanation of
the world, every "Weltanschauung" found in the Church and theology and viewed as a source of Christian proclamation. Barth announced the sovereignty of Christ over all areas of our lives not in
favor of a Christian state or a Christian morality. He objected to the
state's claim of omnipotence and its reference to a collective ethos
that, sooner or later, abolishes every distinction between right and
wrong. The "Christological foundation" is totally different from any
Christian universal formula for the world. A "Christological foundation" does not attempt to bring all things over one denominator;

30. Ibid.

rather, it helps one to perceive the present fullness of Jesus Christ in all of the various aspects of human experience.

In my opinion, the implications of the above for genuine diversity within the Church and theology, and for political plurality, have become visible only to a small extent. The consequences show up most clearly in places where Barth protested against transforming what he considered leading theological basic statements into a fixed principle. Yet this happened, as previously mentioned, in Berkouwer's presentation of Barth's theology, which amounts to a monism of God's electing grace. Or we can consider Hans Joachim Iwand's article "On the Primacy of Christology," read at a meeting of the Association for Protestant Theology in Wuppertal in 1956 and published in the commemorative volume *Antwort*, for Barth's seventieth birthday.[31] Iwand attempted to demonstrate, with respect to the history of recent theology, that theology must unfold out of Christology in order not to fail in its tasks. It is entirely possible to assume that this fits in with Barth in both thought and speech. Yet in the resulting discussion the master and teacher spoke out against the "primacy of Christology" certainly not because the concept of "primacy" struck Barth as risky. He consciously wanted to distinguish Christ from every other theological thought structure that could claim some independent right of its own—even a well-finished, comprehensive Christology.

Whenever Barth came across a "principle," he was firmly saying no to the concept of an ultimate foundation from which all else simply evolves. This opposition did not spring from an aversion to logical thought, to the systematic construction of theology. To the contrary: how expansive and full of inner connections is his dogmatics; how artful is, for example, the doctrine of reconciliation (the composition of which, by the way, developed from one of Barth's dreams)?[32] The systematic nature of his theology is undeniable yet it lacks a systematic principle similar to Paul Tillich's "Systematic Theology."[33] But does there not appear a basic tension in Barth's theology? On the one hand, he exhibited a strict theological logic, a de-

31. Hans Joachim Iwand, "Der Primat der Christologie," in *Antwort*, eds. Ernst Wolf, Charlotte von Kirschbaum, and Rudolf Frey (Zollikon-Zürich: Evangelischer Verlag, 1956), 172–189.

32. Karl Barth in a letter to Hans Joachim Iwand (April 29, 1951; Karl Barth Archives, Basel).

33. Cf. Paul Tillich, *Systematic Theology*, vol. III (London: SCM Press, 1978), 3.

termination to construct theological doctrine, and a theological continuity of argument spanning wide, but nonetheless tightly knotted. On the other hand, Barth's theological thought exhibited ever new starting points, which burst open every "system," according to the postulate of theological freedom, which is valid for the theological presentation as well. In the last analysis, can Barth simply not be taken at his word? Is he unpredictable and therefore draws attention to himself instead of to that which he says and seeks to point out: Jesus Christ himself? While I read Barth, this question enters my mind quite often in the attempt to think with him, to remain open. But must not this question remain open necessarily when Christian theology only retains its continuity, its wholeness, and its capacity insofar as it ever newly expresses the unity of the triune God without the possibility of a definitive presentation?

The First Commandment forbids the presentation of God in any fashion whatsoever. In 1933 Karl Barth interpreted this commandment as a "theological axiom." "I am the Lord your God—you shall have no other gods beside me."[34] This either/or between God and idols, together with the unconditional and irreversible difference between God and humanity—God speaks, humanity listens; God calls and humanity finds its freedom only in faithful obedience—characterizes the structure and, if I may say so, the systematic nature of Barth's theology. This structure is itself Christologically based, namely the unity of true God and true humanity in the person of Jesus Christ. Therefore Karl Barth's dogmatics is a theology of the Second Article of the Creed, which can be faithfully stated only with the help of the First Commandment. The major points within Barth's theology—not all of them but certainly the essential ones—rise out of this partnership of the First Commandment with the Second Article. The First Commandment—the prohibition of idolatry—is applied to theological talk and thought as well as to the theological arguments for our action.

God-talk Adequate to Given Conditions

Can all these remarks shed light on our intial question? Is Karl Barth's theology fundamentally a political conception, perhaps with a certain affinity to Hegel's philosophy of religion?

34. Karl Barth, "Das erste Gebot als theologisches Axiom" (1933), in idem, *Theologische Fragen und Antworten* (Zollikon: Evangelischer Verlag, 1957), 127–142.

I tend to affirm that—with some qualifications: Barth's intention was not a political program, no more than Hegel was interested in a political theory. It would be necessary to extend the concept "political" in order to notice the indirect and nevertheless most effective way of political reflection in Barth's and Hegel's thought. It is political—with the important qualification that it limits a boundless creative impulse by referring to given facts, which can only be *reflected*, not produced in a constructive way (this is certainly true for Barth, but possibly in dispute for Hegel).

In Barth's theology, the given fact—not just a fact among others—in the sense of an *absolute*, unconditional and fundamental event is the reality of Christ: the world reconciled to God in the Cross, the unity between the reconciling God and human being lost in human aversion from God, "Immanuel"—" God with us"—in the person of Jesus Christ, which undividedly is revelation and action. The crucial point—and crucial, above all, for the political character of theology—is the way theology articulates that fundamental condition and is determined by that unconditional fact.

For Barth, God's revelation as "Dei loquentis persona"[35] is the only and sufficient condition of theological talk. In Barth's view, the only way to say this is the refutation of any other possible condition which might be considered fundamental for theology, that is, the world or human being, neither of which is "given" in advance as a presupposition of God-talk. We must notice the almost imperceptible—and yet momentous—shift of perspective: *God talks*, and this is the condition of the possibility of *theological* God-talk. Theological statements and the Word of God, then, can only be perceived at the same level. Human talk will never be able to swing itself up to the Word of God or to drag it down—the Word of God, however, is able to "assume" human words, time and again, depending on God's will. Theology lives on this "assumptive" unity. In the *Church Dogmatics*, theology more and more approaches revelation as a living condition of theology, although Barth (since the second edition of his commentary on *The Epistle to the Romans*[36]) had been concentrat-

35. Karl Barth, *Unterricht in der christlichen Religion*, vol. I: *Prolegomena* (1924), ed. Hannelotte Reiffen (Zürich: Theologischer Verlag, 1985), 67f.; idem, *Die christliche Dogmatik*, 66–68; idem, *Church Dogmatics*, I.1:349.

36. Karl Barth, *The Epistle to the Romans*, trans. Edwyn C. Hoskyns (London: Oxford University Press, 1933), 10.

ing with persistence on the absolute qualitative difference between the Word of God and human words. Unlike other human speech, which is historically, socially, and psychologically conditioned, theology is unconditional. God-talk is an event which terminates all the other conditions: Nobody is disturbed by the lack of further conditions, because the words and statements correspond to reality in a way that there is no need for further criteria. According to Barth, any question for such a criterion would try to submit the knowledge of God to conditions different from the condition created by God: the revelation, again and again transforming the "given facts" of the world and of the human being.

What does that mean for the constitution of theology? Barth's answer is pneumatological—however, it is linked to the concept of revelation in such a way that it certainly explicates that concept, but without controlling its theological discussions. Theology always has to come to the point without digression, that is to the revelation event, duplicated and reflected by the fundamental dogmatic terms. Preliminary considerations belong to the digressions; Barth is alarmed at the possibility that any such "access" might make itself independent and hold sway over theological statements. Certainly, theological talk only *indirectly* articulates its subject. However, it is *immediate*. But in fact—whether intentionally or instinctively—this immediacy attacks all other conditions of knowledge. Any knowledge obtained by a well-tried method may be considered knowledge of "reality," and this reality is not reduced to a pseudo-reality. But Barth's inquiry concerning the *truth* of phenomena—e.g., religious or political phenomena—always amounts to a radical and insurpassable critique, since there is only God's truth. We cannot reach that truth, whereas truth may turn up as soon as God verifies certain phenomena.

In what way are people concerned by God's truth—people who listen to the biblical message, including theologians? In what way does it affect their behavior—their acts and thoughts—towards the "world" to which they belong? Barth, during World War I, wrote in his first commentary on *The Epistle to the Romans*: "Adequate *thought* is the principle of transformation, which will enable you to become new and to represent something new facing the old world. . . ."[37] Paul's formulation in Romans 12:2 is different: "Do

37. Karl Barth, *Der Römerbrief* (1919), ed. Hermann Schmidt (Zürich: Theologischer Verlag, 1985), 470.

not assimilate to this world, but transform yourselves by a new mind." Barth unfurls the formulation from the end and apparently in an idealistic manner: Critical reflection straightens out the world and transforms it by the revision of our cognitive faculty. That does not imply, however, that we must have the true world in our mind in order to change the world we get across! Barth rather introduces a motif which will pervade his whole oeuvre: Thought obedient to faith implies the "permanent struggle and trouble, advancing in a spiral line, aimed at *reflecting* God's thoughts, a continuous *begetting* the truth from truth itself in the permanent confrontation with the 'reality' of this world which is passing away and which has not been begotten from truth itself."[38] Such a way of thinking obedient to faith, Barth maintains, immediately turns into action, so that action corresponds to thinking.

"Adequate Thought," however, is not prior to adequate talk— "at first think the truth, then say what you think" is *not* Barth's motto. Barth does not describe God-talk from without, from a conceptual point of view, which might comprehend theological statements in order to form a definite idea of God-talk and then release it, so that this idea might become a part of our everyday communication. Contrarily, Barth's dogmatic intends to be *adequate talk in action* instead of any reflective suspension of that talk. This is the difference between Barth and Hegel—and the right-wing Hegelians among Barth's students as well. On the other hand, adequate talk is more than just a source of transforming action; according to Barth, action must not be confused with a proof of the statements which inspired it. Therefore, Barth inserted theological ethics into the *Church Dogmatics,* so that the question "what is truth?" is relevant for action, too. In this context, all human action is subordinate to *prayer,* which is the "fundamental act" of "obedience engendered in faith."[39] Prayer is the essential form of action in the freedom of human individuals facing God: "The real basis of prayer is man's freedom before God."[40] This point most clearly marks the difference between Barth and all the left-wing Hegelians even within the periphery of Barth's own theology: Adequate God-talk—with its roots in prayer as talk-to-God—is action in the full sense of the word.

38. Ibid, 471.
39. Barth, *Church Dogmatics,* III.3:283.
40. Ibid, III.4:92.

Words and deeds must not diverge—although it may be necessary to refute wrong action by adequate talk. But then it will also be necessary to resist confused and confusing thoughts.

Barth's repeated opposition to certain actions together with their reasons indicates that he could not resort to interpretations in order to detect and—if possible—to straighten what, in his view, was wrong. But it is equally significant that, all things considered, such opposition was much less important for Barth as soon as he concentrated on the fact that the whole world *has been* assumed by the reality of Jesus Christ. That is what we have to articulate adequately—which for Barth remained the main task of theology. Barth himself, however, would have been the last one to consider his own theological work the ultimate realization of that task.

7

The Concept and Task
of Eschatology

Theological and Philosophical Reflections[1]
The Meaning of "Eschatology"

The term "eschatology" stems from Philipp Heinrich Friedlieb.[2] Abraham Calov entitled the twelfth and last section of his masterpiece of dogmatics, *Systema locorum Theologicorum* (1677),
"ESCATOLOGIA Sacra." This final section, which concludes the
Dogmatics of a leading representative of Lutheran Orthodoxy, deals
with the "last things" (de novissimis), specifically death and the state
after death, the resurrection of the dead, the last Judgment, the consummation of the world, hell and everlasting death, and, finally, life
everlasting. Friedlieb and Calov do not define the artificial term "eschatologia"; they hardly even explain it in the course of their presen-
tations, so that it remains a mere heading. Calov applies it to the eschaton, namely "the end," which, according to I Corinthians 15:24,
comes about when Christ, after subjugating all powers and authorities, delivers over the dominion to God the Father (quaestio 2). In the

1. An earlier version of this chapter was delivered to the sixth European Conference on the Philosophy of Religion, August 29th to September 1st, 1986 in Durham,
England; to a seminar of the theological faculties of Bonn and Oxford, September
29th to October 3rd, 1986; and published in Scottish Journal of Theology 41 (1989):
499–515.
2. The final part of his *Dogmatics* is entitled *Eschatologia seu Florilegium theo-*
logicum exhibens locorum de morte, resurrectione mortuorum, extremo iudicio, con-
summatione seculi, inferno seu morte aeterna et denique vita eterna (Stralsund,
1644).

preceding section Calov had cited New Testament texts which explicitly or implicitly speak of the eschata, the last things, or of the last days as the conclusion of human history.

In his *Loci Theologici* (1610–1622) Johann Gerhard, the most important theological teacher of post-Reformation Lutheranism, refers to, among other texts, Ecclesiasticus 7:36 (in the Vulgate v. 40). This text (along with 28:6 and 38:20 —Vulgate v. 21) warns the reader in all of his words to consider his end (novissima tua), so that he will not eternally sin. In this apocryphal text from the beginning of the second century B.C., the "last things," then, are to be interpreted as death, which should be kept in mind in our lifetime so that our life is not misspent.

This explanation of the meaning of "the last things in general"[3] (de novissimis in genere) is part of the treatise on death. Here Gerhard lists all the biblical references that speak of the end in any fashion whatsoever, seeking to find out what is universally and absolutely (universaliter et absolute) final. In the last analysis the eschata constitute the definitive boundary of human existence for which words and deeds count.

Is Gerhard's doctrine of the last things just a variation of the well-known ancient cautionary proverb, "Consider well, that you too must die"? Does he only discover in the Ecclesiasticus passage the sort of wisdom handed down in the Latin saying, "Quidquid agis, prudenter agas et respice finem."("Whatever you undertake, begin wisely and consider the end")? This could only seem to be the case if Gerhard's treatment of the text were taken out of context. But this very context is nothing other than the mystery of God and the way of salvation. More exactly, it is God's salvation of humanity by calling us into the community of believers, and God's judgment, which recreates the world completely anew by annihilating its present state. The view forward to God's judgment follows on Gerhard's theological ethics, thereby placing all directives under ultimate responsibility before God, the Judge. To this extent, the doctrine of the last things represents an unfolding of the doctrine of justification. Brought to bear on the theologian this means: the theologian is charged to speak of God. Theologians can only do this if God has declared them justified and thereby enabled them in their turn to an-

---

3. Johann Gerhard, *Loci Theologici,* ed. Eduard Preuss, 2nd ed. (Leipzig: J.C. Hinrichs, 1885), tom. VIII, 20.

nounce God's salvation. Whether this has actually occurred, God alone will judge, just as God will sift all that was renewed by this activity yet remains ambiguous, incomplete, not yet patently apparent to all people.

In this theological interpretation the eschata are not merely natural "boundary phenomena" but are what God has irreversibly established and will carry through—a concept that can indeed present itself to us as a set limit. The framework encompasses everything in the Bible which can be understood as delineating the expectations of our faith. So this dogmatic locus was constructed as an attempt to present Christian hope, integrated most often at first under the title "De novissimis" or "De extremis," later, however, explicitly as "Eschatology." Eschatology constituted the finale of dogmatics, whereby it could be unfolded either as a colorful composition of all that will become final both for humanity and for the world, and thereafter pass away—or later, under Rationalism, as a monotonous insistence upon what survives the death of the individual: "immortality." This systematic ordering ties together two questions. First, what is the object of expectation (or, to adopt the most comprehensive perspective, what are the objects of expectation) for the Christian faith? What can we hope for? Second, what limits confront theological reflection? How can propositions of faith which at first glance seem irreconcilable be brought together in the perspective of the end of all things? What reflective implications result for theology from this perspective?

The two examples given from early Protestant dogmatics merit sketching out because they occur at the start of the development of the concept and because their after-effects linger on. The Concise Oxford Dictionary defines "eschatology" as the "doctrine of death, judgment, heaven, and hell,"[4] and in Roman Catholic theology up until the Second Vatican Council, dogmatics was concluded, following the doctrine of the church, with the treatise Concerning the Last Things. At first glance this chapter of doctrine appears to be merely a compilation of theological affirmations about the end and the fulfillment of humanity and the world. On closer inspection, however, systematic issues emerge, relating these affirmations to each other and to other topics of Christian dogmatics. Even the exegesis of the

---

4. *The Concise Oxford Dictionary of Current English*, ed. J. B. Sykes, 6th ed. (Oxford: Clarendon Press, 1976), 353.

"last things" (eschata) or the "final things" (extrema) as end and fulfillment allows for varying possible interpretations. Furthermore, if one (as, for example, Calov does) relates the last things to the human person as "microcosmos" and to the world as "macrocosmos," one must ask what is the relationship of these two to each other. How closely does the world's course correspond to the fate of the human individual? What does the completed totality of the world have to do with the personal future of that individual? Finally, terms such as "universal," "final" (in the sense of end and goal) give food for reflection, as does the concept of time that pervades this doctrine. Does time also belong to the finite world, and how is it confronted with a finality which will never be surpassed and yet is not simply a boundary beyond which nothing further can be said? These are all ontological problems that arise in part from interpretation of the biblical basis, and especially from the need for systematic analysis.

This need is expressed even more markedly in another conception of Protestant theology based on the "analytical method." Introduced in 1602 by the Reformed philosopher-theologian Bartholomaeus Keckermann, it defines dogmatics as a "scientia practica" and concentrates on bringing humanity to salvation.[5] The goal of theology (finis theologiae) is nothing other and none other than God Himself; hence this must be the introductory subject of dogmatics, even, according to Georg Calixt, preceding the doctrine of God.[6]

In this way theology is eschatologically defined right from the start as a movement towards God. Its task is to expound didactically what God Himself has already laid down as theology's finis (or, more precisely, its finis obiectivus): His eternal presence. The slogan of theology is not "respice finem," "think of your ending," but rather: "Open your heart to God: He is the finis—look for Him as your fulfillment and be prepared even now for His coming!"

What is philosophically understood as knowledge of God is assigned to theology as a way. Theology must travel this way within time—that is, in its particular time among its contemporaries, and it will only reach its goal in the fruitio dei, an old term taken over from Augustine that describes eternal life, direct communion with God, existence with God. Theology's hope and that which it must proclaim do not merely trade on a distant future. This hope is called

5. Bartholomaeus Keckermann, *Systema SS. Theologiae* (Hanoviae, 1602).
6. Georg Calixt, *Epitome Theologiae* (Goslariae, 1616).

forth by God's action. Theology must set out in the light of this hope, accompanied by the certainty of this action and led by the expectation of its fulfillment.

There are systematic reasons why this style of dogmatics begins by discussing the "finis." According to the so-called Loci-Method followed by Gerhard and Calov, the chapter concerning the end of humankind and the world comes at the conclusion. This is also the case in Johannes Himmel's Syntagma disputationum theologicarum methodicum, 1621, disputatio 31: De ultimo hominis et mundani systematis fine.[7] These differences, however, become less important if we consider what underlies both theological conceptions and their eschatology. The dry conceptual definitions immediately take on color if we also recognize that these theologians—all pedantry and systematization aside—are moved by the question "Can we hope? Have we a foundation for hope?" They were writing at a time when prospects were particularly gloomy, in the midst of religious wars and political and spiritual revolutions far wider-reaching than the upheaval of the Reformation period. Much appeared to be coming to an end, perhaps the very end of everything was near. In this mood of approaching catastrophe these theologians, by placing eschatology in a prominent position in their dogmatics, gave an indirect but nonetheless clear answer. They summoned their readers—theologians and, through them, congregations—back from escapism, whether of apocalyptic dreams or utopian wishful thinking, and confronted them with God acting to judge and redeem. This explains (if any explanation is possible) the composure of these theological thinkers, a calm that might appear to a superficial glance to be a navel-gazing withdrawal from all external turmoil. Perhaps those theologians who first sought systematically to define "eschatology" did put on blinkers—but only to prevent themselves from being confused and thereby losing their way. They did not simply react to the challenges of their time but gave an "account for the hope" which is according to I Peter (3:15) "in you," because Christians are "born anew into a living hope by the resurrection of Jesus Christ from the dead" (I Peter 1:3).

In the time that followed, this theological line was, on the whole, scarcely maintained, even though the pattern of dogmatics ending

---

7. Johannes Himmelius, *Syntagma disputationum theologicarum methodicum*, 4th ed. (Wittebergae, 1650).

with the "last things" was formally upheld. The question motivating the theologians we have quoted so far—"Why may we hope? What can we hope for in our situation?"—was steadily pushed more and more into the background by reflection on the End (finis) in its all-embracing sense. The relationship of humanity and the world in view of their end; end as annihilation or fulfillment; time and the world: these now came to be seen as epistemological or transcendental-philosophical questions. The question of "the end of all things" was posed in order to establish why people may hope at all, why indeed they must hope. In other words: What does "end" mean in the sense of the framework in which everything else is to be understood?

Reflections on Boundary Questions

In the course of the nineteenth century such ontological questions took on independent status, and in the twentieth century reflection on boundary questions has become more and more important. The concept of eschatology became critical but also ambiguous: it was employed to articulate a range of widely differing perspectives, but was no longer related to a unified field of concern.

The radical shift to boundary questions is signaled, for instance, in Friedrich Schleiermacher's Christian Faith (1830/31, 2nd ed.). Although apparently following traditional lines, when he discussed such questions in connection with the Church's fulfillment, Schleiermacher relativized the Church's doctrine of the last things in comparison to other doctrines and continued (§159.1):

> The phrase, "the Last Things," which has been somewhat generally accepted, has a look of strangeness which is more concealed by the word "Eschatology"; for the term "things" threatens to carry us quite away from the domain of the inner life, with which alone we are concerned. . . . The terms have this in common, that if the beginning of a wholly new and ever-enduring spiritual form of life be represented as from our point of view "the last thing," that endless duration appears merely as the end of a time-life which, as contrasted therewith, is almost a vanishing quantity.[8]

8. Friedrich Schleiermacher, *Christian Faith*, eds. H. R. Mackintosh and J. S. Stewart (Edinburgh: T. & T. Clark, 1928), 703.

141

Schleiermacher was concerned with the relationship of "things" (things in general, not simply the "last things") to the world of the inner life. He could see no possibility of describing things beyond this life. Thus eschatology became a problem of semantics within which all factual issues are superseded. Schleiermacher considered the relationship between time and eternity (in its superiority to time) to be the only question that needed to be discussed; and he had already said what he had to say about *that* in his doctrine of God. Hence, Schleiermacher considered eschatology, at best, to be a stimulus to recall and consolidate fundamental principles, but not a special task for theology.

Admittedly, questioning the description "last things" can also lead to quite different conclusions. Calov thought of the *eschaton*, the final end, as events which terminate human history—but not only that history; rather also the distinction between Jesus Christ and God the Father as far as it is bound up with the world: the Son hands over the Kingdom of God to the Father, he subordinates himself to God with the whole world *so that God shall be all in all* (I Corinthians 15:28). The end coincides with the consummation of God's sovereignty; everything has been taken up in Him and no longer has existence apart from Him. (To this extent, for this theological doctrine, the *last things* are far from being *final*; they are decidedly *penultimate* in relationship to God's kingdom, while "kingdom" itself can only provisionally outline what God Himself is in His complete, all-inclusive fullness.) "Not different any more," "nothing apart from," "all in all": these are the concepts which may also be interpreted as designations for the limits beyond which no more can be said and which consequently delineate what can be said at all. In his paraphrase of I Corinthians 15 Karl Barth wrote:

> Last *things*, as such, are not *last* things, however great and significant they may be. He only speaks of *last* things who would speak of the *end* of all things, of their end understood plainly and fundamentally, of a reality so radically superior to all things, that the existence of all things would be utterly and entirely *based* upon it alone, and thus, in speaking of their end, he would in truth be speaking of nothing else than their beginning.[9]

9. Karl Barth, *The Resurrection of the Dead*, trans. H. J. Stenning (London: Hodder & Stoughton, 1933), 110.

How is this to be understood? It sounds like a transcendental determination of human speech about things as such. Things appear to us to be transitory objects because and insofar as we can only perceive them *between* their beginning and their end. But *beginning* and *end* are themselves beyond experience; hence for our speech they coincide and thereby set a limit to all the distinctions which disclose reality to us. What "exists" beyond them remains inconceivable. This is true not only for remote events but for all things. Those who are aware of this will in the end put their reliance on no object or event. But they will also not hope to achieve a total view of such objects or events in the hope that they will thereby limit and transcend them. Every standpoint and every perspective remains temporal. Only those who accept this have beginning and end constantly around them—whereby it is immaterial whether they see the end before or behind them or the beginning as behind or before. Both remain withdrawn from their grasp, and that means: *they* determine *them*. But then they too will not simply pass away with time.

Barth's statement, however, can also be understood as an attempt to envisage the grounds for all judgments of reality: the existence of everything is not problematic, not even in the light of its end. Rather, its existence is real as categorically limited existence—and only as such real. This "only as such real" must be articulated theologically as indirect speech about God. He alone envelops the whole world by virtue of His sovereignty. We dare *hope* this precisely because *now already God encounters us*—encounters us in such a way that we can only hope in Him; "can only hope" to be sure in the sense that we can *hope in Him alone*. This "only hope" is the outermost limit to which we can really hold.

In this sense the concept "eschatology" marked for the early Barth the problem of speech about God:

> Direct communication from God is no divine communication. If Christianity be not altogether thorough-going eschatology, there remains in it no relationship whatever with Christ. Spirit which does not at every moment point from death to the new life is not the Holy Spirit.[10]

10. Karl Barth, *The Epistle to the Romans*, trans. Edwyn C. Hoskyns (London: Oxford University Press, 1933), 314.

This quotation, too, can be read in various ways. First, it might be an appeal to reason, to the *raison d'être* of the Christian life. In this case it acts as a criticism of existing Christianity: First, Christianity must not appeal to its own traditions but should hold fast to Christ who is not enclosed in these traditions. Second, "eschatology" is here brought into connection with the becoming-present of the triune God; it makes it clear that God is not mediated by the world but breaks through it, and that even now, not just sometimes. Third, eschatological criticism may not be carried out in the name of a future, better world. Christ does not "come" only in the future or in some other subsequent time, no more than do God and the Holy Spirit. Their presence is not still to come but is an incomparable presentness, not derivable from the flow of communication or the continuity of inner and outer life. "Eschatology" (as in Schleiermacher, only here more pointedly) denotes a problem of language: it should express the absolute contingency of the Divine self-realization, and this can only take place in the mode of total anticipation. Terms such as "present," "future," "hope," or "new" can here only be used metaphorically; semantically they must remain vague and only thus do they fulfill their function as theological conceptual aids.

With this we seem to have reached a terminus or, let us say provisionally: the point of no return that at least prevents us from describing eschatology simply as one component of dogmatics among others. Eschatology becomes henceforth synonymous with theology in general; *theology as such is eschatology*—namely, when its dominating, if not indeed its exclusive topic is the *encounter with God,* and when it is trying to express that this encounter *can only be anticipated.* Eschatological theology sees itself as an alternative to any theology which proceeds from a direct presence of God (as in the human spirit or soul) or, conversely, conceives God's reality as the necessary framework for the reality of the world. In contrast to this, radicalized eschatology poses the question "what is reality?" in a completely new way.

An indication of this: God's Day of Judgment, which will definitively separate reality from unreality, salvation from doom, life from death, announced in the New Testament as a future or final judgment, is no longer equated with the end of the cosmos. Instead, in the early dialectic theology of Friedrich Gogarten and Karl Barth and also, in modified form, in Rudolf Bultmann, God's judgment is regarded as the crisis of culture, that is, of socio-historical conceptions of value and achievement. Alternatively we must no longer speak of a "final judgment" because judgment is already taking place within history as a progressive dissolution of the status quo.[11] The absolute end overtakes all conceptions of the end of history. These conceptions crumble if the teleology of history is over-taxed, i.e., if the foreseeable future can no longer promise to meet the claims that are made on a consistent further development. When, for example, Jürgen Moltmann writes today about "nuclear eschatology," he is thinking of the Holocaust of humanity.[12] The possibility of conceiving an absolute end brought about by human agency awakens resistance to its preparation. But this is the only alternative worth talking about (even theologically). Hope in God as Judge and Savior of the world, in Jesus Christ as Redeemer seems by contrast to have no substance left; at least, it seems inconsequential unless capable of changing humanity and thereby preventing the catastrophe.

All this, however, is something quite different from the Judgment which takes place in hearing the Revelation and believing in the Revealer: "He who hears my word," says Jesus in John 5:24, "and believes Him who sent me, has eternal life; he does not come into judgment, but has passed from death to life." Here the judge delivers his verdict and we cannot look for his judgment anywhere other than with him. The verdict pronounced here neither makes the future judgment redundant nor does it anticipate it.

Tasks of Eschatology

(1) The concept "eschatology" must be defined anew. It has been enriched by so many historical and systematic considerations that it appears theologically and historico-philosophically omnipresent, yet as a consequence ambiguous and unclear. "Eschatology" must now be differentiated from adjacent concepts such as utopia (or utopian thinking), Apocalyptic, Messianism, Chiliasm, and Futurology. This requires reduction and concentration in scope. The concept of eschatology must be pointed up as *talk of God which is determined by God's coming*. God's coming means *adventus* and *futurum*, God's

---

11. Jürgen Moltmann, *The Theology of Hope* (New York: Harper & Row, 1967).

12. Idem, "Endzeit oder Adventszeit," *Evangelische Kommentare* 18 (1985): 712.

coming to be present both today and in what still lies ahead. Eschatology would then be extricated from the almost explosive profusion of reflections on the nature of time, conceptions of history, ethical problems and their illustration, hermeneutical questions of the interpretation of biblical expectations and linguistic *aporia*. It would concentrate *on the eschatos rather than on the eschata*: on Jesus Christ as he is described in Revelation 1:17f. (cf. 2:8; 22:13) as "the first and the last and the living one."[13]

The other problems already mentioned should not be abandoned in this process, but must be reformulated. One example: The transcendental-philosophical reflection on the end which is at the same time a beginning can be taken as the context of discovery for the question "What is humanity's lot?" Wherein does humanity exist, conscious of its own temporality, yet at the same time aware that it has "no comprehension of God's work from beginning to end" as the Preacher declares (Ecclesiastes 3:11)? The Preacher's answer, on the face of it quite uneschatological, refers to "his lot": "a man should enjoy his work" (Ecclesiastes 3:22). This joy is open to hope. It is not based on what little remains for one who would otherwise be reduced to despair because he is unable to comprehend the course of events. Confident joy is far more the lot of one who does not seek to comprehend the cause of his life because that is a matter for God alone. To be sure he asks about the proper time for his dealings but he does not try to create the proper opportunity by visualizing the totality of his existence or even of the world and accommodating himself to them. In complementary fashion the teleological question about the aim and purpose of history must be reconsidered. Can it properly wish to sound "the meaning of history"? Are not Martin Kähler's words far more appropriate: "Eschatology opens up for theology sensitivity to history"?[14] This would mean taking seriously

---

13. As variations of such reduction and concentration, see the following: Karl Barth, *Church Dogmatics,* esp. II.1: 631–638; on the Roman Catholic side, Hans Urs von Balthasar, "Eschatologie," in *Fragen der Theologie heute,* eds. Johannes Feiner, Josef Trütsch, and Franz Böckle (Einsiedeln/Zürich/Köln: Benziger, 1960), 403–422; Karl Rahner, "Theologische Prinzipien der Hermeneutik eschatologischer Aussagen," in his *Schriften zur Theologie,* vol. IV (Einsiedeln/Zürich/Köln: Benziger, 1960), 401–428.

14. Martin Kähler, "Die Bedeutung, welche den 'letzten Dingen' für Theologie und Kirche zukommt," in *Dogmatische Zeitfragen,* vol. I (Leipzig: A. Deichert, 1898), 252.

the space-time that God has created and that far outreaches our time for activity—not only temporally.

(2) "Western" theology has for the most part understood "the limitation of theological speech by God's coming" futuristically. We must ask why. One reason was certainly the structuring of dogmatics on the pattern of the history of salvation derived from the sequence of the Biblical writings. This structure corresponded to the teaching methods of ecclesiastical catechesis, also reflected in the creeds of the Early Church. By contrast, Eastern Orthodox theology has remained far more closely bound to the liturgy; for it, God's presence is experienced normatively in worship, and this in turn molds Christians' experience of the world. Here pneumatology and eschatology mesh. In addition, a soteriologically conceived theology rests on the experience of salvation. Such a theology distinguishes between the ongoing redemption of humankind and the still future redemption of the world, and so gains its own perspective.

A quite different approach results if hope is aroused because God gives time, time for repentance and new time for action, determined by God's mercy. This view of time was characteristic, for example, of the Reformers—as imminent expectation of the "beloved last day" in view of the catastrophic condition of the world and of the Church (especially intense in Luther), in view of God's verdict which justifies the godless—"there is forgiveness of sins, there is life and salvation" (Luther); both views are linked to the conviction that God has once more postponed the final Judgment to allow time for repentance, for the proclamation of his Gospel and for action in the obedience of faith. *Hope stands alongside the knowledge that matters could be quite different.*

Limited talk of God, limited by His coming, exposes itself to the Coming One who is still expected (also, but not only in the sense of the temporal not-yet!). Such speech can neither prematurely anticipate its own limitation nor leave it behind. The positive term for this is *God's promise.* This comprises what God has said and done in order that we may look out for and expect him. The question, "What may I hope?" which Kant assigned to religion, can, in my view, only be answered by Christian theology by reference to this promise. In this the emphasis is placed on the "may," on the establishment of hope (*establishment* as *being established*). *Promise* is, in my view, an example of development of a basic theological term. Historically seen it reflects the continuity between the expectations of Israel and the new beginning of hope by faith in Jesus Christ—and theologically: the identity of God's promising word and the living Word of God, Jesus Christ. So, promise is the term of theological reflection on the unity of linguistic symbols of religious expectations like justice, peace, eternal blessing, everlasting life, knowledge of God—and at the same time it signifies the theological basis of these symbols. That means, for example: We cannot understand the longing for justice without being concerned for the justice of God, revealed in Jesus Christ. That means furthermore: We have learned anew to define "justice" by perceiving what had happened on Good Friday and on Easter between God and Jesus for the sake of all humankind, and what is happening now in our struggle for justice in relationship to the justice of God.

Should we then enumerate different, mutually distinguishable promises, or is it a matter of *one* promise? What is to be said here, and how can it be said? These are further questions which replace the linguistic problems mentioned so far.

(3) In the meantime the above question cannot be answered without posing yet a further one: How does eschatology come at all to its assertions? Certainly not in collecting and harmonizing biblical texts which in some form or other express hopes or include future perspectives. Even the authors of the treatises "Concerning the Last Things" or similar theological *loci* did not proceed in this fashion, although it may now and then seem as if they did. In fact, a biblicistic systematization does not emerge until the attempt is made to construct a context of universal history and then to enter in it the biblical references which seem to be useful as evidence. This was the case e.g. in Reformed Federal Theology, especially worked out by Johannes Cocceius[15] then in the historico-theological writings of Johann Albrecht Bengel and in the Lutheran Theology of Salvation History of the nineteenth century (Johann Christian Konrad von Hofmann).[16]

---

15. Johannes Cocceius, *Summa doctrinae de foedere et testamento Dei* (Lugduni Batavorum, 1654); and idem, *Summa theologiae ex scripturis repetita* (Amstelodami, 1662).

16. Johann Albrecht Bengel, *Erklärte Offenbarung Johannis oder vielmehr Jesu Christi*, ed. Wilhelm Hoffmann (Stuttgart: Fr. Brodhag'sche Buchhandlung, 1834). Johann Christian Konrad von Hofmann, *Weissagung und Erfüllung im alten und im neuen Testamente* (Nördlingen: C.H. Beck'sche Buchhandlung, 1841–1844); idem, *Der Schriftbeweis* (Nördlingen: C.H. Beck'sche Buchhandlung, 1852–1855).

They all attempted to draw out God's revelation from the whole Bible. They all tried to spell out this totality in the continuity of an historical retrospective upon fulfilled predictions and a prophetic anticipation of promises still unfulfilled. Hence the problem lies in the comprehension of what can be said from God about the world, presented as an organic history. The aim here is to grasp totality through temporal mediation as the whole which is disclosed from its conclusion as a unity. Of this motif in the philosophy of history Reinhard Wittram states "the end of world history" is "in no way the object of historical enquiry, but the question of that end is decisive for our perception of history," because it enables the assumption of a world-history, and "without a world-history, history has no meaning."[17] The inability of *historical* study to determine what the end of world-history is does not, of course, of itself signify that *theology* has this responsibility, even if Wolfhart Pannenberg has attempted to prove just this in numerous articles.[18]

The question "What is the end?" can be posed from quite different frameworks of discovery. It is always presupposed in connection with understanding—whether when one is driven into a corner with no apparent means of escape or, by contrast, finds oneself in a situation experienced as open, yet not indeterminate, but rather pressing purposefully forward. Both are highly complex perceptions which anticipate a possible alternate state in order to be able to sight their own position at all. Looking for what is to come is no epistemological luxury, not an extension (or even over-extension) of the field of vision which, if need demands, can be done without. It belongs rather to the perception of what exists, if it is really a question of perception and not simply of a dissociated impression.

At this point one of Luther's aphorisms from *De servo arbitrio* is appropriate:

> What is there in any creature at all that any human being at all could understand if "understand" means "perfectly know and see"? For then it would be impossible for anyone to understand something and yet at the same time fail to understand it. If he had grasped only one thing he

17. Reinhard Wittram, *Das Interesse an der Geschichte* (Göttingen: Vandenhoeck & Ruprecht, 1958), 135.

18. Wolfhart Pannenberg, *Grundfragen systematischer Theologie*, vol. I (Göttingen: Vandenhoeck & Ruprecht, 1967).

would have grasped everything—namely, in God. Whoever does not understand God can never understand even a part of creation.[19]

"To understand in God" does not mean to trace something back to God or (which would amount to the same thing) to place it within the widest conceivable context of meaning. Only that which is present as coming from God can be understood in God in such a way that, in its recognition, God is Himself simultaneously perceived. This is what is meant by the concept of "promise" if (with II Corinthians 1:20) we interpret it as the embodiment of what God has confirmed as finally valid, so that we can assent to it and our "Yes, so be it" determines all our expectations. "He is the yes pronounced upon God's promises, every one of them. That is why, when we give glory to God, it is through Christ Jesus that we say 'Amen.'"

Hans Conzelmann once said in his lectures that the concept of "promise" is like a sausage hung from a car to tempt a dog; every time that the poor animal thinks it can snatch the delicacy, the driver accelerates and delays the fulfillment of the wish. This may well be a caricature of the pattern "promise and fulfillment" that seeks to explain the historical extension of Jewish and Christian hope. However, Conzelmann's bizarre picture laughs itself out of court if we realize that "promise" is meant to designate what we are given to recognize as God's action and how we can recognize it. The promises of peace, justice, life, and rest in God express what God has established so that human beings can align themselves with it. Likewise, it is only in the hope that "God is all in all" that it can be said that these promises constitute a unity.

I think that this is the key to the so-called Scripture principle of the Reformation, according to which all theological statements should be derived from the whole of the Bible without any kind of systematization. *The Christ-event allows everything that is biblically recounted, attested to, and announced, to be understood as promise.* God is present as *Deus promittens* in a final manner which encompasses and elucidates everything before and after. He acts in the death and resurrection of Jesus Christ. Eschatology speaks of God's reality which realizes itself in promise.[20] This is a reality which es-

---

19. Martin Luther, *De servo arbitrio* (1525), WA 18:605, 9–14.

20. Ingolf Ulrich Dalferth, *Existenz Gottes und christlicher Glaube. Skizzen zu einer eschatologischen Ontologie* (Munich: Chr. Kaiser, 1984).

tablishes itself— it is up to us not to interrupt it. Methodology can only make approximate preparation for this: horizons of understanding, contexts of meaning, and elementary questions must continue to exist alongside one another, not necessarily to generate mutual tension between them, but to allow such a tension to arise.

The reason: God is present in His acts, yet these acts are at one and the same time His hidden work. It is hidden because God becomes present as Himself in His own way and in His own time but remains beyond human grasp. He remains hidden even as He reveals himself. His acts take place *sub contrario* of that which humankind expects of Him (instead of waiting for Him and hoping in Him!). This two-sidedness of speech about God, upon which Luther laid such stress, also belongs to the sphere of eschatology. Eschatology must distinguish what in God is a unity: His indivisible presence. Human language, however, is incapable of reflecting this. Any attempt to do so will effectively shut itself off from reality. God's reality manifests itself in human language in that it is spoken of as promise, because such language grows out of solidly based hope. It is also hope that we may yet recognize as unity what at present still appears to us as divided, shadowy, even contradictory, and that includes ourselves.

(4) "We may (still) hope because God gives us time"—"We have hope because we are born anew through the resurrection of Jesus Christ from the dead"—"We can do no other than hope in faith because the revelation of God's acts which are at present hidden can be expected." These are various intuitive accentuations that state theological axioms but cannot be otherwise established. They can best be described as *Gestalt* perceptions.

From this arises *various emphases* in eschatology. They are often described misleadingly, thus giving rise to spurious problems, especially when confused conceptions of time are drawn in or even played off against each other. "Consistent eschatology" competes with a "present eschatology," "thorough-going eschatology" (Albert Schweitzer)[21] is superseded by "realized eschatology" (Charles Harold Dodd),[22] or Christology is called "perfect eschatology"

---

21. Albert Schweitzer, *The Quest for the Historical Jesus,* 5th ed. (New York: Macmillan, 1956).

22. Charles Harold Dodd, *The Parables of the Kingdom* (London: James Nisbet & Co., 1935).

(Gerhard Ebeling).[23] Should we not first ask why "time" (and its modalities—past, present, and future) has become a problem? As I see it, Christian theology has from its beginnings been faced with the question *why there can continue to be any history at all* after Good Friday and Easter. Or put another way: in what sense *is* there history? Eschatology attempts to answer this question theologically.

Eschatology differs from other *topoi* of theology in that it directs attention specifically to *what is to come* as what still remains to be realized in a temporal sense. In other thematic contexts it touches on the doctrine of God, Christology, and pneumatology. Eschatology ought not to make itself independent of these; but it gives them more precision and is indispensable for them. For example, the relationship between God and humankind is formulated by eschatology in temporal terms and by pneumatology in spatial ones.

Not the least of the contributions eschatology has made is that it has taken up into theology significant *philosophical problems*. As outstanding examples of this I have mentioned the problems of totality, universality, and time. "Individuality" could also be considered, as also the general relationship among the human individual, humanity, and world.[24] Considering the abundance of these themes Ernst Troeltsch in 1891, in his doctoral disputation at the Faculty of Theology, University of Göttingen, put forward the thesis: "As far as it is at all advisable to systematize the Christian conceptions of belief, eschatology must constitute the focus of their interrelations."[25] Later he approvingly quotes a contemporary: "Today the office of eschatology is usually closed. It is closed because the ideas upon which it is founded have lost their roots."[26] It seems that the work of this office at the present time is partly being made redundant by futuristically steered rationalization, partly

23. Gerhard Ebeling, *Dogmatik des christlichen Glaubens,* vol. III (Tübingen: J.C.B. Mohr, 1973), 399.

24. Cf. Wilfried Härle and Eilert Herms, *Rechtfertigung: Das Wirklichkeitsverständnis des christlichen Glaubens* (Göttingen: Vandenhoeck & Ruprecht, 1979), 205ff.

25. Published in *Troeltsch-Studien,* vol. I: *Untersuchungen zu Biographie und Werkgeschichte,* eds. Horst Renz and Friedrich-Wilhelm Graf (Gütersloh: Gütersloher Verlagshaus Gerd Mohn, 1982), 300.

26. Ernst Troeltsch, *Glaubenslehre.* Nach den Heidelberger Vorlesungen aus den Jahren 1911 und 1912, ed. Martha Troeltsch (München/Leipzig: Duncker & Humblot, 1925), 36.

being expended through negotiations with advertising agencies. Eschatological thought can only begin to put down roots again if the question which calls it forth regains its urgency—the question "Can we hope, and why? Can we, when all is said and done, do anything other than hope?"

8

Current Issues
in German Theology

Before turning to some points of interest currently being discussed in German Protestant theology, I should like to make some general remarks about the circumstances under which theology is studied in Germany today.[1]

The study of theology was confirmed as a part of the classical educational system of German universities by the reforms that took place at the end of the eighteenth and beginning of the nineteenth centuries. As late as 1961, the plans for a new university at Bochum (in the heart of the largest industrial area in Germany) included a Protestant and a Catholic theological faculty, despite the existence of well-established theological faculties at near-by universities. Not until the creation of an entirely new breed of university in the last 20 years is a department of theology absent. Even these have a religious education course for teaching "Protestant" and "Catholic religious education." Students who intend to teach "religion" are also required to take a second subject, such as German, English, French, biology, geography, or chemistry. In the Federal Republic of Germany the majority of universities offer this combination; these students are outnumbered by theology students who intend to be ministers by at least three to one at universities with theology faculties, though some faculties have more. Catholic faculties have a special problem these days: relatively few students are seeking ordination. Many of them are interested in theology as a single subject, although they do not feel called to live a life of celibacy. These students try to find some

1. This chapter was presented as a first introduction to students of the Faculty of Theology, University of Oxford.

154

other form of church work for which priesthood would not be required. In addition there are a few students who take theology as a second subject (along with sociology or art history, for example) as a supplementary qualification for a career in a different field. Apart from the state-run universities, theology may be studied in church seminaries (Kirchliche Hochschulen) or at priests' seminaries (the Catholic name), but only for a few semesters.

For some years now there have been more students of theology willing to become ministers than the church is able to employ as future ministers. Both, the state of theological education at German universities and rather poor job prospects, contribute to the shaping of those issues that are currently discussed and on which I would now like to focus.

Ecumenical Theology?

I have already mentioned one important characteristic of theological studies in Germany: the coexistence of Catholic and Protestant faculties at many universities. An administrative union is legally impossible because of the different contractual agreements between the various church authorities and the state. This does not, of course, prevent Catholic students from attending lectures and seminars by the Protestant faculty, and vice versa. Many universities have also established ecumenical institutes, concerned with promoting understanding between the two traditions. Cooperation at the professorial level progressed most among exegetes. Catholic theology has become much more Bible-oriented since Vatican II, and Catholic exegesis uses the historical-critical method unreservedly. A common translation of the Bible has sprung from this cooperation, as well as a joint Protestant-Catholic commentary on the New Testament.

Has ecumenical development given rise to particular topics of discussion? Not so obviously in theology as between the churches themselves, where the problem of mixed marriages and our understanding of the ministry are continually being discussed. Yet the practice of the churches does affect theology. The "Küng case" exemplifies this. A conflict has arisen between the autonomy of critical theological research especially in historical questions, and the authority of the church with its responsibility for theological tradition. More recently Eugen Drewermann—due to his depth psychological exegesis of the Bible—has come into conflict with the authorities of his church.

There has also been a Protestant parallel in the doctrinal disciplinary action against the Hamburg minister Dr. Paul Schulz who had presented radical views in his sermons that were no longer compatible with the Bible or with Lutheran confessional documents which he had accepted as binding at his ordination. These cases are more than signs of a tendency favoring "restoration" in the church. The problems in the Catholic and Protestant churches may not be the same. However, in the Protestant church—and theology—the memory of the *Kirchenkampf* in the national-socialist state stays alive and reminds us that there can be no "independent theology" without a recognition of the theological authority *(Verbindlichkeit)* that is also binding for the faith of every Christian. Of course, it is by no means always easy to distinguish the authority of theological doctrine from the mere perpetuation of church or theological traditions. Nonetheless, one of the important issues of contemporary theology, I should suggest, consists in the question of church doctrine: the consensus of the church in the confession of faith to which theology makes its contribution and upon which theology itself depends.

Ecumenism of Christians and Jews?

Most recently the question of Christian doctrine has become a matter of debate from quite another point of view, that of Jewish-Christian dialogue. In 1980 the synod of the Protestant Church of the Rhineland (its parliament, so to speak) issued a resolution, "Toward a Renewal of the Relations Between Christians and Jews."[2] The resolution includes a confession of the church's share in the guilt and responsibility for the holocaust. It states: "We confess the common hope of a new heaven and a new earth, and the power of this messianic hope for the witness and work of Christians and Jews for justice and peace in the world." A close study of this declaration and its accompanying texts reveals that an ecumenical relationship between Jews and Christians is being contemplated. Here, to be sure, this relationship is viewed not as a united "church," but as a communion of faith which is based on the election of Israel, on whose history the history of the church is grafted. The text explicitly speaks of the common Bible of Jews and Christians (so a hermeneutical priority of the

2. "Synodalbeschluss zur Erneuerung des Verhältnisses von Christen und Juden," *Evangelische Theologie* 40 (1980): 260-262.

New Testament for Old Testament interpretation is excluded); Jesus Christ is understood as Israel's Messiah, although the common significance for Jews and Gentiles ends with his death; the traditional distinction of synagogue and church as "old" and "new" people of God is criticized: "We should . . . only [speak] of the *one* people of God, which as God's Israel follows the call into God's future."

The two most important questions that arise from this declaration, and from the discussion surrounding it, are: first, what are the insights on which this "confession" rests and, second, what is now the role of the New Testament and its exposition?

Jewish-Christian dialogue is very much concerned with historical experiences. This not only includes the horrors of anti-Semitism and the mass executions of Jews and, in addition, the foundation of the State of Israel, an event which is interpreted as a fulfillment of the continuing promise of the land. It also sees Christians and Jews as common groups in a "salvation history" that begins with the election of Israel for the salvation of the nations and that will, without interruption, with no dividing line inserted by the existence of Jesus Christ, reach its goal in the redemption of the world, of all humankind. But what does the application of "salvation history" mean in this regard? Since the seventeenth century German Protestant theology has undergone the influence of Dutch Reformed traditions, later of pietism and finally of the philosophy of history of German idealism. This complex influence led theologians to conceive the relationship of Old and New Testaments as historic continuity. According to this conception Jesus Christ is considered to be the fulfillment of salvation history. Actual history must then be interpreted in terms of the meaning of history as fulfilled in Jesus Christ, and this interpretation further illuminates history "after Christ." Jesus Christ is the center and turning point of history! The new Historical Theology— "salvation-history theology"—of the Jewish-Christian dialogue, if I may call it that, says with Martin Buber: "We do not perceive a caesura in history"—like a dividing line created by Jesus Christ. "We do not know a center of history."[3] From this point of view the New Testament cannot be more than a commentary on the Old Testament,

3. Martin Buber, "Kirche, Volk, Staat, Judentum. Zwiegespräch im Jüdischen Lehrhaus in Stuttgart am 14. Januar 1933," in Karl Ludwig Schmidt, *Neues Testament — Judentum — Kirche.* Kleine Schriften, ed. Gerhard Sauter (Munich: Chr. Kaiser, 1981), 159.

the commentary of the Christians, who have separated themselves from the Jewish people in order to take on a task of their own within salvation history: a task which cannot contest the election of Israel but at the most assumes a salvation-historical function for the Gentiles, which is not (or is no longer) concerned with Israel.

This understanding of the New Testament, moreover, sets out to be radically historical, even more radical than traditional historical-critical research. Jewish-Christian conversation must revolve around the course of the history of Israel; it lets itself be guided above all by the impression of this people's suffering, by their real political hope and its realization in the state of Israel. "Theology" sees itself here as an answer to the challenges of history. This "challenge and response" model of Arnold Toynbee's philosophy of history is taken up (albeit unconsciously), reflecting a general trend in recent theology: theology is a reaction to history. As such it seeks to learn from historical events in order to avoid mistakes of the past and thereby, to carry history closer to its goal, unbounded humanity in a sanctified world. This is a controversial issue in current German theology as it can probably be found elsewhere as well.

Church Practice and Practical Theology

The example of Jewish-Christian dialogue brings us to a characteristic feature of the relationship of the German Protestant church to its leadership and decision-making bodies and to academic theology. Since the end of the last war "the church" has often pronounced on theological questions. Yet even more it has pronounced on questions of ethics and of communal, and even, foreign politics. Church leaders, synods, and, not the least, individual Christians have been seeking to realize their faith through social responsibility. To a significant extent this was a reaction to the failures of church and theology in times of testing in the past, especially in the 1920s and 1930s. In the last few years the *Evangelische Kirche in Deutschland* (the administrative union of Protestant Landeskirchen, that is, of the established Protestant churches in the "provinces" that were once part of Germany) has issued statements, based on the work of specially appointed committees, on such topics as: Jewish-Christian relations; reconciliation with our eastern neighbors; property; sexual ethics (and abortion); the prevention of war and the protection of peace; democracy and ethics of the economy. Those statements are called "Denkschriften." Although theologians were involved in writing them, these statements are by no means simply an application of theological insights to questions of church and society. They are plainly a product of the pluralism that is to be found in the church, especially in ethical matters. Generally official church statements need to find a compromise between conflicting positions, or at least (as far as the question of war and peace is concerned) to leave room for the various parties within the church so as to prevent ethical and political controversies from leading to schism. Occasionally, however (such as in the "Denkschrift" on reconciliation with our eastern neighbors, particularly Poland), the leadership of the Protestant church has acted independently and published a position several steps ahead of public and church opinion, committing the church (at least for a time) to an unambiguous party line on the way forward to foreign politics.

Thereby a new type of theology emerges. It is not at all similar to the traditional "church theology" that defends established traditions against the innovations of critical theology. On the contrary, it sees the church's ethical and political statements as expressions of a process of social change affecting the church, sometimes even furthered and intensified by groups within the church. From time to time the representatives of "academic theology," the exegetes, church historians, dogmaticians, ethicists, and practical theologians, are prepared to add to the pluralism in the church by taking up extreme positions. This was the case, for instance, in the discussion that surrounded the anti-racism program of the World Council of Churches over twenty years ago. By general consensus, racism was sharply condemned as a sin against God; the memory of the horrors of racism in one's own past made this a particularly sensitive question in Germany. It was and remains, however, controversial whether solidarity with the liberation movements of the third world is an imperative of faith. Many theologians, influenced by social and political conflicts in other parts of the world, saw the world on the brink of a great struggle between the kingdom of God on the side of the oppressed and the hordes of the antichrist—led by Wall Street, the multinationals, and the military strategists of the major powers. They saw the anti-racism program as a call to decision, to division, even in the German church. Other theologians saw the controversy as posing a question to the church: the question of her mandate in the world; of the possibilities of political action that avoid the danger of a friend-or-foe mentality; and of Jesus' peace, which may indeed lead to conflicts but does not see conflict as such as the proper means by which the truth should be established.

The question remains: what is the work of the church? Is the church one group within a pluralist society, a secular state, trying to defend its interests and achieve its goals? But what are the church's goals, what are her tasks? As I see it, German theology has for some years been wandering dangerously between Scylla and Charybdis on this issue. Danger threatened on the one hand from the "theology of the *Zeitgeist*": current events and urgent concrete problems are not seen as tasks to whose performance theology has its own contribution to make. Rather, they are expected to provide a reason for changing theology. The aim, to be sure, is to enable theology to react better to to the needs of the day, but in fact this approach renders theology unable to give a theological answer and, in extreme cases, turns it into a reflection of fashion. It is beyond dispute that several more recent theological conceptions in Germany, which seek to express the whole of theology in terms of one modern, "relevant" concept, have at least partly succumbed to this temptation; I am thinking, for example, of Jürgen Moltmann's "Theology of Hope,"[4] also of some contributions to a *theologia crucis* or to a "Theology of Revolution."[5] On the other hand, the work of the church in recent years has been felt increasingly to revolve around the problems of the individual within society: communication problems, isolation (especially among young people), the "crisis of meaning" brought about by the loss of an authoritative framework, and by growing fears for the future *(Zukunftsangst)*. These are doubtlessly highly important tasks, for which German theology used to be inadequately prepared (due to the lack of attention paid in its recent history to psychology and social psychology). A danger lurks here nonetheless, that theology could end up with a new self-understanding as (wholly) a theory for coping with life. This is what gives the question of "meaning" such importance that, to a large extent, it dominates religious education in schools, pastoral work, and preaching. Church and theology, it is said, must combat the ubiquitous growth of nihilism by giving meaning, by "making sense" of the

---

4. Jürgen Moltmann, *The Theology of Hope* (New York: Harper & Row, 1967).
5. Trutz Rendtorff and Heinz Eduard Tödt, *Theologie der Revolution*. Analysen und Materialien (Frankfurt a.M.: Suhrkamp, 1968).

world. They are expected to give isolated individuals a new sense of fellowship in community by encouraging them to share their personal problems and to take themselves seriously, in every aspect of life. Theology is thus turned into a cultural phenomenon of self-analysis and of sensitivity for oneself and one's fellow beings. All communicatory signs, body language as well as words, the whole "atmosphere" of social living, are regarded as centrally important. Not what is said but how—the communicative effect, not the propositional content—is what matters.

This leads, however, to a radical transformation of the "practical theology," studied at German universities as a compulsory subject in academic theology alongside the traditional disciplines. It is still relatively young in German theology, introduced by both Catholics and Protestants only about 200 years ago; on the Protestant side, especially due to Schleiermacher "practical theology" has been understood as theoretical reflection on the church's work.[6] The student is supposed to learn how to carry out his or her official duties responsibly (preaching, church teaching, pastoral care, and social work). This part of the university education is then effectively continued in the "Vikariat," a two-year internship in a particular congregation which is the final phase of a minister's education before ordination. What actually happens today, however, is that practical theology is mainly concerned with the young theologian him- or herself: the theologian's personal questions, experiences in communicating with others, the search for meaning and reflections on the role of the profession in a changing society. Still, in my opinion, the question is whether it would not be preferable to treat the challenge of the church within present society as a theological problem rather than to translate it into personal issues which would only affect the individual minister. The theologian's own self has—I must say, unfortunately—become a major topic of theology. This is a revival of the traditions of pietism and the revivalist movement, of philosophical idealism and existentialism—of their good and bad sides. What we may hope for is a rediscovery of that self-discipline and *Selbstvergessenheit* which are essential and indispensable for academic study as well as for the work of the church.

6. Friedrich Daniel Ernst Schleiermacher, *Die praktische Theologie nach den Grundsätzen der evangelischen Kirche im Zusammenhange dargestellt*, ed. Jacob Frerichs (Berlin: G. Reimer, 1850), 12.

9

The "Image of Humanity" and the Question of Development

A Christian Viewpoint

In general, the term "development" denotes a continuous, unbroken transition from one condition to another. That which was still incomplete in an earlier form develops as it changes. The later form is already prefigured in the earlier and, conversely, the earlier stage is not annulled by the later but is contained in it. Nature is the model for this type of development, where the plant emerges from seed, the fruit from flower. Seen in this way development is a natural unfolding.

Nature offers models for the developments which take place in other areas of life as well. Charles Darwin inquired into the conditions for development in the society of his English homeland during the Industrial Revolution and found his answer as a scientist on the South Sea Galapagos Islands. However, it is debatable whether one can speak of development in culture, history, and society in the same way as one speaks of it in nature. Nevertheless, with respect to the development of the forms of state, social structures, and technology, the terminology "unfolding" and "natural growth" are used even when humans beings intervened in the course of events. A development is said to be "natural" when a reality develops out of a previous condition without the need for any external influence other than the stimulation of forces which in the past lay dormant. Just as every plant needs light and warmth so every person needs the fostering of gifts within him- or herself, so that he or she might develop as independent persons. Thus "development" means, on the whole, a development towards the higher and the better; in short, an advance.

The idea of development as it has been described so far is foreign to the Christian faith—not on account of a conflict with modern science and its theory of evolution—but because Christianity, like Judaism and Islam, does not experience God and humanity as an eternal cycle of becoming and decay, and because it is therefore not a religion of nature. When the Bible and Christian theology speak of "becoming," they speak of the miracle of creation and new creation. They speak of an activity of God without presupposing a precondition in nature or in human beings. The Gospel of John says, "The Word became flesh and dwelt among us", God became human. It does not say that a human being developed out of God, or that the incarnation was so prepared in the divinity of God that it was inevitable. God has not developed into a man but has become one in complete freedom: He entered into history without being taken up into it and its development. God's becoming human, His incarnation of Jesus of Nazareth, is decisive in what can be said from the Christian point of view about the becoming of humankind, and therefore, "becoming" means the beginning of a new life.

I said previously that the idea of development in the sense of an "origin by development from earlier forms, not by special creation" is foreign to Christianity. However, the Bible speaks uninhibitedly of development in the sense of "gradual unfolding" or "growth." God's word is said to be sown in order to die and thus produce fruit. This growth is not automatic but depends on whether the seed falls on fruitful soil, whether the sun dries it up or weeds choke it, or whether men destroy it. Indeed, Jesus himself is a seed which dies, that is, must lose its solid form in order to gain new life and produce fruit. Therefore, "development" in this sense means that human beings and the world are not complete but yet have a future for which and in which they change. Persons and the world are called to this change, and to this extent they themselves contribute to their own development, which, however, is thereby made no less dependent on what happens to them. Thus, development cannot be an automatic process and certainly not a progression that obviously leads to a better, more complete life.

In that language of the Bible "growth" means that life thrives and is passed on. Life means to produce fruit, indeed good fruit. If a life-form, or part of one, grows only in order to extend itself, to claim light, air, and space for itself alone, the result will be that it restricts or suffocates other life—like the weeds that in the Bible are a simile for the rampant power of evil in the world. Expansion, concentration of power, centralization, and all-embracing power claims are therefore, for the most part, seen as a sign of the development of evil in the world, the accumulation of the high-handedness of humankind. For example, in Daniel's vision of the unfolding of history (Daniel 7) four world empires in the form of beasts follow one another in succession, each being greater and more voracious than the last, until the whole world is under threat of being devoured. It is not only the fear felt by a small nation in the face of the empires of the ancient world that is being expressed in this vision; nor is it only the fear of the excesses of an imperialism that concentrates its power in the hands of a few in order to increase and consolidate that power. Rather, the concentration of power is seen as both threatening to life and antagonistic to God because such concentration inclines to self-glorification and concern only for its own survival. The tendency of imperialism to expand and to concentrate power threatens the welfare of those who are subordinate to the power. Their lives become merely the means for the self-preservation of that power.

In contrast to uncontrollable, imperialistic power and its claim for total mastery is the image of the growth of "the body of Christ," as the church is called in the New Testament. The "body of Christ" could not come into being until Jesus Christ, the seed of God's new world, died. The death of Jesus brought life for all humankind, not only for one nation or one religious group and not only for Christians. Christians are convinced that the death of Jesus Christ is the root of life for all humankind, and, more than that, the only root of our life with God. Christ gave up his life in order that others might participate in the communion with God which is the energy of life, and might thus be fruitful. In this way Christ brought to an end another solidarity of humankind, the solidarity of guilt and the fate of death. It is common to all of us that we must die because of our separation from the life of God. This solidarity is repeatedly confirmed anew when an individual exhaustively pursues the possibilities offered in life at the cost of other lives or of nature. In this way the individual and the world are bound together in the destruction of our own life; the one is sacrificed to the expansion of the ruling power;

the ruling power itself oversteps its sphere and thus comes to an end. This solidarity of death is opposed by the promise of life for all through the death of Jesus. This is a life that grows by the unfolding of its vocation for the peace of God and does not assert itself at the expense of others or of the environment. Now solidarity comes into being and grows, in that both the individual together with others and humanity, together with the world, grow towards peace.

There can be no question of growth, expansion, and development in themselves. Development in and for itself has no value in the light of Christian belief because survival in and for its own sake cannot be justified. Development must be oriented to the goal that chooses between what is valuable in life and what is not. We must therefore ask in what direction something is developing—and this applies as much to the life of nations as to individuals, to the structure of communal life and the relationship between humanity and nature. In the same way, the type and way of development are also dependent on the goal. The critical questioning concerning the goal and rationale of development checks the misunderstanding that development is always to be qualified by continuity, permanence, and expansion.

The question of the goal of development must be put radically. It cannot be satisfactorily answered from provisional perspectives. The Christian view of humanity asks: Can the individual and humankind as a whole develop towards God in such a way that they become God? The answer is to be found in a somewhat obscure passage of the New Testament which is, however, of particular importance to the Christian view of humanity, and has been taken up especially by the Greek Orthodox Church:

> See what love (God) the Father has given us that we should be called children of God; and so we are . . . We are God's children now; what we shall be has not yet been disclosed, but we know that when it is disclosed we shall be like him because we shall see him as he is. Everyone who has this hope before him purifies himself, as he is pure (1 John 3:1–2).

For our investigation concerning the image of humanity and the nature of development that statement is both pioneering and bold. It speaks of a future that far surpasses the present: believers are already God's children but, at the present, they do not yet know what they are to become. They are still incomplete. Something essential has yet to happen to them. But even though they cannot foresee their future in detail they can know that their way leads them into the immediate presence of God: "We shall see Him as He is." This recalls the ancient story of the Fall in Genesis in which it was insinuated to the first human couple: "You will be like God" and thus they were tempted to try the fruit of the tree of life. Eve and Adam wanted to leave the last level of creation, to burst out of their creatureliness, so to speak. They wanted to stand above the last antithesis of the world, on the other side of the distinction between good and evil, but in so doing they fell into futility. The thirst for knowledge by which humanity seeks to exceed its creaturely limits is described in this story as an acquisitive greed, a striving after a satisfaction that incorporates the guarantee of life. The hedonism with which we seize everything, because we fear that otherwise we will die, is now set in contrast to the vision of God. Even when humankind "sees" God "as He is" and thus comes before Him directly, they will always be faced with Him though they are no longer estranged.

The endpoint of the development of the individual and of humanity cannot be God. Although the theological authorities of the Greek Orthodox Church spoke of the "divinization" of humankind they did not mean divinity in itself but a progressive approach to God or, put concretely, to God's rationality. Individuals are enabled through their divine kinship to overcome their fall into the natural cycle of becoming and decay. They are no longer ruled by their sensitivity, impulses, and drives. Instead they give heed to reason and the spirit of obedience to the will of God.

I have emphasized Eastern Christianity's view of humanity because the Eastern Church is the neighbor of Islam in many countries and has the closest contact with it. The idea of perfectibility has been pushed aside to too great an extent in the Western churches. They feared a naturalistic misunderstanding, that is, that perfectibility would be understood as a development towards the spiritualistic, a gradual overcoming of the material, the temporal, and the transitory. The theologians of the Eastern Church have always emphasized this view that the divinization of humankind can raise him above the natural conditions of his life. The divine kinship in which humankind participates through the Son of God, Jesus Christ, is like a seed which sinks into our nature, dies, and then grows. On the other side there have always been voices in Western Christianity repeatedly speaking of a development of the mind that leads to a complete mastery over nature. In their view a person's humanity is only fully developed when he or she is no longer blindly subjugated to nature. These are two of the sources—and often independent of Christian faith—of the technological development of Western civilization: the idea of freedom; and the concept that individuals must progressively understand the whole world in itself in order to be able to develop an environment from it that is suitable for humankind. To draw from Karl Marx, this means the humanization of nature and the naturalization of humanity.

The latter understanding of development causes a severe conflict for Christianity, one that determines its stance with respect to progress—both in technology and civilization—and the changes associated with it.

On the one hand, viewed from a Christian standpoint, individuals are not perfect but are in need of deep-seated change. Indeed, they are in need of new life. However, this life cannot be created by change in the external conditions; rather, it was given to us by God the Creator and Redeemer. Thus we can say that development is only possible when people know themselves to be God's children, and therefore abandon the self-glorification that only appears to enrich them but which, in fact, destroys the environment and finally our lives. The possibilities of life which are granted by the Creator can only be developed, can only grow if the right to life of all created things is protected. In the Bible the condition in which life can flourish is described as "blessing": through blessing, life increases and thrives, producing fruit for many. In this sense even Israel's social ordinances took an interest in development. The economic concentration of power in the latter days of the monarchy and the consequent social restructuring were sharply criticized by the prophets. They viewed this development as disastrous because it led to exploitation of the land and the people. The Sabbath commandment was and remained an important criterion for the development of a "blessing": human beings and beasts, and among them, even the slave and the sojourner who is outside the protection of the law, all must, on one day of the week, be totally free creatures in order to be able to praise God and to show that they have Him alone to thank for their lives. The Sabbath is the sign of the solidarity of all creatures. It stands, therefore, under the sign of the promise of blessing.

Thus, in this respect the biblical view of humanity is open to the notion of development. However, on the other hand, Christianity cannot adopt the idea (and utopia) of development according to which a person does not start as a fully realized human being but has first to *become* human by creating perfect living conditions in which needs and wishes can be satisfied. Ludwig Feuerbach conceived of such a "humanization" taking place within the history of humankind—Karl Marx followed him, in his own way. Along with Darwin, Feuerbach belongs to the fathers of the modern theory of development.[1] He is particularly important for our subject because he is dependent upon religious ideas. In his understanding, the goal of development is the deification of humankind, that is, the historical realization of qualities which in theology have been ascribed to God: infinity, omnipresence, omnipotence, and perfection.[2] Feuerbach understood these as the determining features of humanity, which are to be realized through formation in the world and the perfection of the social community. In the place of God becoming human in Jesus Christ, Feuerbach thought of a human being becoming a god.

As if he had foreseen this, Martin Luther once said in criticism of the conception of the divinization of humanity mentioned earlier: God became human so that we, who ourselves wished to become gods and thereby became arrogant and wretched, could at last become true persons. We are to become nothing more than real persons, God's creatures in his creation. Certainly we must first become such individuals: people who live in communion with God and who give recognition to the right to life of all other creatures and are only therefore capable of genuine solidarity. But we can only *become human* because we *are* perfect persons on account of God's action. We are creatures whom he has created "in his own image" (Genesis 1:26). This means that every person is so formed by God that he or she may look to God. He or she can praise and thank God for his or her life and for the life of all other creatures. Humanity is called to be for God, in and for the world, and to worship him. This is not self-evidently the case, either from the standpoint of humanity or as seen from the history of humankind. The world is not fulfilled by an in-

---

1. Ludwig Feuerbach, *The Essence of Christianity* (New York: Harper Torchbooks, 1957).

2. Idem, *Grundsätze der Philosophie des Zukunft* (1843), 6–9, in idem, *Kleine Schriften* (Frankfurt a.M.: Suhrkamp, 1966), 146–153.

dividual's praise of God. For that to happen much that is fundamental must be changed. Nevertheless, persons are not the "image of God" only on account of a stage of development in the history of humanity. They are the "image of God" despite their culture, race, the technological development in their society, or the form of the political community in which they live. This has been recalled in recent decades by Christians in Africa and Asia; with full justification they have asserted their humanity over against the Europeans and Americans who were all too easily inclined to tie the concept of humanity to a certain stage of cultural development. To think in this way is to run the risk of speaking about "under-developed" and "developed" peoples as if there were indeed a lower and higher humanity. This would not only destroy the solidarity of human beings as the "images of God" but would also destroy their solidarity with the whole creation. For such "higher persons," on the way to self-divinization, would use all that is in the world—other persons, animals, plants, water, and air purely as a means for their self-development. In doing so they would misuse all that is in the world.

What then are the consequences for the political task of developing living conditions, if it is to be carried out in the spirit of true solidarity? The answer that can be inferred from the Christian point of view sounds very simple and yet has far-reaching consequences, even with respect to the assessment of technical and social developments. It runs as follows: we were created to praise God, to let God be the Lord of the whole world, and to live in communion with Him and His creation. The politics of development, in my opinion, can only meaningfully wish to provide the opportunity for *this* for all people. Many—indeed all too many—cannot praise God because they have to suffer in such a way that it seems impossible to them to look to God. Individuals and peoples are so entangled in their concern for day-to-day survival that the time for thankful stillness before God is taken away from them. The faces of many people are so marked by hopelessness and desperation that they no longer suspect that they also bear within themselves a trace of the Creator. Yet it is precisely they who are "images of God," that means figures of the suffering Christ who, before all peoples, is called by the New Testament the image of God and the New Humanity. Therefore, the question of solidarity and development does not lead us to the utopia of similarly expansionist living conditions for all. That would demand the spread of the lifestyle of a civilization that is on the brink of destroying its environment all over the world, a consequence that destroys the solidarity of creation. We are faced with the question of defining optimal living conditions in the light not only of human solidarity but also the solidarity of creation. If it is the criterion of the Christian view of humanity that each individual may thankfully praise God in all the expressions of their lives, because their lives are both blessed and a blessing, then this will give us a new view of both the standard and the goal for desirable development.

10

Eschatological Rationality

"Historicity" (*Geschichtlichkeit*): I used to run into this magical word all the time in my university studies, and it has dogged me—for the most part with reproach—from the beginning of my own theological work. It requires that we fully understand ourselves in the cultural, social, and political milieu of our time, that we consider the relativities of where we are placed, and that we conduct ourselves accordingly. But is the attempt to make "historicity" such a comprehensive perspective possible at all? Do we not have a hidden self-contradiction here? "Historicity" can consist only of learning the limitation of one's own perspective on equally limited questions, pursuing these questions, and then seeing the extent to which the proposed solutions are provisional. This *scientific-ethical* reflection, it seems to me, is crucial in a situation in Christian theology in which general concepts and universal terms promise an orientation that corresponds less and less to the actual state of theological communication. It is this discrepancy, therefore, that I should like to use as my entry point.

The impression is often created that theology develops in a series of overall conceptions and focuses on basic theological questions, whether these fundamentals be sought in the relationship between faith and reason, church and society, or theory and practice. Such an interest in fundamentals stimulates, at regular intervals, a revision of theology as a whole. It does not reckon with the fact that on a universally recognized basis individual problems can be independently investigated, in which the result—perhaps by exposing an aporia—might possibly lead to a basic crisis, though not with the intention of unhinging the whole structure or having it fit with new hinges. But could such an approach focus attention on the foundation on which Christian theology rests and, on account of which, claims have to be made? How does it become clear what keeps theology going, what provokes it to counter- questions, and then, perhaps even against its tradition-saturated preferences, produces new insights?

Let me try to clarify this with the attractive title of a book by Eugen Rosenstock-Huessy, *The Christian Future or the Modern Mind Outrun.*[1] The author sees his slogan as a future-oriented reminder of the Christian hope of salvation, which became, as it were, the driving force of Western humanity by getting going a static spiritual and social order and by continually proving vigorous enough to break up calcifications, overcome anachronisms, and make possible social and intellectual structures that accommodate the struggle for justice and peace. So understood, theology should be a consciousness that is ahead of its time and that pushes people forward to action just as much as it necessitates subsequent reflection.

One can also read Rosenstock-Huessy's formulation (the first and less pretentious part, at any rate) in another way, however: as an answer to the questions of the horizon of the Christian life. This horizon is formed by the promises that God confirms in the life and death of Jesus Christ (II Corinthians 1:20), promises that He has so fulfilled in the crucifixion and resurrection of Jesus that all of human history is decided in this event. "Decided" does not mean, however, that here something is enclosed, possibly even entombed. On the contrary, life is opened up, since it finds its foundation not in its own depths but in God's future.

Promise and Expectation

If "eschatology" is thought of as discourse about this future, it is then a particular topic in Christian theology. Yet at this very point theology is asking paradigmatically about the nature and grounds of its own knowledge. It must distinguish between that which is simply given to human discourse by God and that which we take upon ourselves to investigate. Within this tension the future, too, is perceived as that which is yet to happen in time—with the question of what we humans have to expect from God and how this relates to the pattern

1. Eugen Rosenstock-Huessy, *The Christian Future or the Modern Mind Outrun* (London: Jarrold & Sons, 1947).

of experiences that take the form of our longing hopes. Eschatology provides an exemplary opportunity for extracting basic determinations of what theology is from the inner structure of theological statements. With respect to the absolute necessity of theological discourse, its feasibility, and its difficulties, it is imperative to clarify what is given beforehand to theology and what there remains for it to do.

I return to II Corinthians 1:20: "All of God's promises are 'Yes' in Him (Jesus Christ); so through Him the 'Amen' is also spoken by us to the glory of God." That is a key proposition not only in Pauline theology but in Christian theology in general. It refers to the divine promises given to Israel and shows them to be grounded in Jesus Christ. What is more, it characterizes Christendom as the congregation of those who respond to this action of God. They say, "Amen," that is "Yes, this is the way it is and no other." The historical course of Christianity could then be judged on the basis of that response, glory to God, which joins in the action of God. At the same time some light could be shed on the eminently theological problem of why and in what sense there *can* be a history "after Christ" at all—which I regard as the least obvious fact in the world. If Jesus' coming, suffering, dying, and resurrection are not just an historical intermezzo; if world history did not just pass over the sealed tomb of Jesus to the next item on the agenda—and indeed that is what Christian faith lives by—then the question of how to label subsequent history becomes all the more pressing. The theological answer to that question cannot consist in "explaining" the factual development of history in such a way that church history, at least, is understood as the continuation of the story of Jesus and of the spread of his influence: for example, as the successful coping with the catastrophe of his death, or as a compensatory activism towards the return of Christ, expected in the near future but not yet happened, or as the hope that Jesus would suddenly break in and transform all things, sublimated in a consciousness of innermost security in God in the midst of unchangingly miserable outward circumstances, which this consciousness and a strong determination can at least mitigate. Even the idea that, possibly, gave rise to the so-called Christian Era, namely, that the birth of Christ signified a decisive turning point because the "prophecies" of the Old Covenant and, generally speaking, the whole intention of the covenant of God with His people found their "fulfillment" in Jesus Christ, is also inadequate if only because it does not make allowance for the coexistence and frequent opposition of the Jewish and Christian expectations of salvation.

The crucial point seems to me to be that the concept of "promise" that Paul obviously picks up on in this passage as something already known was formed first and foremost in reference to the Christ event. Yet it is not so much a matter of the philological observation that the word "promise" increases in the New Testament in comparison to the Old Testament and is the characteristic expression for God's future-oriented Word. What is more important is that in the New Testament the concept of "promise" stands for God's Christ-oriented Word, that it is adapted to this meaning, and that this happens in such a way that at the same time we learn how it can be "used" from now on. All of this belongs to the process of theological *concept formation*. Such formation does not, for example, add up the total of God's proclamations for His Covenant people; nor does one sift out of the Jewish Scriptures those prophecies that are not yet, or at least not completely fulfilled, or that point beyond themselves and therefore can be claimed for Jesus Christ; nor also are divine promises so detached from their former historical concreteness and, as it were, dematerialized that in this new meaning they appear to refer to Christ. New Testament concept formation differs from all of these attempts to explain it in that it sets about to state knowledge of the definitive action of God for the whole world. This action of God is filled with promise, since it inserts both humanity, which has been affected by Him, and derivatively the world bound up with humanity, into the history in which God is glorified, that is, in which He redemptively penetrates all reality and absorbs it into His divinity.

If "promise" becomes the basic category of faith, then the dimensions of Christian hope can be more sharply delineated than is suggested merely by its anthropological character (the relation of the person to the world, in the face of the passage of time). In a radio discussion in 1954 on the subject "Christian Hope and the Problem of Demythologization" Günther Bornkamm asked Rudolf Bultmann what he had to say about the expectation of the cosmos in travail, which (according to Romans 8:19ff.) longs for the revelation of the freedom of the children of God. Bultmann replied that this longing did not affect him; he could only say with Luther, "Christian hope knows that it hopes, but it does not know what it hopes for."[2]

What Luther says in the passage cited by Bultmann (*Lectures on Romans, 1515–16*), however, is that hope inserts the hoping one into that which is hoped for but that which is hoped for is not apparent. Rather, hope leads one across "into the unknown and hidden, into inward darkness so that it does not know what it hopes and yet does know what it does not hope for,"[3] namely, that which it can expect naturally, that which begins in the visible. Luther is describing here the birth of hope in the suffering that submits to God's action. It is action of the hidden God, which calls one doomed to death and staring death in the face to believe in "hope against hope" (Romans 4:18).

The hope of faith, therefore, is oriented toward the action of God. This action is not "hidden" in the sense that it is concealed in an inscrutable sphere or that it is accessible in a deeper, broader, or higher vision and can become visible to another mode of seeing. "Hiddenness" means, rather, that God acts and becomes present in His own way. The way of suffering, which Luther pointed to, is the painful process of becoming aware of the divinity of God in His action, becoming aware of the Divine contradiction to human longings and wishful imaginations, to God as the projection of that which we are not, but would definitely like to expect for ourselves and for humanity, so as not to have to submit. Over against exactly such a projected future, hope is introduced into not-knowing. Hope has no leg to stand on, just where it thinks it might move beyond all provisional knowledge by its wishful thinking. Humanity must abandon these levels of expectation in order to be able to rely fully on God. Hope does not thereby become devoid of all "content"; it does not become a pure act or movement that finds satisfaction in itself. Rather, it is extended towards its fulfillment.

The way of suffering and hope, then, is the process by which faith comes to knowledge, for "fulfillment" relates not to wishful

2. Günther Bornkamm, Rudolf Bultmann, and Friedrich Karl Schumann, *Die christliche Hoffnung und das Problem der Entmythologisierung* (Stuttgart: Evangelisches Verlagswerk, 1954), 57f.

3. Martin Luther, "Scholion," Romans 8:24, WA 56:374, 14–17: *"Ergo spes transfert in speratum, Sed speratum non apparet. Ideo transfert in incognitum, in absconditum, in tenebras interiores, ut nesciat, quid speret, et tamen sciat, quid non speret."*

imaginations but to the action of God. Therein can be perceived, as God's promise takes place, how the God of Abraham, Isaac, and Jacob, the God who raised Jesus from the dead, acts in divine fashion with the world and with us. By reaching out for what He promises us and for how He binds Himself to us in that promise, we step out of the self-reference of our own acting, seeing, and thinking; we live in an "ecstasy" that is worlds apart from all mere rapture and enthusiasm, since it long ago lost its arrogance and exuberance in the face of all that which makes up the reality in which we live—a reality which is perceived as all the more miserable the less one allows oneself to be wistfully distracted from its distress. The one who hopes becomes continually (though not progressively) aware of what God did for the world in Jesus Christ and what He intends to do for this world on behalf of His own people. Thus hope can express what it does not know by leaving behind that which does not originate in God. It can express that, and therein is found the difference between a "pure" act of hope, which soars beyond any of its materializations, and a hope that claims nothing for itself, that does not even know what it desires but can desire only what God desires. Hope can only express such things, however, by remaining oriented to that which happens by virtue of the promise of God, has happened, and is going to happen. It confidently knows what it hopes. This is not contrary to what Luther was saying but the very same thing, if one rightly understands this "knowledge" as the declarative discourse of faith which says "Amen" to God's action and with this Amen testifies to the action of God, action that precedes it and never comes under its control. In order to assert something (and not, let's say, to express one's own transcending emotion), this discourse must limit itself to what God communicates in His promises: His justice, His peace, His life. That alone is what hope engages in, and with that it says all that it can know, by saying it hopefully, expectantly.

If justice, peace, and life as the essence of the "salvation event" are understood and interpreted strictly as promissory concepts, then the usual question about what they mean "concretely" is of no concern. They are not empty dogmatic forms that can be "filled" with ethical illustrations. Promissory concepts are not linguistic substitutes for realities of a heavenly or earthly nature, but they are signs of God's action itself. That means that whatever we perceive with their help is an indication of God's reality, which stands over against both our conceptualizing and our concepts.

The theological translation of promissory concepts into expressions of human action must reveal the special semantic incommensurability (*Gebrochenheit*) peculiar to hope, which knows, at any rate, that it "does not know what it hopes and yet does know what it does not hope for" (Luther). To use some examples, such translation will not seek to make God's justice plausible with conceptions of equality that match the culturally developed desire of humankind for equal treatment, for compensation of natural differences, and for the overcoming of acquired differences. God's peace becomes manifest in the unity of humanity, not based on natural ties, on sympathy, on biological, intellectual, or elective affinity, or on convention. The unity demonstrating God's peace will rather become apparent whenever human individuals agree to God's promise-filled action, a unity that thereby establishes unanimity and consensus. "Life" from God is displayed in fellowship with the suffering Christ, which despite every threat, injury, and actual destruction of human vitality and spirituality, does not let humanity perish but—often imperceptibly to those afflicted—brings to light the power of God, made perfect in weakness (II Corinthians12:9). The unavoidable semantic incommensurability of a "theology of hope" is shown precisely in the fact that it finds terms for Christian ethics different from those that appear to "correspond" to promissory concepts. All analogizing, all seeking after correspondences can only lead to the question of how in fact our actions are related to the actions of God.

I should like at this point to explore a bit further the question of the translation of the promissory concept of "justice" in the context of eschatology. Two other key terms, "peace" and "life," will be discussed later.

The *justice* with which God binds himself to humanity in the fate of Jesus Christ is and remains God's justice. The reformers saw in its reception the all-decisive event of salvation: humanity is accepted by God, called into fellowship with God, and snatched from the power of sin, death, and hell. By God's love they are freed to look up to God and to devote themselves to their neighbors in need, since they no longer lapse into self-justification; their turning in upon themselves is broken apart in the hope of the life granted them by the gospel of Jesus Christ. The concept of "justice" was defined theologically—in the Reformation doctrine of justification's fresh and illuminating interpretation of Pauline theology—as the saving action of God which overpowers human forgetfulness of God and overcomes selfish resistance to God and His creation. Justice, therefore, neither has to do with correct measurement that allocates to individuals their due by what they have or have not done (*iustitia distributiva*), nor does it mean the golden mean between too much and too little of all that we expect and can claim for ourselves. God's justice does not lead to the balance between that for which He demands payment for Himself and that which we do or do not accomplish. Rather God exercises His rights in such a way that He relieves us of the burden of guilt of our past, indeed first of all breaks the grip of our past by confronting us with it. This past no longer dominates the horizon of the future but really does become the past: removed from our assessment, it is now God's business: God transforms the continuing effects of our past into a new living space. To be declared righteous means to receive comfort for life and death from this forgiveness, not to exhaust one's energies through worry about the need to gain a life that one precisely wastes on one's own efforts.

The crucial point in the translation of God's justice into human righteousness and political justice is, as Luther and Augustine recognized, that God contradicts every conception of justice as *iustitia activa*, the assertion of one's own righteousness. The only ones, says Augustine (*City of God* 21.24), who experience the gracious gift of God's righteousness are those who do not assert their own righteousness, indeed neither wish nor are able to do so at all in face of the action of God that makes things right. Justice as an ethical matter, therefore, means common submission to the will of God, listening to His commandments as the promise of life for all people. It does not look first of all at "just" proportions, that is, at a distribution of goods that supplies the individual with neither too little nor too much of what he or she needs and desires. Rather, it creates the expectation of the eschatological justice of God, in which some day all humanity will submit to God's will alone and therein find their complete happiness, the right view of each other and their social needs. Precisely if a state avoids making divine justice its own concern and thus sooner or later an instrument of its own preservation, it will concern itself properly with prosperous conditions for all those entrusted to it. Justice as an ethical task of Christian hope is sought and tested in the resistance to that all-too-human selfishness of both the "haves" and the "have-nots" who want nothing more than to join the "haves." The semantic incommensurability (I could now also say the eschatological rationality) of justice comes to expression not in the definition "to each his own" but what can be ethically defined "as the agreement of reasonable beings concerning the objects of their love."[4] So believed Augustine. The same thing could be found in Luther's political ethics in his two-kingdoms doctrine, which for polemical purposes is often completely misinterpreted (misunderstood as a withdrawal into themselves by believers concerned only about the salvation of their own souls). Applied to our contemporary situation and the world-wide demand for social justice, which is the motivating force in the ecumenical movement, God's justice reigns where His love gains ground, a love that can be roused, as it were, possibly by basic pity, definitely also by sympathy and like-mindedness, but in such a way that it does justice to the requirements of political organization. Not less but more rationality is necessary to help people to a life truly filled with expectation, a life not so consumed with worry about basic necessities that no petition or thanksgiving to God is voiced. For the sake of the promise of justice, God's free gift of salvation must be kept distinct from all human yearning after what is just. Theological rationality has to apply this distinction and thereby call attention to the foundations of the polis, the commonwealth.

Contexts of Discovery and the Context of Justification in Theology

The relationship between eschatology and ethics requires a scientific-theoretical clarification of theological discourse. For what circulates as "eschatological" in theology—and this has been especially true of the hope-impulse generated since the 1960s—is often such that it is necessary to ask about its theological substantiation. This question is raised precisely because the turn to the future is occasioned by present-day challenges more strongly than need be the case with other themes of theology. Theology is supposed to legitimate the answer to these challenges. It is indeed striking that the eschato-

---

4. Paul L. Lehmann, *Ethics in a Christian Context* (New York: Harper & Row, 1963), 255.

logical "awakening" about twenty years ago did not occur, for example, in pastoral care but to a large extent had its origin in social ethics.

What brought me to eschatology? It was, first of all, my wish to reflect on biblical-theological insights (especially from the hermeneutical discussion concerning the Old Testament) from a systematic theological perspective, in response to impulses from the Jewish tradition of hope. The problems of Messianism confronted me first in my acquaintance with a Jewish Christian, then in books on Jewish philosophy of religion and sociology of religion, and still later in the transformation in the Neo-Marxism of Ernst Bloch and others.

Another major factor was the question of what lay behind the category of *promissio* in Reformation Theology. In Dialectical Theology's adoption of the Reformation term "Word of God" I thought I detected fundamental differences with the Reformation usage. In both cases the time factor is absent, or at any rate is not constitutive. Beyond that, however, in Dialectical Theology (at least in its early form) the factor of the "not yet," of the eschatological reserve, was emphasized in a way that was foreign to the Reformers. For them *promissio* was the Essence of the Word, of the promise of God, hence a personal relation and "speech act" *("Sprachhandlung")*, a deed-word. By *this* Word (not by any mere "linguistic event," *Sprachgeschehen*!) time is constituted. And this *"Sprachlichkeit"* has great communicative import as the foundation of the consensus of faith.

That was *one* occasion. A second is one I have become fully aware of only in retrospect. When I was vicar in the parish, I was impressed by ethical mobilization as a response to the political and ecological "challenge" to the Christian hope. "We live as we hope"— so went the motto already back then. Here was, so to speak, a locomotive ready to move full steam ahead, but there were no train tracks and the "gears" of spirituality were all jammed. The question of "concreteness" destroys the perception of what has been "given" and what has been "commissioned" to us. What in God's promises is concrete? This—that they are God's promises: God's justice, God's peace, life from God. These promises become perceptible to us not through analogies based on fictitious univocations. Rather, they stand in judgment upon such semantics. Should we not see that the translation of biblical promissory concepts into exhortation and paranesis begins first of all with the shattering of linguistic analogies and the introduction of other terms for ethical orientation such as "unity" and "consensus" in respect of the promised peace? Connected to that is the fact that God's promises are not, as it were, behind us, as a divine fait accompli, which we somehow have to bring into our reality. Instead they are realities in front of us, anticipating us; we encounter them and have to discover them, and this happens in conflict with whatever we already do, desire, and contemplate! Thus we must sharply distinguish between the responsibility of Christian ethics, its accountability before the judgment of God, and a motivational context or framework, in which divine truths are supposed to move us to action. Eschatology has much to do with unsettled problems of Christian ethics, with the lack of clarity about what ethical instruction can accomplish (which is why scientific-theoretical clarifications are imperative here), and with the priority of the (anthropological) question, "Who are we?" over the question "What should we be doing?"

We also have to clear up the misunderstanding of eschatology as essentially the treatment of contextual problems, hence as a phenomenon of the sociology of knowledge: eschatology as a breakout, an awakening, a seizure of open space in opposition to what presently exists. It is not a matter here of old or new suspicion of ideology. But it can be asked and considered how it came about that in the mid-1960s, when political alignments had long been stable and economic-ecological problems could be evoked but not yet attacked, Christian theological interest turned so intensely to social and political changes on such a grand scale. Was it not really already an escape movement? When its "object" slipped away, the search for a tangible reality, a reality to grab hold of, so to speak, led then to a journey towards the interior. Should not decisions be postponed and life lived in this postponement while all the while preaching the permanent overhaul of reality? The resignation that we complain about today and that has actually already been preprogrammed in this way, shows itself now as the flip side of this behavior.

Socio-political and intellectual changes in the 1960s gave a powerful boost to interest in eschatology. The same is happening today under the impression that we are living in an apocalyptic world situation. How do such occasions relate to "giving an account of the reason for the hope," which according to I Peter 3:15 is demanded of every Christian? It is a matter of framing this question theologically, that is, of arguing in such a way that the "reason for the hope that is in you" is unmistakably expressed. Precisely because this reason cannot be produced by any human act or rational activity, it allows for a substantiated discourse that contrasts with all forms of theoretical or practical self-substantiation, and with supposed "substantiations" that end up justifying in the public forum only their own intellectual existence or the motivation of their own action or inertia.

In order to explain this difference and its very practical effects, one must distinguish between the theological *context of justification* and the *context of discovery* (or various contexts of discovery, as the case may be) of theology. The context of justification may be described as a set of basic statements which enables us to decide whether certain theological chains of reasoning are valid as *theological arguments* in a strict sense. Theologically, they can be *substantiated* only by their connection with the context of justification. This might be demonstrated with an example from the history of theology:

Augustine's theology of history, which he developed in his work on the *City of God*, is, of course, perfectly intelligible in the flow of its own argument, but it takes on sharper contours in the context in which it originated—the sack of Rome by Alaric in 410. This catastrophe was given a religious interpretation by the Romans, namely the turning away of the gods from the metropolis that had been infiltrated by Christianity and thus had become "atheistic." This interpretation was based on the ancient theory that the cosmos moves in unending cycles, remaining secure as long as its orbits are not disturbed by impiety. In contrast to that, Augustine posited a view of a history that is fashioned by God, stretched out between creation and consummation, and thus directed toward a goal; a history in which decisions and divisions between faith and unbelief take place; a history whose quality of salvation and calamity cannot be gathered from the course of history itself but is assessed in the tribunal of God from beyond the world and time.

The "context of discovery," then, can be renamed for the totality of pretheoretical elements out of which such views have developed. That is the way the term is also understood, for the most part, in scientific-theoretical usage: the ensemble of a wide variety of psychological, social, religious, and other factors that affect our thinking in more or less uncontrolled form, but that help to reveal how this thinking is embedded in "life."[5] I most often use the term "context of discovery," however, for a theoretically structured model, which suggests conclusions (or at least the rudiments thereof) that are theologically possible, without being able at the same time to substantiate them. Augustine's view of history was formed out of the traditions of Jewish and Christian prophecy, the Aristotelian concept of time, and other elements and was solidified under the pressure of a particular life-context (which we can reconstruct only with the help of theories of society and history). None of this, however, could substantiate his theology of salvation history; that occurred in confession of the action of God, who time and again had intervened in human life and society, had entered them before people could begin to speak about it and theologians could begin to reflect on it. That God comes to meet us from amidst the reality in which we live is an axiom of faith, however. If it is expanded, theoretical models of history can be constructed. One talks then quite differently about time and the world than, for instance, in a cyclical view of world and time. Dogmatically speaking, the axiom is based on the hiddenness of God and on His presence as Spirit, that which creates and sustains life. This presence of the Spirit might be what is meant in I Peter 3:15, when it says that one is to give a reason for the hope "that is in you." This reason is not merely a personal source of that reason deep inside one but the "intervention" of God through the hope that directs the hoping one to that which God has made ready.

What does this mean for "doing theology"? First and foremost, that theology must be understood as an activity that simply follows

5. Cf. Hans Reichenbach, *Experience and Prediction: An Analysis of the Foundations and the Structure of Knowledge* (Chicago: The University of Chicago Press, 1938), 6f.: " . . . and the well-known difference between the thinker's way of finding this theorem and his way of presenting it before a public may illustrate the difference in question, I shall introduce the terms *context of discovery* and *context of justification* to work this distinction;" Hans Albert, *Traktat über kritische Vernunft*, 2nd ed. (Tübingen: J. C. B. Mohr, 1969), 38; Wolfhart Pannenberg, *Theology and the Philosophy of Science* (Philadelphia: The Westminster Press, 1976), 321; Gerhard Sauter, *Wissenschaftstheoretische Kritik der Theologie: Die Theologie und die neuere wissenschaftstheoretische Diskussion*. Materialien-Analysen-Entwürfe (Munich: Chr. Kaiser, 1973), 356. For the research in the natural sciences, the structuralist concept of theories of J. D. Sneed and W. Stegmüller emphasizes that various theoretical concepts nonderivable from each other must be connected in a complex way. Cf. W. Stegmüller, *Hauptströmungen der Gegenwartsphilosophie*, 6th ed.(Stuttgart: Kröner, 1979), vol. II:468–494.

the substantiation established as hope. Christian theology has to identify the arguments that respond to God's promise and do so for every reality that is affected by this promise. Theology is a particular *activity,* a praxis *sui generis,* and an experience *sui generis,* not a reflexive superstructure imposed on other experience but the experience of theological reasoning, an "experience with experience." Such a theology can indeed be distinguished from one understood as *conduct,* conduct towards one's environment historically, culturally, socially, and politically.

This distinction between *activity* and *conduct* can, once again, be made especially clear with respect to eschatology. Understood as theological conduct, eschatology adamantly refuses to become involved with the "existing." If God, according to this "logic," is the radical future, then hope can be convincing as continuous movement, as constant transcending, and as unchecked contradiction. It would be unimaginable that anything really definitively arrives or is fulfilled, even symbolically and temporarily, for that would rob such hope of its elan. The Jewish sociologist of religion Gershom Scholem writes about this conduct in looking back at Jewish Messianism:

> Living in hope is a great thing, but it is also something deeply unreal. It devalues the importance of the person, who can never be fulfilled since the imperfection in all one's undertakings devalues the very thing that affects one's central worth. Thus the messianic idea in Judaism forced a life in postponement, in which nothing can be done and completed in a definitive way.[6]

It is no accident that this conduct of pure hope can best be described sociologically: as the manifestation of the actions and reactions of people who relate to their environment in a common way, namely, in a process of continuous self-differentiation and resistance to any assimilation. The periodic awakening of Christian hope could and can be understood in similar fashion: as a departure from conventional ties of every kind, from a history of Christian culture weighted down by tradition, with the fetters of an outmoded way of thinking. All of this *can* happen. But it may not become the leading cognitive principle of theology, for then theology would be ex-

6. Gershom Scholem, "Zum Verständnis der messianischen Idee im Judentum"(1959), in idem, *Judaica,* vol. I (Frankfurt a.M.: Suhrkamp, 1963), 73f.

plained and substantiated out of the structures and mechanisms of a context of discovery. The theory of theology then becomes patterned after the philosophy of history proposed by Arnold Toynbee, who fashioned a dialectic of "challenge and response." This approach seems to me to be far more characteristic of the recent development of theology than it should be, even if theology might like the potential results.

It is not as though there are not constant challenges that theology has to face! Augustine's conception of the "City of God," his view of the overlap of salvation events and world history, was a response to the challenge brought on by the breakdown of the ancient world of meaning under the onslaught of the barbarians from the north. Or take Luther's doctrine of justification: it was provoked by corruption in the exercise of spiritual power in the penitential practice of the Church of his day. But neither one of these examples explains what the two men had to say theologically, let alone that it could be substantiated thereby. For then Augustine's theology of history and Luther's doctrine of justification would still be noteworthy but no longer theologically memorable. The theological context of justification is different in kind from the historical, cultural, and social contexts of discovery, for in both cases above it did not present something to which theology could simply react, but rather contained a response *that was not indicated in the question.*

In other instances these distinctions are blurred, as, for example, when liberation (a political context) is experienced as an indication of the "glorious freedom of the children of God" (Romans 8:21). As happened in the Greek Orthodox Church after centuries of subjugation and as can be heard today from many of the oppressed, the confession of freedom bears in itself the traces of the challenge in which an oppressive situation is confronted with the promise of faith. But in these traces the extent to which such a discovery as the perception of faith leads to theological discourse—discourse about God—must be just as clearly discernible. Theological substantiation has to develop this discursively, in step-by-step argumentation.

This distinction between the context of substantiation and the context of discovery calls to mind two conceptual forms of Christian theology that, in the last two centuries, have frequently been played off against each other, nowadays often as the confrontation of "dogmatic" and "contextual" theology in ecumenical discussions. This conflict, which is widely considered to be the antagonism between the Western rational tradition—indeed rationally dominated faith—and a new situational piety, will be treated here only insofar as it may support the following thesis: in this confrontation there recurs a very old, if not always sufficiently obvious, problem of theology, namely, the relation of its "time-conditioned" insights to the permanent questions that belong to the character of theology.

Here there emerges in a new form a problem that for the last two centuries has been treated as the question of the "historicity"—*Geschichtlichkeit*—of theology. This question was specified by Ernst Troeltsch, who confronted theological dogmatism with the historical method.[7] The attempted solutions provided by the historico-critical thinking of Western theology after many conflicts—such as the hermeneutical responsibility of theological tradition before the forum of a general consciousness of truth, a procedure that makes the unique character of theological tradition stand out all the more sharply—have lost their persuasive power or are at least limited to representatives of a cultural consciousness, which is losing more and more ground, both sociologically and culturo-geographically. For that reason dogmatics threatens to become the subject matter of the sociology of knowledge; it loses its character as a theological way of thinking and becomes a normative system of principles required by religious groups to regulate themselves as social systems.[8] In fact, recently emerging "theologies" can often be only approximately described as intellectual expressions of the conflicts of religious groups with their environment (including their own traditions). The statements of a dogmatic tradition as normative first principles then reduce the religious group-consciousness to a common denominator, which certainly might claim the highest communicative validity for those participating in this discourse. I have in mind here not only very different forms (depending on the situation) of a "theology of liberation" but also, for example, forms of "feminist theology," or even earlier the "death of God theology."

7. Ernst Troeltsch, "Über historische und dogmatische Methode in der Theologie" (1898), in *Theologie als Wissenschaft*, ed. Gerhard Sauter (Munich: Chr. Kaiser, 1971), 105–127.
8. Cf. Niklas Luhmann, *Funktion der Religion* (Frankfurt a.M.: Suhrkamp, 1977), 126, 174–181.

The chasms that have opened up between these new forms of Christian self-understanding and the theological context of justification in the form of "classical" theological dogmatics are substantially deeper than the "ugly broad ditch" that Lessing deplored between a contemporary, current religious reason and the biblical-theological truth claims developed by dogmatics.[9] Most importantly, it is no longer just one ditch that is created here, but ditches upon ditches between communities, groupings, and alliances, all of which are apparently claiming only one thing: to give expression to their own specific "experiences." They never do this any longer in the expectation of accepting step by step other experiences as well and thereby, as through the elimination of unsound impressions, arriving at a universal recognition of truth. They do so rather in the belief that it is a matter of being on the side of God, or to put it another way, of having God on one's own side—thereby, however, theologically sanctioning the battle lines of our world society.

All of this adds up to a serious theological challenge of dimensions that we were hardly confronted with before. Not only are institutional church relationships at stake here, not only does the idea of a world church (even in the limited form of the ecumenical movement) seem more and more like pure fiction, but the unity of faith loses at least its common language. In this situation, analytical thinking is imperative, that is, a precise determination of the location and limits of problems. In a complex situation of dialogue and conflict the point in question must exactly be defined. Otherwise the discourse will become slippery, so that apparent problems arise that can no longer really be solved.

It is possible to analyze discourses like that, but the diagnosis would only bring socio-psychological factors into the picture, which, while considerably important, nevertheless do not apply to the question of the substantiation of theological statements. Rather, the *theological substantiation of faith in God's action* must designate the grounds that are "given beforehand" through God's presence in the death and resurrection of Jesus Christ and that fix us upon the hope that awaits God even in the very places where the reality accessible to us contradicts what we ascribe to God: His realization of jus-

9. Gotthold Ephraim Lessing, "Über den Beweis des Geistes und der Kraft," in *Gesammelte Werke*, vol. VIII: *Philosophische und theologische Schriften* 2, ed. Paul Rilla (Berlin/Weimar: Aufbau, 1968), 14.

tice, peace, and life. Theological argumentation has to speak about God's acting in *His* way. Human experiences are opened up to God's action by not remaining fixed on yearning expectations. That can happen only if theology does not cover the world with a net of interpretations that explain everything in advance but rather states what can be expected with good reasons as filled with promise, and what is available to human knowledge only piecemeal, in disjointed form, and at best by way of sign.

If time-and-situation conditioned problems are fashioned into enduring theological questions, into the basic questions of theology, then there is always the danger that insofar as answers are found, they only echo a particular situation instead of listening to the answer that first and foremost enables us to ask theological questions. To be sure, there is no definitive stock of dogmatic principles that determines these basic questions once and for all. Theological dogmatics, which has to state the context of justification, originated and developed in the midst of urgent problems. If one views the history of dogmatics in this way—and that is the task of an analytical reconstruction of its history—then it presents a much more complex picture than is generally conceded when one looks only at the doctrinal tenets once considered binding and when these are interpreted only as norms for newly appearing questions. This analysis has to show in detail how much and how far situational formulations of questions led to theological conclusions *that distinguished themselves as theological knowledge by not being able to be explained as functions of the problems that provoked them.* Rather, they overcome these challenges. They prove to be substantiated statements—even when they have to be formulated as permanent questions—as it becomes clear that these questions are not contrived but are seriously being raised, not by the situation but by the existence of people under the call and promise of God. Therefore, the knowledge expressed in a theological substantiation cannot be more than substantiated hope.

There is yet a further respect in which theology occupies itself with the distinction between substantiation and discovery. I mentioned before that "context of discovery" is usually understood scientific-theoretically as simply the atmosphere of elements not yet within theoretical grasp, which somehow precede any theoretical endeavor. Theology, however, encounters additional contexts of discovery that have already been theoretically analyzed. That is the case today at any rate, where, for example, a sociological or psychological explanation of human behavior is provided, purporting to discover things that are important for the work of theology. Questions about what constitutes community (and I shall return to this in just a moment when I deal with the catchword "consensus") or questions about standardized experiences of human social conduct must be considered by theology. But how do they relate to what theology has to say on its own ground? I shall attempt to explain these by looking at the theological codeword "consensus."

For Christian theology *"consensus"* originally meant humanity's joining in the action of God by the power of the Holy Spirit, who inserts us into the promissory history of God with humanity.[10] The consensus of faith is thus an integral part of the work of God itself which unifies human individuals divided by nature, religion, and culture, and who are indeed, because of these different traditions and convictions, hostile to one another. God brings them together in the unity of the Spirit, so that they "may be of like mind among each other according to Christ Jesus, so that with one accord they may with one mouth glorify the Father" (Romans 15:5f.).

Consensus in the form of unanimity of human individuals is a sign of the speed and manner of God's having reconciled the world to Himself. In the consensus, the *promise of God's peace* is fulfilled, which, to be sure, extends considerably beyond the foundation of a new community of people but which is not meant to take effect without them or pass them by. Accordingly the Christian congregation, in which Gentiles and Jews have been brought near to God and "have become near [to each other] through the blood of Christ, who is our peace" (Ephesians 2:13ff.), is called upon "to preserve the unity of the Spirit through the bond of peace" (Ephesians 4:3).

The ethical task consists in remaining freely in the unity bestowed by God and in doing, speaking, and thinking that which leads to peace. The "dogmatically," or better yet doxologically, expressed oneness ("there is one body and one Spirit, just as you were called to the one hope that belongs to your call, one Lord, one faith, one baptism, one God and Father of us all, who is above all and through all

---

10. On the following cf. Gerhard Sauter, "Consensus," *Theologische Realenzyklopädie*, vol. VIII (Berlin/New York: de Gruyter, 1981), 182–189; idem, "Hypothesen in der theologischen Ethik, erläutert an der Frage nach der Einheit der Kirche," *Evangelische Theologie* 40 (1980): 285–302.

and in all"; Ephesians 4:4–6) is articulated in correspondence to the ethical task in the fashioning of precisely a new and different concept for what is ethically necessary: the preservation of unity in the *consensus* that confesses the oneness of God. Communal human action is tied to the action of God, but in such a way that it does not simply "correspond" to it, even linguistically—a heavy restriction when compared to analogy building, which supposedly "translates" promissory concepts like justice, reconciliation, and peace into ethical terms by reproducing a dogmatically developed strategy as an ethical task. But is it not of critical importance, in the face of every hasty directive to translate into action what has already taken place from God, that we first of all consider of what the "unity of the Spirit" consists in any given situation of discord, conflict, and hostility? Must not consensus of faith and hope be found ever anew, an agreement that does not arise out of the recitation of old formulas of Christian unity but one that in view of the threatened situation of the world and humanity must be obtained and expressed anew in full accord? This consensus is more than just applying old truths in the form of traditional insights to a new situation; that puts one on the wrong path either to an interpretation that already knew all things beforehand (since it views the whole of the world and history ostensibly "from God") or to a reduction (often hardly noticed) of tradition to that which it permits to be acquired in a given situation. The knowledge content of Christian consensus refers instead to what God does to humanity here and now—even in such a way that He makes humanity look out and cry out for Him, albeit without their knowledge, and because other people or even the church do not find the peace of God, because their energies, ideas, and words are consumed by discord. But these predicaments, too, can be perceived only if—even in an entirely inconspicuous way and in hidden places—oneness with God becomes an event. There will also appear, wholly unconstrained, unanimity and agreement that no longer embraces only those who think and talk alike, that does not make people speak uniformly or in unison, but which enables them to accept one another (Romans 15:7), "to bear with one another in love" (Ephesians 4:2), as a sign that they bear the truth. Consensus is expressed, therefore, in a dialogue full of tension—a fruitful dialogue, appropriate to the consensus, which gains in discernment through the incorporation of representative experience; it does not limit itself to the smallest or (better still) largest common denominator of various opinions.

In consensus the church communally takes on and "processes" present-day challenges and situation-conditioned problems, as they are brought before God and lead to an answer of faith, which, in the light of the knowledge of God's action, says what we can do and may expect. To cite just three examples: (1) In the fellowship of the body of Christ in the *Lord's Supper* there emerges a unity created anew from an existence broken by humankind—the existence of Jesus broken down into his body and blood. This fellowship founds a new community in the midst of a world that is passing away, a communion that does not have to claim to build the new society in which life becomes worth living. (2) In the *proclamation* of the free grace of God we experience freedom beyond the false problems posed by the alternative "heteronomy and autonomy." Thus a truly free response is made possible to that which must be said to us and is given to us in advance without leading us into false dependencies and limiting responsible action. (3) In a *diakonia* that is focused entirely on the needy, one finds out that human effort and divine help are as "unconfused and unchanged" but also as "indivisible and inseparable" as true divinity and true humanity in the person of Jesus Christ, according to the Formula of Chalcedon. From this we can learn today how we should speak of divine action and human activity in the oneness of the Spirit.

In the consensus of the church there becomes evident in a very practical way what was said above in a scientific-theoretical view about the relationship between the theological context of justification and the contexts of discovery. Consensus often forms, as it were, the hinge between these two, that is, when doxological unanimity and agreement in argument meet and blend together. Agreement here as a rule must remain relative to the situation, historically open, and flexible in formulation. What in theological terms and creaturely knowledge (what can at best be termed a *docta ignorantia*) is considered to be assured knowledge, now and then will enter into the theological context of justification which consists of binding statements of faith that one can hold to, in all the fluctuations of history and in changing communicative circumstances. As consensus, however, these statements do not remain impervious to historical and social change, no more than they may, on the other hand, become a quarry from which each generation mines the raw materials for its own housing. With regard to the constitution of consensus and the possibilities of critical self-examination contained in it, it can be shown how the question of truth can be stated and must be answered theologically. Whoever today seeks to trace this out is bound to come into conflict with the consensus theory of truth, as advocated under the influence of a sociological reconstruction of social reality. It has made the catchword "consensus" interesting but also obsolete, because it has dislodged the "classical" philosophico-theological theory of truth (as agreement between knowledge and that which is known, between consciousness and its object) with its promise and claim of objectivity, in favor of a merely social validation of facts: they are "real" only so long and so far as they can be communicated within the framework of human communication and in such a way that they can really be perceived. If, however, "truth" only consists of what is socially valid, then "knowledge of truth" threatens to be given over to an unpredictable group-dynamic process; truth itself becomes a matter for a plebiscite, the result of majority decisions. A theory that embraces this corresponds all too closely to our real politics of communication not to attract the attention of theologians who are somewhat sensitive to the atmosphere in which opinions and judgments are formed, even in ecumenism. But it is not because "consensus" has become a shibboleth in social philosophy and communication theory that theology should work out a theory of ecclesiastical consensus, but because the history of this term in the church and theology shows that "consensus" is the necessary, though not sufficient, condition of theological truth in human language. "There is" theological truth only in that which "the church" has to say unalterably—and that is why theology is *ecclesiastical science.*

That leads me to one last scientific-theoretical aspect. If a Protestant theologian refers expressly to "church," one not only easily (as always) falls under suspicion of paying tribute to the institutional church, which might be detrimental to the freedom of theology: the suspicion also immediately arises that one is abandoning the responsibility of theology to say what is generally true and thereby to represent the universality of the Christian faith in its relation to God, the Lord of heaven and earth. If God, so it is said, is the all-determining reality (and Christian faith cannot speak about Him in any other way if it does not want to revert to other gods), then theology too can acknowledge no boundaries between human views and convictions without simultaneously crossing them, and consequently becoming a universal science.

I have often had to listen to the objection that concentrating on ecclesiastical consensus drives theology into a ghetto and is satisfied with the self-understanding of those faithful to the church. Thus it does not do justice to the doubts of their contemporaries. It immunizes the responsibility of faith instead of sharpening it in argument with the general consciousness of truth. All of this sounds plausible, but it seems to me to exhibit a typical confusion in the way the question is formulated, creating problems that are only apparent. Corresponding to the concept of consensus outlined above, the consensus of faith is not only spatially distinct from a public consensus (concerning the values and goals that hold a society together to the same degree as they are followed) or even from the *sensus communis.* There is a spatial distance, because the church and even religion long ago have become a partial system of society. But, what is more, there is an *essential* difference: In the *sensus communis,* even if this can only be conceived of ideally as a transcendental condition of social understanding, the logical range of its assertions is tied to that which, in each case, at the most, can be brought up for discussion as a concrete universality. "Generality" and "General validity" then, must be determined in their social relation to each other. The church and theology always became painfully aware of this relationship over the course of their history, when they came into conflict with other authorities procuring and controlling knowledge. The relationship between "faith" and "reason" can *as well* be described as the consequence of these conflicts. As a result, however, Christian theology also had to develop a way of thinking that pointed beyond the sociologically describable aspects of the problem area. Whenever theology tried to portray the oneness, uniqueness, and totality of God conceptually, it became totalitarian. In the effort to grasp the oneness of reality rationally, theology practically, or at least theoretically, excluded not only those who thought differently (or, what really amounts to the same thing, assumed that the critics, doubters, and outright unbelievers could not think correctly or broadly enough, or that they were limited in their conduct); it also excluded hope from its thinking, degrading it to an outlook on the universal.

Whoever claims to think of God in any way as totality, as the all-for-
mula, must deny the hope that focuses on the expectation "that God
may be all in all" (I Corinthians 15:28), and that statement is expressly eschatological. If it is thought of as already realized, then
concepts of totality arise (as especially influential examples today I
mention only: the *one* history as the history of liberation and, in that
respect, of salvation; the "other" life as the "true" life, made plausible under the assumption that we live in a perverse world; the totality
of meaning as a universe of supporting relationships, a net that as individuals we must, more and more, fasten on to so as not to lose our
grip on the common world). For a number of years now, all of this
has no longer been a matter of the special interests of theologians.
The intense search for that which is universal, that which represents
the oneness of reality by binding all people together (now or in the
future), has long affected, for example, pastoral care and religious
instruction. For pastors and religious educators the personal integration of those entrusted to them has become paramount, and for the
sake of that goal they prefer not to encourage maturity of faith, an
independence that is also prepared to endure loneliness. Years ago
William W. Bartley pilloried the "retreat to commitment" of theologians and church people who sought to overcome both doubt and
life's most difficult problems through activity and communal action.[11] Bartley also attempted to show, however, the indispensable
connection between commitment and rationality. In the meantime,
if I see it right, the retreat into totality—whether this totality be conceptual, sympathetically experienced, or allegedly "meditatively"
disclosed—has become a far greater danger. It is not merely in view
of the vast appeal of the irrational, an appeal that is associated with
such a retreat, that we should strive for rationality; this holds true
even more where the striving after universality and totality is defended with the highest claim to rationality, as if by supreme effort
it were possible to grasp and describe that—according to the faith
that truly awaits God's Lordship—which cannot be grasped at all
without being completely missed!

11. William Warren Bartley III, *The Retreat to Commitment* (New York: Alfred
Knopf, 1962); idem, "Wissenschaft und Glaube: Die Notwendigkeit des Engage-
ments," in *Neue Anthropologie*, vol. VII: *Philosophische Anthropologie 2*, ed. Hans-
Georg Gadamer and Paul Vogler (Munich: Deutscher Taschenbuch Verlag/Stuttgart:
George Thieme Verlag, 1974), 64–102.

The Hidden Life

With that the *ethics of theological knowledge* again enters the picture. It has not played a significant role in German Protestant theology since the middle of the nineteenth century, although back then important proposals were put forward especially by Friedrich Schleiermacher and Richard Rothe. They proposed conceptions that not only transplanted theology into a cultural-ethical context of discovery (understood as an essential part of the representative action of European culture) but also intensively questioned how we could work theologically, how we could "do theology." How can we precisely, as theologians and not just as human beings like all others, in and through our work submit ourselves to critical scrutiny? This question cannot be satisfactorily answered with such motifs as "devoutness," "existential concern," "subjectivity," or "commitment"; it must be described in terms of the conduct that goes with the theological statements.

In seventeenth-century Protestant dogmatics this conduct was referred to as the *habitus theosdotos:*[12] the theologian is enabled by God to do what God asks of him or her and in so doing is enabled to exist. A certain demeanor is acquired with this activity, a demeanor that must be tested by what the theologian has to say theologically. Thus the theologian is held responsible by his or her God-talk which substantiates the theological profession and, moreover, his or her whole existence. In 1933—a decisive hour for the German Protestant Church—Karl Barth spoke in a comparable sense of "theological existence": the Christian situation before God, a situation which must be accounted for before other people as well, not only in what the Christian confesses but also by the way in which the Christian makes known the foundation of this confession; in short, how attentive this person is to the authority one has to listen to amid the bombardment of all kinds of other voices.[13] Professing as a hearer—that is essential especially for the dogmatician, and by that the dogmatician represents, as Martin Kähler once said, the "laity"

---

12. Carl Heinz Ratschow, *Lutherische Dogmatik zwischen Reformation und Aufklärung*, vol. I (Gütersloh: Gütersloher Verlaghaus Gerd Mohn, 1964), 40–43.
13. Karl Barth, *Theologische Existenz heute!*, ed. Hinrich Stoevesandt (Munich: Chr. Kaiser, 1984), esp. 29–32.

in theology.[14] When I speak of the theologian as an agent of the laity, I am not thinking in the least about the differences between "clergy" and "laity" (that would be most inappropriate for Protestant theology!). I am also leaving aside the question of the ecclesiastical office of theologians, the *ministerium verbi divini* according to the Protestant understanding. The theologian may be understood as an *expert,* who is in a certain way "experienced" and helps other people share in this experience to the extent that they show a basic interest in it.

What is the theologian experienced in, or should become so at any rate? Is it incidents that stand apart from the daily routine, perhaps frontier situations, life crises, a "Damascus-road experience" in the form of radical shake-up of an innate and acquired religious commitment, or a Reformation "breakthrough"—in all of which those who look for the assurance of salvation, and who are moved by the deepest of spiritual trials concerning the meaning of their lives, cast off the fetters of an ecclesiastical mediation between God and the world and go as individuals directly to God? Or are theologians examples of those who are at the intersection of traditional religious ties, with all their uncertainties, and life in a world obviously estranged to religion, so that the theologian's professional task is to clarify, first for one's self and then for others, how one can be simultaneously "modern" and "religious"? Or finally—to embody a broader and more widespread conception of the theological profession today—in a society dominated by specialists and guided by an insular perspective on others, where egoism in private life, in the workplace and in politics is celebrating some frightening victories, would it be the singular concern of the theologian to learn and to teach how to give attention to "the whole"?

I listed these common contemporary descriptions of professional theology (for they are what is at issue, even if they form the guide for theological projects) because here once again contexts of discovery appear. Another example has already been given in the explanation of eschatology by the sociology of science: opening up to the future

14. Martin Kähler, "Jesus und das Alte Testament," (1896) in his *Dogmatische Zeitfragen. Alte und neue Ausführungen zur Wissenschaft der christlichen Lehre,* vol. I.2: *Zur Bibelfrage,* 2nd ed. (Gütersloh: C. Bertelsmann, 1937), 117. Cf. also Gerhard Sauter, "Der Dogmatiker als Anwalt des Laien in der Theologie," in *Vom Amt des Laien in Kirche und Theologie.* Festschrift für Gerhard Krause zum 70. Geburtstag, ed. Henning Schröer and Gerhard Müller (Berlin/New York: de Gruyter, 1982), 278–295.

arises out of opposition to "things as they are," out of resistance to a world regarded as perverse. Such a posture, unlike a mere uneasiness with the dominant culture or, even, an unhappy consciousness in retreat from a vexing environment, can be nourished by critical insight. Here sensitivity to the creaturely yearning for freedom can come to the fore. Along with that, however, it is crucial to know whether theologians who express themselves that way thereby express a real understanding or are only displaying themselves. How is theology different from the self-presentation of people who are mainly concerned with finding their way in their environment and who use words like faith, love, hope, and liberation for that search?

I was asked this some years ago at an ecumenical consultation by a psychiatrist who had discovered anthropological features behind theological statements, features that he rightly supposed ought to be thought of not only psychologically but theologically. This overlap of personal behavior and theology is a coefficient exercising an influence on theological thinking, theological discourse, and the action that follows from them, and it rarely appears in expositions of the theological locus of anthropology. Over the course of time I have learned more and more to pay attention to this, not least in dialogue with students who have wanted to view their theological studies as training in a certain way of acting. What develops out of that goes far beyond what is usually discussed as the necessary existential concern of the theologian, the unavoidably subjective side of theology, and the intertwinement of doctrine and life. What is at stake there is the objectivity of theology, hence its epistemological quality, and connected with that is my impression that today it is extraordinarily difficult in theological dialogue to draw attention to the questions of the "laity."

If one wishes to concentrate on such questions, then theological existence must be perceived as the vocation of every Christian and must be considered in light of how the profession of the theologian is involved with one's being human.

To exist theologically is to be a person under the promise and in the expectation of new life. Under this promise one is called, one is inserted into the situation before God that is opened up by God's condemning and saving judgment. One is inserted into the hidden history of Jesus Christ in the world. That *is* the living space in which our being human is "located" and "takes place." "For you died, and your life is hidden with Christ in God" (Colossians 3:3). That is a categorical indicative, the content of the judgment of God upon our existence and at the same time the communication of new life. *"Life,"* the third theologically fundamental promissory concept, is thereby described as a new beginning, an origin from God. It is an absolute beginning in the sense that no person can return to a point before that beginning, which implies that no person can take an absolute point of view of his or her own self, in order to project their own existence and the givenness of the world as a possibility and then, step by step, to measure its realization. In addition, the origin of life cannot be sought in any nebulous beginning that we can reconstruct and hypothetically define by going back through the history or life history known to us, in order to show the direction of the further unfolding of our lives. The age-old question about the absolute beginning, which Western philosophy first asked and which today has sound currency in the scientific-theoretical critique of definitive substantiative claims in society and research, is asked of theology in a peculiar way:[15] not as the initial boundary of an experience within space and time, but as the decisive turning point for a life already lived, for a history already long lasting, for a world already existing. God appeared in Jesus Christ in the midst of time. As one born of a Jewish woman, he belonged to the people of Israel. He died, excommunicated, outside of the Holy City and thereby became the equivalent of a Gentile. God's "yes" to this death in the resurrection confirmed him as the Savior of all humanity.

To be able to begin here, Christian theology will have to return again and again to the cross on Golgotha and to the empty tomb, which finally puts Jesus of Nazareth beyond all human harm and turns the gaze of humanity "above" (Colossians 3:2) to the side of God. Christian theology begins with the "yes" of God to His promises in Jesus Christ. Theology, therefore, has stood from the beginning in the middle of a world of other religions, other ways of believing, other hopes. Thus it cannot be understood as one (perhaps by its own estimation the highest) stage of development in the history of religion, or as an exemplary, optimal (it is hoped) realization of the possibilities of "religion" in general. I am suggesting by all of this

---

15. See also Gerhard Sauter, "Hermeneutisches und analytisches Denken in der Theologie," in idem, *In der Freiheit des Geistes. Theologische Studien* (Göttingen: Vandenhoeck & Ruprecht, 1988), 152–165.

only that from the start Christian theology concerned itself in a special way with the problem of the beginning, of being able to begin, because it arose out of the contingency of God's act in Jesus Christ, because it continues to be based on this contingency of the action of God.

Life from God and before God means being able to begin anew. That is what the reformers meant with their doctrine of the justification of the godless without works of the law, without any "basis in one's self" or self-substantiation, without a first or final word that one can say concerning one's self—only by faith, only by receiving the work of God, and by listening to His life-creating will. The anthropological scope of this fundamental theological idea, it seems to me, must still be discovered, with Christology as the starting point. Jesus Christ is the justified one in the form of the suffering servant of God. He accepts God's will for him. He becomes the new person by having God alone act upon him, even where only other people seemed to have their hands on him—on the cross. Suffering here proves to be the birth of new life, one which manifests itself for others. In the suffering of Jesus Christ any picture of humanity is shattered that divides into activity and passivity and sees death as the moment when action is finally at an end. From now on suffering means *doing* what *God* wills, and this doing goes beyond the usual differences between actives and passives.

People learn and know that this is so only by virtue of the promise of life. Here again appears that noteworthy semantic incommensurability that I had to talk about earlier in the interpretation of the promissory concepts of "justice" and "peace." That "life," stated religiously, is more than vitality, has long been known. That "life" is not coincident with a spiritual sphere (as distinct from a corporeal), cultivated only, if at all, through conflict with corporeality, is something that Christendom had to learn in long and tiresome conflicts. In the face of life's manifold handicaps, the decline in the quality of life, and the constriction of living space, to which many people and other creatures in our world are subjected, Christendom today confronts with the question of the extent to which suffering can be overcome, or at least diminished, by the struggle against such afflictions. Or if mere liberation from the limitations of life is understood as the experience of the salvific new beginning, to what degree is suffering transferred to other areas of life or possibly even increased? Suffering is certainly not a "putting up with" that resigns itself to the way the world is. But there is also, by the same token, no indication to the Christian faith that suffering gets its power of hope from resisting the world as it is and from (falsely) describing the world as first of all perverse, in support of such resistance. Suffering, as acceptance of that which happens from God to and through people, is something other than the experience of the limitation set on the hearts and desires of one's own life. It is not death that is first suffered but the beginning of life, birth. Whoever accepts his or her own life, whoever does not reject it (either by blaming others for it or by seeking to bring about some other set of circumstances whereby one's life might once again be lived completely differently), gives God the glory as the Creator. Another person can also be "suffered" as the creaturely boundary of one's own life, by which each person experiences his or her own finitude and which is missed if one views and treats others only as possibilities for benefiting one's self. Finally, our thinking is also a "suffering," insofar as it is not a luxury but belongs to the creational make-up of humanity. Every human individual is called to think from a point beyond his or her own self and to grasp his or her personality from there alone: not by a vague transcendence of one's present state of consciousness, but rather in relation to God, who cannot be grasped by human thought, and for that reason, sets us to thinking about what we need for life.

Name and Subject Index